My Remembrances of

LIFE AT

TOMPKINS

BARRACKS

By
SP4 Kirk

MISSION: TWO FOLD, PRODUCE MAPS FOR THE EUROPEAN THEATER IN PEACE TIME, BUT BE READY TO MOBILIZE IN TWO HOURS TO MAKE MAPS IN THE FIELD

My Remembrances of

LIFE AT

TOMPKINS

BARRACKS

By

SP4 Kirk

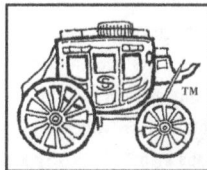

SWEETWATER STAGELINES™

SAN ANTONIO, TEXAS

My Remembrances of Life At
TOMPKINS BARRACKS
© 2006, 2015 by Donald Keith Kirk
SECOND EDITION

Published by Sweetwater Stagelines™
an imprint of The Old West Company™
5118 Village Trail, San Antonio, Texas 78218

TRADECLOTH EDITION
ISBN: 978-0-9801743-9-7

TRADEPAPER EDITION
ISBN: 978-0-989800402

Printed and bound in the United States of America

STORY SUMMARY:
An autobiographical sketch of one soldier's experience in the
United States Army during the Vietnam war.

A MEMOIR
Photos by Donald Keith Kirk except where noted otherwise.
Contributing photographers:
Frank Dulfer, Paul Balcavage, George Taylor, John T. Young, Mike Kilman,
PSG Tokuhisha, Jim MeKay, Michael Lovely

This novel has not been approved, endorsed or authorized by the United States Army or the Engineer Topographic Center. The story, names, characters, and incidents portrayed in this memoir are real as far as the author's memory will allow it. All events described herein actually happened between 1971 and 1974, though on occasion the author has taken some liberties with the sequence of events and some dialog has been added for dramatization. Any resemblance to persons living or dead should be plainly apparent to them, and those who know them, especially since the author has been kind enough to provide their real names. Fictional names were used for those characters engaged in serious criminal activity and for those soldiers whose names the author simply couldn't remember. If there are any errors or omissions, the author will be pleased to correct these in any subsequent reprintings. This story is for those who were there.
Contributions and corrections welcome (kirkwest@sbcglobal.net).
Copies available at Lulu.com/sweetwater and Amazon.com

My Remembrances of Life At

TOMPKINS BARRACKS

TABLE OF CONTENTS

DEDICATION

To my father, Colonel Samuel K. Kirk, US Army, Ret.
who raised me right, but after that I was on my own
to make my own mistakes.

PREFACE

This book was written to express the author's feelings about the military that wrenched him from his planned direction in life, sadly, a path that he was never able to return to. His rage, though tempered now, was never completely neutralized, unfortunately, because his memory of Tompkins Barracks could never be completely erased. His complete distrust for the government began here as he witnessed the lies and waste that permeated the system during the Vietnam war. The author was never sent to Asia, but the drug culture, frustration, and feelings of worthlessness by soldiers fighting in "Nam" also existed in military units in Europe. In fact, it existed in all of the American military around the world. Lets hope the Iraq War doesn't rekindle those feelings.

–ENTRANCE GATE TO TOMPKINS BARRACKS–
TO SOME SOLDIERS, IT WAS THE ENTRANCE TO AN
AMERICAN PRISON IN A FOREIGN COUNTRY

SP4 Kirk
B Co., 656 Engr. Bn. (Topo) &
A Co., 649 Engr. Bn. (Topo)
APO 09081

My Remembrances of

Life At

Tompkins Barracks

By SP4 Kirk

(Selective Service Number 41-9-48-199)

PROLOGUE

A light snow fell on the crisp, brown grass of the quadrangle and the steep slate roofs of the four-story barracks buildings were peppered with glistening snow. The roofs were punched with dozens of dormers, creating possibly, some fourth- and fifth-story space. Looking across the parade field, I could see large, faded, red medical crosses on the gray roofs.

I stood before a large casement window peering through a hole I had wiped clear of cold wet condensation. The dull, stainless-steel flagpole in the center of the field tethered a garrison-sized American flag that fluttered lightly in the breeze. Six large buildings, plastered in a rough-gray, rock-stucco finish, surrounded the parade field like

TOMPKINS BARRACKS QUADRANGLE
–BOTTOM LEFT: NINE-PIN BOWLING ALLEY–

steep canyon walls. Battalion headquarters stood at the north end, and over the central doors, a large white sign read, "USAREUR ENGINEER TOPOGRAPHIC CENTER." A bridge-building company was housed in the barracks across the parade field and the structure at the south end accommodated the post Service Club and its recreational facilities. Just beyond the quadrangle stood a ten-foot tall chain-link fence crowned with concertina wire, and beyond that I could see neatly furrowed agricultural land with a city's fog-shrouded skyline just a few miles distant. I had just arrived here from Frankfurt am Main, the processing center for troops coming over from the states. I was given a crate of paperwork to fill out, was issued more uniforms, and attended various orientations about Germany. I was issued a yellow card (printed with a red flag containing a hammer and sickle) that told me what I was to do if I sighted a SMLM (Soviet Military Liaison Mission) vehicle. It said I was to get a description of the vehicle and its activities and <u>detain</u> it if I saw it near a military installation. Detain it? How, I wondered?

This was Germany in the winter of 1971 and the Vietnam War was still being fought thousands of miles away. The Berlin Wall was still standing strong, with communism's tentacles slithering and creeping around the world like the alien's appendages in the War of the Worlds.

TOMPKINS BARRACKS, SCHWETZINGEN, GERMANY
INSTALLATION MAP, 1968

The SMLMs where the eyes of our Russian allies (authorized by the NATO WWII peace treaty) and they could drive around in Germany and spy on our activities as long as they used the official red license plate. But, I felt lucky, very lucky, that I was being sent here instead of that horrendous, sultry jungle of Vietnam without so much as a front line in a war without a mission, a war run by politicians of arguable scruples

MY DRAFT CARD

instead of generals with an edict to win. And it wasn't exactly luck that got me here. I had made a deal with the devil: a shameless recruiting sergeant. I agreed to sign up for a third year, instead of the draft's required two, with the recruiter's assurances I would not be sent to Nam. Not really a hard decision to make, though I hated the decision throughout my military "career," especially during that third year of confinement.

I was an architectural student, in my fifth year, soon to graduate, in fact only a week away from wearing my black cap and gown, and the sergeant wanted me to take the OCS (Officer Candidate School) exam in Houston, 120 miles away. They wanted me to take the exam on the same Saturday that I was to take my last two final exams— exams that would determine whether or not I'd get that hard-earned diploma. So the decision was again easy, and I couldn't imagine being a uniformed officer in the military. I had weathered one awful soul-searching semester in the Corps of Cadets back in '66, and I wasn't going to give up five years of college work for Lieutenant's bars. A private's wages would have to suffice. My professors had frowned on architectural design students who were in the corps, not just because they didn't believe there was time for both (there wasn't), but because they believed men in uniform weren't really committed to becoming architects and saw no reason to waste energy teaching them. The army was not for me, I was the creative, artistic type with several architectural firms in San Antonio already ready to hire me. But that wasn't going to happen because two years before, in 1969, I had the unfortunate luck of drawing the high number "47" in Tricky-Dick Nixon's first annual lottery, a lottery, I was sure was designed to divide and conquer—which it did appallingly well. Those who got low numbers, cheered, took a gargantuan sigh of relief, and no longer fought the fight to get us out of Vietnam. It was the nation's first draft lottery in twenty-seven years and a "luck of the draw" would decide which of 850,000 young Americans of military age would be called into service. At the selective service's national headquarters, the 366 plastic

TRICKY DICK'S "DIVIDE AND CONQUER" STRATEGY

Luck of Draw Decides
Lottery Tells Military Fate of 850,000

capsules, each containing a slip of paper with a month and a day written on it, were drawn, one by one, from a huge glass laboratory jar. We all listened with fixated ears and bated breath as the drawing was aired live on the radio. Under the new lottery system, a registrant's birthday would be the key to the order in which he would be subject to a draft call. Basically, it was first drawn, first called, last

CADET KIRK, ROTC, A&M, 1966

drawn, last and probably never called. To put it simply, some of us became Draft Card Lottery winners while the others were freed from their shackles to go on with their lives.

The negotiations with this over-enthusiastic, less-than-forthright recruiting sergeant, with his starched and finely creased uniform, continued. Sitting behind a gray, steel desk, he said I had to decide in what occupation I wanted to spend the next three years. I was asked to make three choices in order of any preference I might have. He handed me a rather short list of MOSs and I ran through it carefully trying to visualize what each Military Occupational Specialty might actually do. None of them seemed to require my talents and artistic skills. I could be in a frontline engineer battalion who's job it was to span gorges and rivers with steel float bridges and shepherd earth movers to clear roads through jungles, or I could be an infantry grunt encumbered with a seventy-pound backpack and a locked and loaded M16-A1. I liked motion picture photography—shot two short films in college—but a Combat Photographer MOS didn't seem like the thing to ask for in the middle of a war, so I chose the designation "Map Compiling" as my first choice and left Combat Photographer as the third. I don't recall my second choice, cook maybe, not likely though, I hated cooking, but the sergeant made it very clear that I might not get my first choice, I would get what was needed at the time of my graduation from boot camp, maybe even something not on the list. Great! I'm volunteering for I don't know what. Then he asked me where I wanted to serve. My god, <u>where</u>? You mean I have a choice? Then, by god, Vietnam—that god-forsaken jungle somewhere in the South China Sea—would go at the very <u>bottom</u> of my list.

War movies like Catch-22, Patton, and M.A.SH. had recently come out—I had seen them all—and now it looked like I was going to join those soldiers for real.

MY BROTHERS AND MYSELF WERE GROOMED
FOR THE MILITARY BY MY GUNG-HO MILITARY FATHER

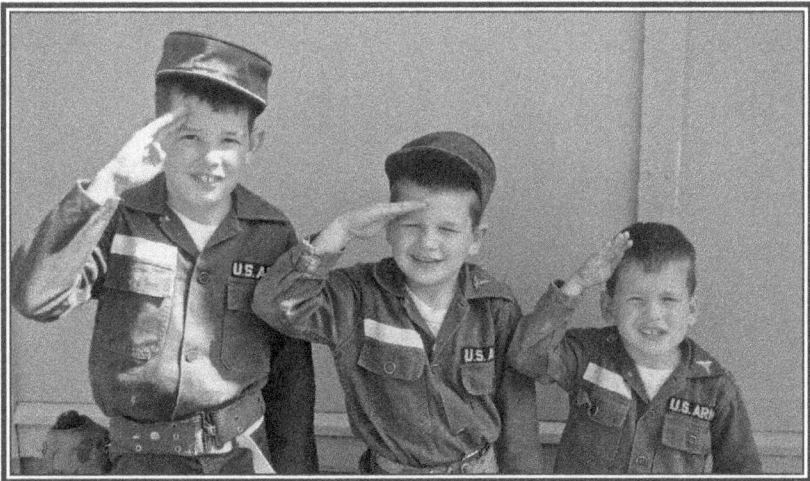

Well, I took my last two final exams, graduated, and was sent to Fort Lewis, Washington for my basic training. I was given a Government Issue haircut (all your hair—and your identity—comes off) and a half-dozen vaccination shots with some kind of high-powered pneumatic syringe. I slept in an open-plan wooden-trussed barracks building with fifty other white-side-walled new recruits—most of them young and wet behind the ears—I was one of the oldest in the lot having received a college deferment at Texas A&M University, while the less fortunate went fighting and kicking off to war. What I would do and where I was to go, was still unknown to me. After learning to shoot, clean, and reassemble my M16A1 in the dark of night, after

WEAPONS TRAINING, CLASSROOM INSTRUCTION, "MORE
P.T. DRILL SERGEANT," AND SLEEP WHEN YOU COULD GET IT

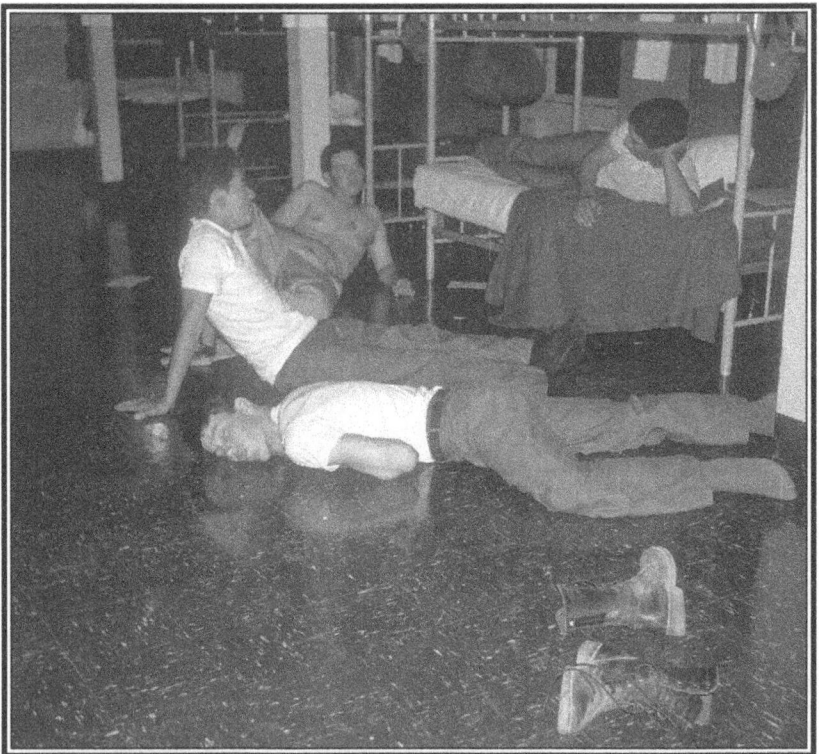

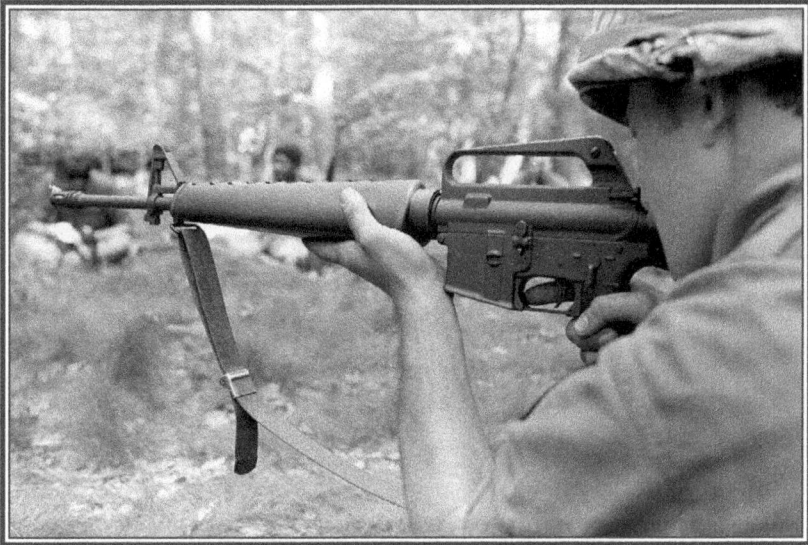

LEARNING TO LOVE YOUR M16-A1
"THIS IS MY RIFLE, THIS IS MY GUN.
THIS IS FOR FIGHTING, THIS IS FOR FUN."

learning how to pick out an enemy soldier in a valley while sitting guard on the military crest of a hill, after learning how to cover your buddy while shooting down range at plastic, human-shaped pop-up targets, after learning how to march and sing Jody's about girls you never knew, after learning how to administer first-aid to a plastic dummy, after learning how to avoid Punji-stick booby traps, after learning rifle and bayonet combat with Pugil sticks (giant Q-tips), after learning how to cross a long run of monkey bars before being allowed to enter the mess hall, after painting landscape rocks white and pulling KP duty washing greasy pots and pans, and finally, after witnessing the shooting of a drill sergeant by a deranged recruit on the firing range, I boarded a C-5 cargo plane bound for Fort Belvoir, Virginia. I had been awarded my first choice: I would be a cartographer and make maps; I was assigned MOS 81D20.

OUR PLATOON SIGN OUTSIDE THE BARRACKS
TOO BAD THERE WERE NO FEMALE SOLDIERS IN BASIC
IT WOULD HAVE MADE THE DRAFT LOTTERY UNNECESSARY

DEPARTMENT OF THE ARMY
U.S. ARMY CAREER COUNSELORS OFFICE
701 San Jacinto Street
Houston, Texas 77052

USAROC-RSA   8 April 1971

Mr. Donald K. Kirk
PO Box 1577
College Station, Texas 77840

Dear Mr. Kirk:

The Chief, Office of Personnel Operations, Headquarters, Department of
the Army, has directed me to inform you that your request to attend the
Map Compiling
Course Number   411-81D20   commencing on   27 Aug 71
has been approved under the Army's Service School Enlistment Option.

In order to complete required processing and basic training prior to class
reporting date for the above course, you must enlist ████████ on 24 Jun 71
so that you may begin basic training on   5 Jul 71 .
In the event you do not enlist during the above period, the authority for
you to attend the course listed above is cancelled.

Please keep this letter with you until you have completed the schooling
authorized above. Should this course be discontinued for any reason
prior to the class for which you are scheduled, you will be afforded the
opportunity to select a related course or any other course for which you
are qualified and for which quotas are available.

Your application for this training indicates an initiative which should
enable you to make rapid progress in a successful Army career.

I am pleased to welcome you as a future soldier of the United States Army
and trust your period of service will be a rewarding and honorable one.

Sincerely,

MAX ENGLISH
MSG
Career Counselor

USAREC FL 24-R
REV 10 Apr 69   (PREVIOUS EDITIONS OF THIS FORM LETTER ARE OBSOLETE)

LETTER AUTHORIZING TRAINING
AS AN 81D20 MAP COMPILER

The Jodys (cadence calls) I heard in Basic rattled around in my head as I sat strapped in that cavernous fuselage of the C-5:

"They say that in the Army the food is mighty fine, but I once dropped a biscuit and killed a friend of mine...They say that in the Army the pay is mighty fine. They pay you one-hundred dollars and take back ninety nine. Sound off, one two, three four, one, two..."

Before long, I was stepping carefully down the long stair run of the huge C-5, and driven to my new duty station. Again, billeted in an open, warehouse-type barracks, I was told it would be another eight weeks before I was assigned to my duty station. Here in Belvoir, I would study my MOS in what they called AIT, Advanced Individual Training. I learned how to make maps using the latest WWII technology, like quill pens and press-on lettering, when map-making techniques in the civilian world had already encompassed such labor saving devices as Rapidiograph pens and photo-reproduction techniques (the

11

personal computer had not yet been invented). Our job would be to take land survey information and aerial photographs, rectify them, make a photomosaic, trace over the details—like roads, rail lines, rivers, airports, and bridges—and scribe them with metal tools on a plastic medium called <u>Orange Peel-Coat</u> to produce a negative flat. The titanic amounts of lettering required for a map would be typed on a desktop phototypesetting machine and then each word stuck-up with beeswax on Astralon (clear plastic sheets). These color separation layers could then be chemically etched on lithographic plates and run on offset presses to produce full-color maps. As a college graduate, with good hand-eye coordination, I finished the course at the top of my class and was promoted from Private First Class to the equivalent grade of a corporal: a Specialist Four (SP4), a non-command position. I would get a raise to $206.00 a month! My orders were cut for my PDS, the Permanent Duty Station, and I was driven, along with several others in my class, to a plane bound for Europe.

MAP COMPILING DIPLOMA
November 4th 1971

United States Army Engineer School

Be it known that

Private Donald K Kirk

is an Honor Graduate of the

Map Compiling Course

He is therefore entitled to receive this

Diploma

Given at Fort Belvoir, Virginia

this 4th *day of* Nov *19* 71

Captain, WAC, Assistant Secretary

THE BEAUTIFUL, HISTORIC HEIDELBERG
MANAGED TO AVOID BOMBING RAIDS IN WWII

ARRIVING AT THE DUTY STATION

Germany was indeed a fine place to be stationed, especially in the small 250-year-old village (population 17,000) called Schwetzingen, just fifteen minutes (about 12 km) from the beautiful old river city of Heidelberg, a city that had been spared much of the bombing in WWII. The 656th Engineer Battalion was stationed in a military complex known as Tompkins Barracks. It was built in 1937 and used as the headquarters for Nazi Field Marshal Lieutenant General Erwin Rommel in the early years of the war. His 7th Panzer Division tanks were maintained in these very garages. We called them "The Ramps" because a ship-gray boardwalk provided access to the 1940s five-ton expandable vans we worked in. Yes, WWII vintage all the way). The tank's movements were kept hidden from the Allies by driving them through a tunnel to a forest of tall pine and birch trees just outside

HEIDELBERG– A MEDIEVAL TOWN ON THE NECKAR RIVER
WITH MEANDERING COBBLESTONE STREETS

HEIDELBERG'S ORIGINAL TOWN GATE
WITH CASTLE RUINS AND BAROQUE ARCHITECTURE

"THE RAMP," HEIDELBERG SKYLINE IN THE BACKGROUND
ROMMEL'S TANKS WERE REPAIRED IN THESE VERY SHOPS

the compound where they could come out of the tunnels unseen. The compound, of course, was dressed to look like a hospital, the sacred Red Cross painted on the roofs with a few gray German ambulances parked outside. Tompkins Barracks was named after PFC George S. Tompkins of the 397th Infantry Regiment who earned the Silver Star and the Purple Heart for bravery. In the face of heavy artillery and mortar fire on the third of April 1945 near the village of Heilbronn, Germany, he refused aid for his wounds and held his exposed position allowing his comrades to withdraw, regroup, and then retake the lost ground. Private Tompkins proved that one man could make the difference between victory and defeat.

I signed in that blustery, dreary, November afternoon after a hundred kilometer ride in the back of a deuce-and-a-half (M35, 2-1/2 ton cargo truck) from RheinMain Air Base. I lugged my ninety-pound OD-green duffle bag with my newly issued clothing up the concrete stairs to a large billeting room on the second floor of building 7284. Steel-framed "cots" lined the walls, most covered with olive-drab wool blankets carefully stretched over the mattress and tucked in with "hospital corners." Battle-ship gray steel lockers, not more than a foot wide, stood between each of them with barely enough space for me to stand. My bed had an old, stained mattress on it. I had been issued two blankets, two sheets, a pillow, and a mattress

cover. I now understood the need for the mattress cover. I threw them all down on the bed and tried to squeeze my duffle into the locker because I had been warned of a high incident of theft, but no cigar, I had to stuff it under the bed, a place where I knew it wouldn't pass muster. After wiping the frost from the window and peering

out at the beautiful white snow covering the gray plastered buildings under a very low-hanging gray sky, I collapsed on the bed, still dressed in my Class-A dress uniform with an iron-cross-with-silver-wreath Army Weapons Qualifications Metal and a red National Defense Service ribbon pinned on the left pocket. A spade-shaped Specialist Four patch with a gold eagle was sewn to each sleeve.

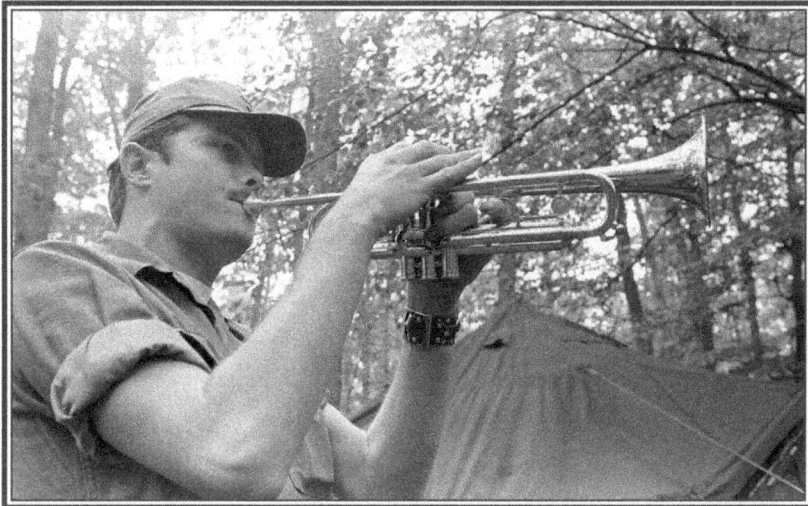

PRIVATE KAMMERMAN OF A-COMPANY BLOWING REVEILLE

Above those, a blue USAREUR patch with rainbow and firey sabre. I felt far away from home and quite lonely, but fell dead-away asleep.

THE MESS HALL

Reveille blared on a brass trumpet and a large hairy hand shook me until my brain bouncing against my skull knocked me into consciousness. "Go get breakfast, son. Formation in fifteen minutes."

I staggered to my feet, realized I was still fully dressed and was cognizant enough to ask, "Where's the chow line?"

"In the basement, follow your nose."

Yes, the chow line was as pictured in the movies. A grungy, unshaven cook—with enough dried food on his "white" apron to make anyone upchuck this early in the morning—dropped a slice of charred bread on my tin plate and slapped a ladle of creamed chipped beef over it. That must be the SOS, I thought, Mayday! Mayday!—

"Did you sign the book?"

"Huh?"

"At the door, sign it. That's how we get our allotment of food."

"Oh, I'll do it, sir."

"Don't call me, 'sir.' See them stripes on my shoulder. I work for a livin'."

"Yes, sir, I mean . . ."

"I'm Billy Wallow, I do the cookin' roun' hare. Get yoself some cow. I'll fatten your skinny ass up."

I was still skinny as a rail, even after five years at A&M, and figured nothing could ever fatten me up. I was just shy of six foot and even with baggy fatigues, I still looked as lean as a toothpick. Even my high-school acne lingered on.

I held my tin cup up to a white plastic tube that looked much like a cow's utter, and foamy white milk gushed forth. As I grabbed a set of heavy well-worn (meaning "bent every which way and that") silverware with the letters U.S. stamped on the handle, a tired-looking young man in fatigues—it was clear he had been pulling night duty—pulled me aside and said I was to take my duffle and go to the firehouse. He had one lonely stripe on his sleeve and I figured he

TOMPKINS BARRACKS–SECLUDED FROM THE WORLD

ROAD BUILDING EQUIPMENT VIEWED FROM MY WINDOW
–THE 541st ENGINEER COMPANY WAS ALSO AT TOMPKINS–

hadn't even graduated from high school, much less ever had a need to shave.

"Can I eat my breakfast first?"

"You don't want to," the clerk replied in a resolute voice and grabbed the tray from me and lay it on the table. "Come with me."

THE FIREHOUSE

I spent the next two weeks in that firehouse (located just off the quadrangle) having not yet met any of the people in my assigned photomapping platoon, not even the company commander. I spent much of the time laying on my bunk in the second floor attic, right near the brass fire pole, ready at a moment's notice for a conflagration on the post, a post so small you could see almost every building from one vantage point. On that bunk, I read John D. McDonald, Nero Wolff, Adam Hall, Rex Stout, and Perry Mason mystery novels between the wiping down of our lone WWII vintage fire engine (an engine that had probably never seen a fire), the rolling and unrolling of flat canvas hoses, and sitting around talking to the fire chief, the only other man on duty. It wasn't one of those usual shift things with twenty-four hours on and thirty-six hours off, it was just the two of us, two straight weeks on. We played some checkers and he, Gunter Schmidt, a large-framed, slightly over-weight, salt and pepper-haired man who could have passed for a U-boat commander, was more than willing to talk about his military past. He said he was a Nazi and informed me quite matter-of-factly that there was still a Nazi organization thriving underground and he was still a proud member. "Vee stash weapons, 'ave combat training. Vee 'ave units in every country of Europe, even Britain. Vee 'ave good purpose. Vee prepare for Soviet invasion. Zhey come. Mark my vord."

Christ! Chills ran up my spine. He was working for us, sitting here, living here in our fence-encircled compound.

"Vee follow Mein Kampf," he said, "Hitler not so bad, verrückt, little crazy maybe, ideas they good. Vee 'ave inflation and deflation same time, deutschmark no worth scheisse. Towelheads pouring into Deutschland, take jobs, take power from us."

He said he didn't hate us, the Americans, we were good to him; it was the British he wanted to boil in hot oil.

"I 'ave nothing for English. Zhey should die thousand deaths. Torture me, treat me like sewer scum. I 'ave no bitch with Americans, treat me vith respect. The Limeys should all go to 'ell, zoz filthy lice should be exterminated. Britain one big pile of die Kuh dung. I no talk, they no like answer, snip off der fingers."

He held up the fingers of his left hand, some finger tips were missing and a whole finger completely gone. Schmidt was apparently trying to tell me about his delightful stay in Britain during the war.

"I spend last year of vor in P.O.W. camp. I learn English zare. After vor some Germans stay in Britain. I brought up under Hitler and I volunteer at seventeen. I vas P.O.W. at age venty-three."

I kept wiping down the only engine we had as he sat in a chair eating a large #3 can of military issue peaches, no paper label, just the contents stamped in black on the lid.

"I no like Limeys, no. P.O.W. horrendous, zhay interrogate me, torture me, think I know military plans. I sergeant, no nothing. Zhay don't feed us. Not let us sleep. Extract teeth."

Hans raised his lip to show some missing teeth. I said nothing. I didn't know whether to believe a word he said—could have just lost his teeth from poor oral hygiene, but the fingers?

Klaus was on a roll, I didn't dare interrupt, "Zhay pride itself for human rights. No respect for Geneva Convention. I vas stripped necked, kicked in gut, doused with ice water, valk in circle for hours, throw down stairs."

I had just gotten to Germany and now I was fearing for my life.

Why am I here, I thought.

"Some beat senseless until beg to be killed. Say if vee complain about conditions, be made to disappear."

I was beginning to feel ill and wondered why I was put in the firehouse as soon as I had arrived at my PDS.

"Vee never get news of family or vhat is happening in home country. I no like English, never go back zhare."

"Never been there myself," I said.

"Vest talk about American prisoners in Germany and Japan, never hear vhat Limeys do to us—here you miss, clean ladder."

I moved my rag to the varnished oak ladder.

"Ever have a fire on this base?" I asked.

"Grease fire, basement building 4235, kitchen."

"How did you survive?" I asked.

"Not big fire."

"No, I mean the P.O.W. camp."

"Ah, vee vorked. Geneva Convention say can't force us to, but vas better'n' sittin' roun' camp. Vee volunteer, dig latrines, repair concertina wire, clear bomb damage."

"You followed Hitler and his ideas?"

"Yeah, I salute Hitler. Zhat is vat you did."

"You told me you are part of Nazi party now."

"No, not me. I say there is group shall rise again on zuh vings of national socialist party. I not loyal to Nazi doctrine. Vhat I speak of, everybody know."

This made my skin crawl. Upstairs I was reading a fiction novel about a Nazi treasure sunk in a Swiss lake.

"Americans give me this job. I loyal to Americans."

I wasn't so sure.

DAILY MORNING FORMATION AND ROLLCALL
(SSG TOKUHISA ORDERING OUT PF2 WADDELL)

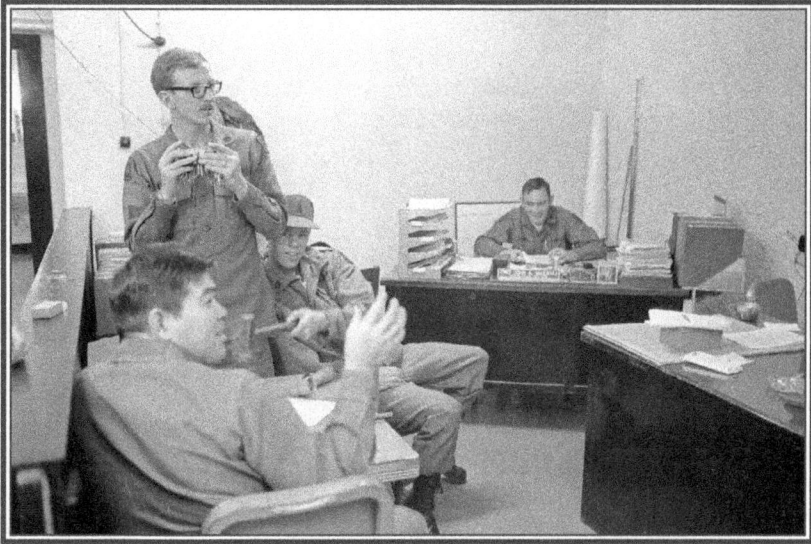

OPERATIONS—TOKUHISA, JOHNSON, EDDY, MAXWELL

THE RAMP

Two weeks in, I signed the mess log and took my burned-to-a-crisp, stone-hard, bread roll (it would qualify as Civil War hardtack) and oozing SOS to a dining table covered with a real tablecloth, though it didn't look as if it had been washed in a month. My first day back from reading ten or so paperbacks, I was shaved and dressed in clean and pressed green fatigues for my first day at the Ramp. I fell into formation, yelped a "here" when my name was called (at least I finally knew I was where I was supposed to be), then we did a little PT by double-timing it around the parade field. We then marched route-step to the place where I would be working. ("Route-stepping" was my word for the slack, slovenly marching skills of our platoon, nothing like the strack, highly motivated training we had received in the Corps of Cadets at A&M.) The I-don't-care attitude of the EM's was woefully apparent. I would soon find out my first impression of this unit was an understatement.

M292 EXPANDABLE VAN

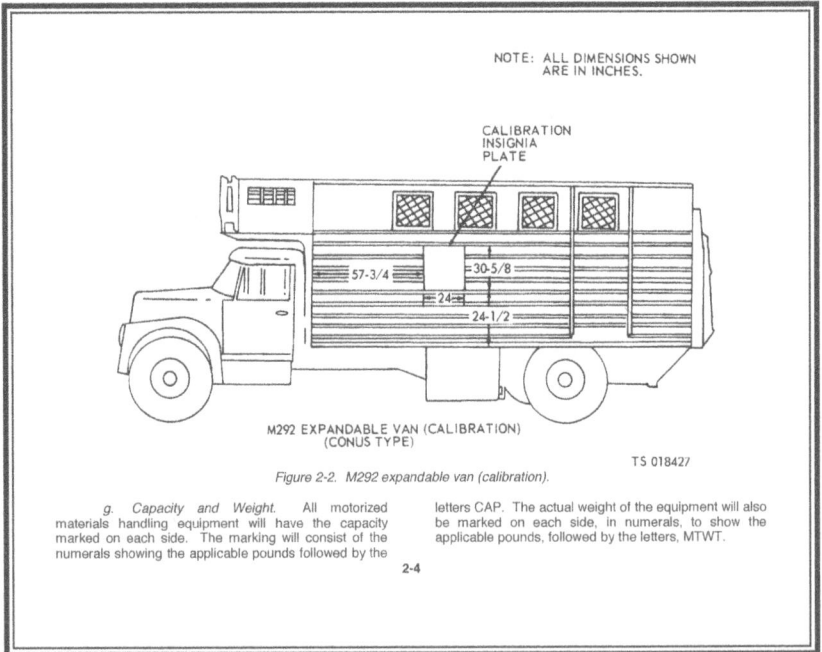

NOTE: ALL DIMENSIONS SHOWN
ARE IN INCHES.

CALIBRATION
INSIGNIA
PLATE

57-3/4   30-5/8
24
24-1/2

M292 EXPANDABLE VAN (CALIBRATION)
(CONUS TYPE)

TS 018427

Figure 2-2. M292 expandable van (calibration).

g. *Capacity and Weight.* All motorized materials handling equipment will have the capacity marked on each side. The marking will consist of the numerals showing the applicable pounds followed by the letters CAP. The actual weight of the equipment will also be marked on each side, in numerals, to show the applicable pounds, followed by the letters, MTWT.

2-4

Source: TECHNICAL BULLETIN TB 43-0147, DECEMBER 1975

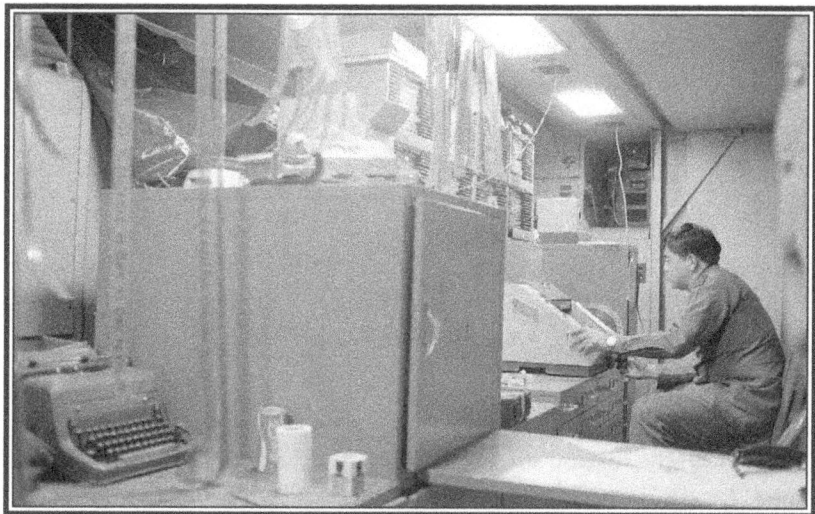

FILM-PROCESSING DARKROOM IN A VAN–TOKUHISA IN B.G.
(Frank Dulfer Photo)

It became clear we had two missions, one to make maps of potential combat areas in western Europe and two, to be ready to work
on those maps anywhere we might be sent, in other words, to be
mobile at all times. To accomplish this, we worked out of 5-ton
M292 expandable vans—heavy duel-wheeled, four-wheel-drive trucks,
painted OD-green, with sides that would crank open to provide floor
space around a central desk with all the required equipment to do our
job. Each van was a self-contained drafting room with lights, heaters, stools, drawers, and cubbyholes for all our supplies, including
those quill pens and beeswax. These vans were backed up against a
long wood walkway so the rear doors could be opened and we could
walk from one van to the next. The vans were lined up in a long row
of enclosed bays (just a very long garage any muffler shop would
love to get their hands on) in a warehouse-like building with transom
skylights and large folding doors, like you might see at an old fire
station. We had to be ready to move out at a moments notice, our

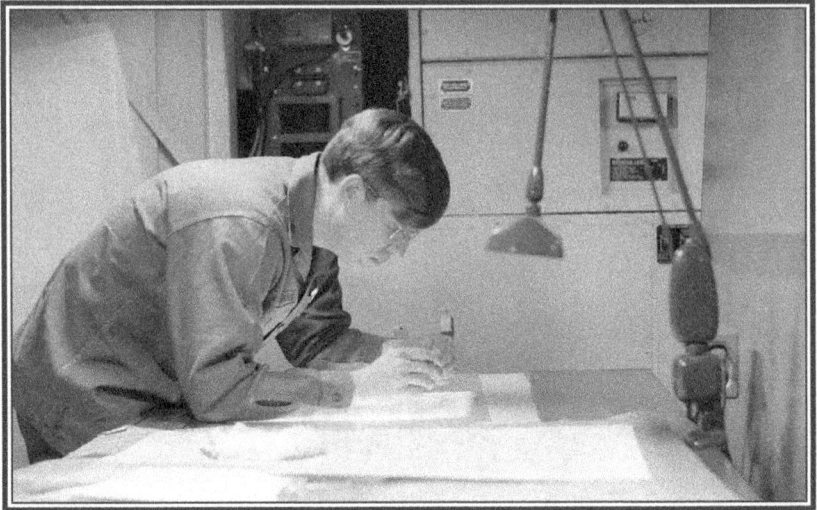

PFC VAN MALSSEN HUNCHED OVER A DRAFTING TABLE
(Frank Dulfer Photo)

vehicle's gas tanks kept full, tires checked and engines started once a week. To hit the road, all we had to do was put our work in horizontal file cabinets, push our chairs under the tables, crank the van's sides closed, drive out, and then hook up the generators and the trailers that contained our tents, field equipment, and personal duffel bags packed with clothes and personal gear.

Warrant Officer (CW2) John A. Maxwell ran the photomapping platoon in A Company. A tall, lean man who stood confident and proud, he gave orders with authority, but would remove his jacket and party with the enlisted men like one of the boys, in fact, he used to be one. He had been extremely overweight, but was loosing it at a brisk clip. It seemed that he was committed to improving himself—and getting that next promotion. Platoon Sergeant Tokuhisa—the same man I was privileged to have as my instructor at Ft. Belvoir—was the go-between, the man who's job it was to keep both the officers over him and the men under him happy, not an easy task. I was quickly assigned the job of section map editor because of the quality of my work and got a position crouched over a light table in the interior of the warehouse-like building. No windows here either, just three other tables for the editors. The operations officer's desk sat in a corner facing out so Chief Maxwell could see the goings-on while he spent his day doing paperwork. PSG Tokushia—a Hawaiian we nicknamed "Pineapple," (but we called him "Toke" to his face), had a desk next to the chief and spent his time on his feet, choreographing the day's jobs and activities. When I first arrived at the Ramp, little work was actually being done; guys listened to music on the radio (the Armed Forces Radio Network), solved crossword puzzles, and cleaned and trimmed their fingernails with a pocketknife. But, Tokuhisa—shiny black hair, powerful wrestler-like build, and always cheerful—was not a sit-and-strum-a-guitar kind of a guy. He wanted to work, wanted to accomplish something, so he and Chief Maxwell put out the word to USAREUR command that they were looking for projects to do. And projects they soon got.

SHAPE UP OR SHIP OUT

With all the new work coming in, I became Toke's "sidekick," exhibiting enthusiasm and energy that Toke would use to help get the men off their rear ends and do some real work. I would "set an example," he said, an easy assignment for me since I was born to be a workaholic. But that didn't go so well with some of the diehard goldbricks. And ironically, the men who took me to task were the college educated ones, those who where just marking time and had no career ambitions in this man's army—like myself. Within weeks, I was brought into the room of two like-minded college-student draftees that had lost their deferments and managed to get a room together, and like the M.A.S.H. characters, Hawkeye Pierce and Trapper John,

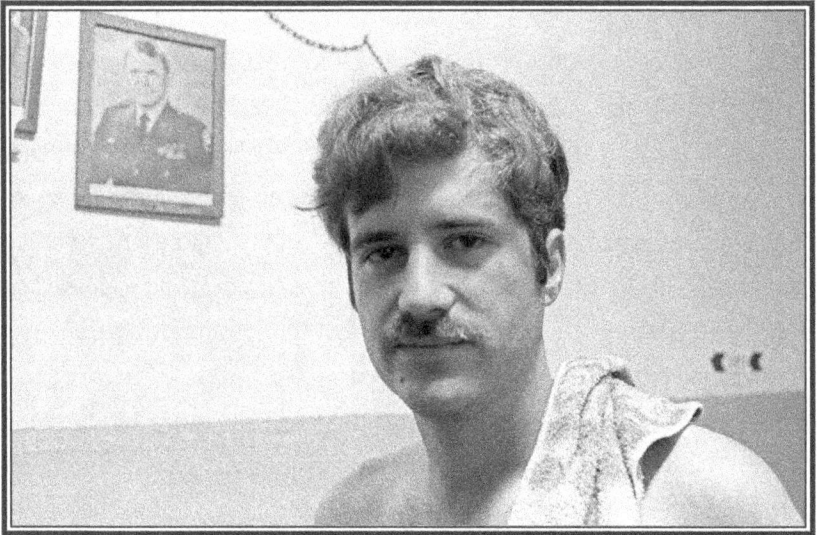

SP5 PICKLO ON THE WAY TO A 6:00 AM MORNING SHOWER

spent their evenings in their room having purchased their own coffee pot, hot plate, and refrigerator on "The Economy," trying as best they could to stay away from mess-hall food. They bought and prepared their own food and drank the best German beers and wines available. They even hung curtains on their windows! Keep in mind, this is a small barracks room with two, three or four steel bunks with O.D. green wool blankets stretched tightly on top. SP5 "Big Al" Picklo was the tall, dark-haired, good-looking ringleader (Hawkeye)—a drink always in his hand—and the light-haired, bushy-mustached SP5 "Flash" Lilburn played the part of Trapper. (Flash got his handle because of the sudden, without any warning, upchucking he did after drinking a bit too much.) Because the college educated Picklo was drafted, he oft repeated his attitude toward the army, "You can have my body, but not my mind." He had two signs over his desk in the Edit section of the Ramp: "This Office Has Eager Leavers," and "Work Like a Horse and Everybody Rides You."

"We'd like to have a heart-to-heart talk with you, Kirk," insisted Picklo as he sat me down on his bunk bed. He moved up close to me, getting squarely in my face.

"You're rocking the boat, Kirk," said Picklo matter-of-factly.

"We'd like to suggest you quit working so hard," continued Lilburn, "The enlisted men are quite upset."

"You're making them look bad," added Picklo.

I just sat there dumbfounded.

"You're screwing them around, don't you get it," said Lilburn with some intensity.

Fear was growing in my stomach—and they weren't Nazi's as far as I knew.

Picklo continued as he got up and went to the refrigerator and poured a shot of liquor, "We went to college like yourself and we know what's going on. I did the same thing when I got here, tried to work, but they straightened me out. I realized all the jobs we were

SP5 LILBURN–TWO YEARS HUNCHED OVER A LIGHT TABLE
BURNISHING PRESS-ON LETTERS FOR A SIGN, NOTHING TO EDIT
(Frank Dulfer Photo)

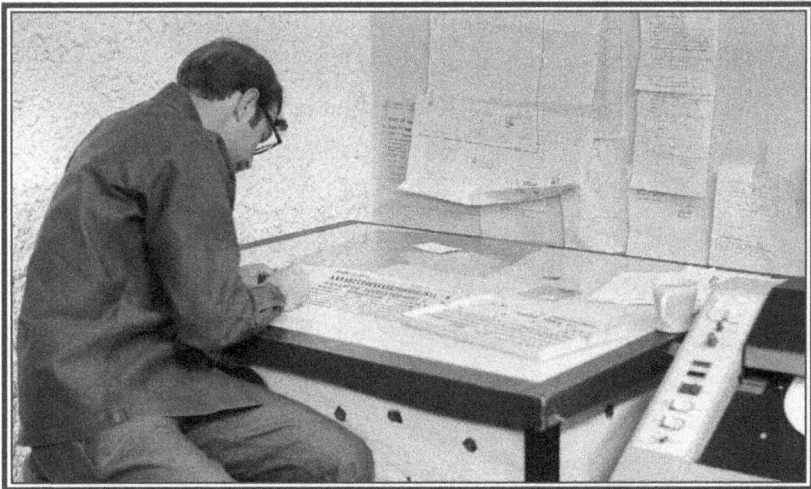

given were useless, worthless crap, no damn purpose at all. You'll see it, mapping projects just to keep us occupied."

"We're just here to stand ready in case of war with the Russians," added Lilburn.

I had heard that one before.

"What he says is true," said Picklo. We're just warm bodies to meet the NATO agreement. That's it."

"If you look into it," added Lilburn, "you'll find there's no due dates on the jobs. Why do you suppose that is?"

I just stared at them, disbelieving what was happening.

"It's simple, you have to learn to be lazy," said Picklo, "it's not that hard."

"That's gonna be your job, Kirk, understand?"

I replied in a muffled voice, "I guess so."

"You guess? Better decide what it's going to be," said Lilburn.

"You wouldn't want a late-night ride into the forest would you?" asked Picklo, "We'll strip you down, stuff you into a duffel, and leave you on the side of the road." Picklo took a sip from his glass of liquor. "Have fun trying to find your way back here, now get out, and heed what we said here tonight."

They escorted me out of the room.

That night I wrote a letter to my parents, thinking it might be my last—that I might actually be dead tomorrow. That's how scared I was.

Luckily, the trip to the woods never happened, but they tried one other thing that caught me off guard: Picklo invited me to play a game of Rugby with them. Rugby was basically tackle football with no uniform and no rules—or so I was told. Picklo rounded up about a dozen players and a pigskin. Sports were not my thing, but they didn't let me turn them down. The game got underway and I found myself getting blocked and tackled awfully hard. Thrown, flipped, landing on my face, I could see some of the guys staring at me hard and saying lets go again. I was not good at catching a football, but they seemed to want me to receive or carry the ball. I took a few more hard hits, plummeted into the dirt, and then I staggered off the field. There was a condescending smirk on Picklo's face. It wasn't until I got back to the room that a light bulb went on: They were warning me.

THE BARRACKS

We were A Company, two photomapping platoons of "map compilers,"—cartographers. The rest of our battalion included Head-quarters Company with its survey platoon, mess hall, supply, motor pool, armory, and B Company, with its reproduction (22nd) and map distribution (24th) platoons. They had trucks outfitted with heavy printing equipment, though most of our everyday printing was done at the "Base Plant" with huge Heidelberg offset presses

A HEIDELBERG OFFSET PRESS AT TOMPKINS BARRACKS

ENGINEER TOPOGRAPHIC CENTER

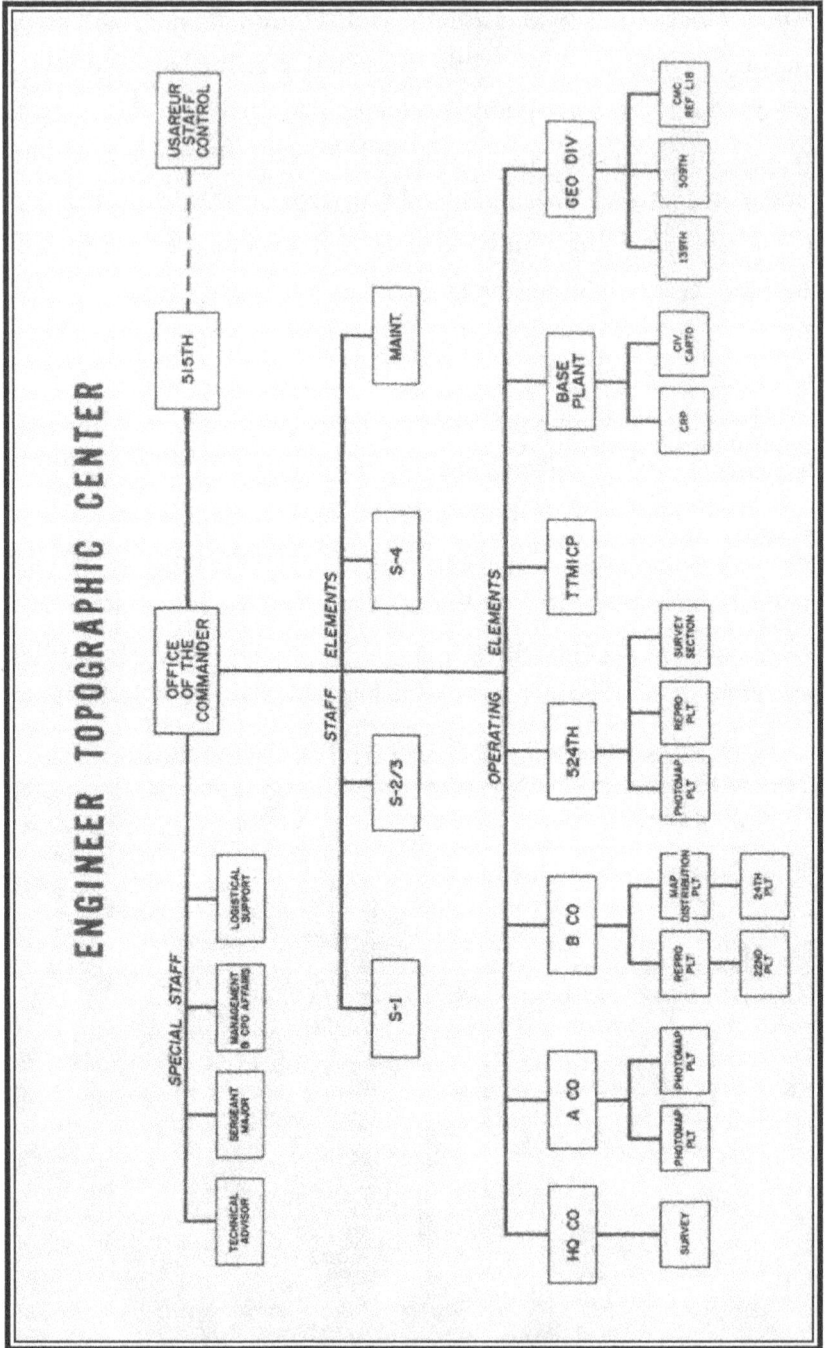

Organizational chart:

- USAREUR STAFF CONTROL
- 515TH
- OFFICE OF THE COMMANDER

SPECIAL STAFF
- TECHNICAL ADVISOR
- SERGEANT MAJOR
- MANAGEMENT & CPO AFFAIRS
- LOGISTICAL SUPPORT

STAFF ELEMENTS
- S-1
- S-2/3
- S-4
- MAINT.

OPERATING ELEMENTS
- HQ CO
  - SURVEY
- A CO
  - PHOTOMAP PLT
  - PHOTOMAP PLT
- B CO
  - REPRO PLT
    - 22ND PLT
  - MAP DISTRIBUTION PLT
    - 24TH PLT
- 524TH
  - PHOTOMAP PLT
  - REPRO PLT
  - SURVEY SECTION
- TTMICP
- BASE PLANT
  - CRP
  - CIV CARTO
- GEO DIV
  - 139TH
  - 509TH
  - CMC REF LIB

permanently located in a large warehouse space similar to ours. I noticed immediately that most of the lower-ranking enlisted men in Repro were black and all but three guys in our platoon (SGT Jesus "Randy" Easter, Willie McCrory and Junious Hayes) were white, and the "Depo Dudes" lived in large 13-man rooms at one end of our barracks while we were billeted at the other end, in the smaller two and four-man rooms. Rank, indeed, had its privileges. They used the common shower at their end; we used the one at our end. Our barracks was a large building, with a long central, noisy hall built for military troops, the floors of stone tiles etched with rows of ridges like a washboard to reduce slipping by troops running in combat boots. Wide runs of stairs ran between floors to handle large numbers of scrambling German troops loaded with guns and gear. A and B Companies were billeted on the second floor, Headquarters Company on the third. The walls were plastered and painted across the bottom half in wainscot fashion in what would become my most

WALKING THE SLIPPERY SECOND FLOOR HALLWAY
WITH COMBAT BOOTS COULD PUT YOU ON CRUTCHES

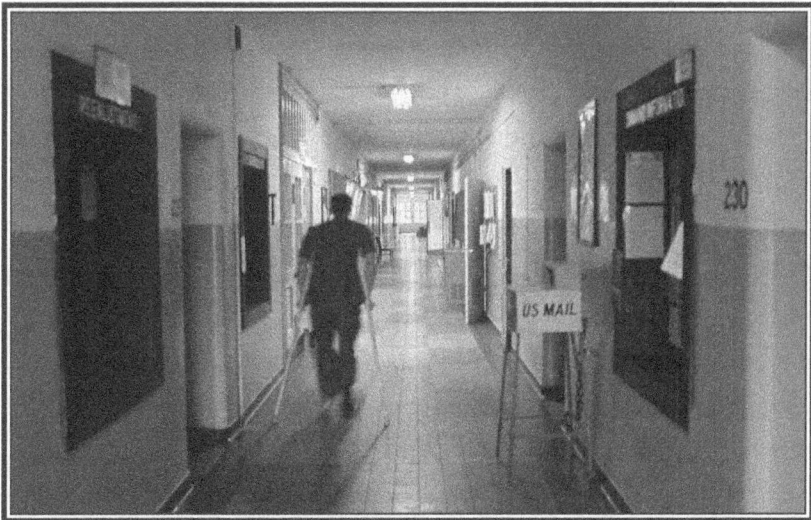

favorite color: O.D. (Olive Drab) green. The only other colors in the military supply chain were battle-ship gray and jet black. The color black was used on vehicle tires before IGs (Inspector General's inspections). The trucks were green, fatigue uniforms green, and our socks green; only the truck tires, combat boots, fatigue insignia, and the Heidelberg presses were painted black.

For the single guys living in the barracks—like myself, we had almost daily inspections of our rooms. Blankets tight with hospital corners, everything dusted down (including the tops of windows), trash cans emptied, and drawer contents neatly organized. We felt like we were still in Basic Training.

DOPE HEADS, JUICERS, AND STRAIGHTS

This was the early seventies and drug use was running rampant in the military. Hashish was the drug of choice in Germany, available on the Economy at very affordable prices. The stuff was passed around the barracks like cigarettes, and those who used it, hung together after work hours, and stayed high until formation the next day, some stayed that way all day, like fellow Texan SP4 Jim McKay who was in basic and AIT training with me. A petite, baby-faced kid, he kept his fatigues pressed and gig line straight, happy to be in the US Army (maybe the hashish just made him appear that way). A cocky sort, he sported the ugly standard military issue black-rimmed glasses known as BCGs—"Birth Control Glasses" because one could forget about getting a girl if he wore them—and tussled with his long, stringy black hair that was always falling down in his face. He smoked cigarettes like a steam locomotive on a steep grade (the army was nice enough to provide cigarettes tax free). These happy-go-lucky boys sat around in their rooms—Pink Floyd, Lead Zeppelin, or The Doors blaring (sometimes at the same time), smoke seeping from under

SP4 McKAY—ALWAYS WORE A PAIR OF DILATED EYEBALLS
(Mike Kilman Photo)

their doors—feeling as if they were Beethoven creative, strumming on a guitar and attempting to write the lyrics to a Grammy-winning song. We referred to them as the "Dope Heads."

A second group of men were tagged the "Juicers." Drug use was, of course, frowned on in the Army, but alcoholism seemed to be condoned—apparently a long-standing tradition. Some of the men, enlisted and officer alike, would spend their evenings drinking beer or hard liquor, whatever their propensity. PFC Norman "Scotty" Scott, a short, lovable, but aging, single, career man who worked in the darkroom at the Ramp developing aerial photos, was a fifteen-year veteran who wore various ranks, not necessarily in order (he'd been busted several times). He downed a fifth of gin alone in his room almost every night, and almost every morning he was late to formation—and who knows what he kept in the darkroom where he worked most of the time (maybe it was just the fixer he was drinking). He looked old for his age with graying hair and leathery skin, either

A GET TOGETHER IN FATIGUES TO WORK
(A LEADERSHIP CLASS PHOTO FOR THE BATTALION NEWSPAPER)
(Michael Lovely Photo)

A GET TOGETHER IN "CIVIES" TO DRINK
(ON LEFT: PICKLO, ODINGA. ON RIGHT: WOODBURN, SGT EDDY,
CHIEF MAXWELL AND MAXWELL'S WIFE)

from a hard outdoor life or well-fermented corn liquor. He was from Sandia, Texas and secretly kept a raccoon named "Suzy" in his room, one that he smuggled in from back home (he had declared it as a "cat" for shipping purposes). He put it outdoors in a cage when word of an inspection was rumored. Inspections were seldom a surprise: the clerk in the Company Commander's office—just down the hall on our floor of the barracks—was one of ours.

Just outside the front gate of Tompkins Barracks, the Army had provided an EM Club for enlisted men where anyone, including Germans, could hang out and drink and try to pick up German girls, an easy task since they aspired to marry "wealthy" GI's and get a ticket to the states; their most common come-on line, "I'm tipsy, can you take me home." Some GI's took them up on their offer. On weekends, the club had local live German bands playing American rock music. German youth had embraced American culture to the chagrin of the older generation. Hard acid rock, disco music, and

COMPANY COMMANDER'S OFFICE IN OUR BARRACKS
–OFFICIAL COMMUNICATIONS WENT THROUGH THIS OFFICE–

WASHING A DEUCE-AND-A-HALF AT THE "RAMP"
ACTUALLY PRODUCING MAPS WAS A SMALL PART OF OUR DAY
(LOVELY, BALCAVAGE, WOODBURN, AND WHITFIELD)

PREPARING FOR A "SURPRISE" IG INSPECTION
(AREY, TOKUHISA, AND O'NEILL CLEANING UP A 3/4-TON)

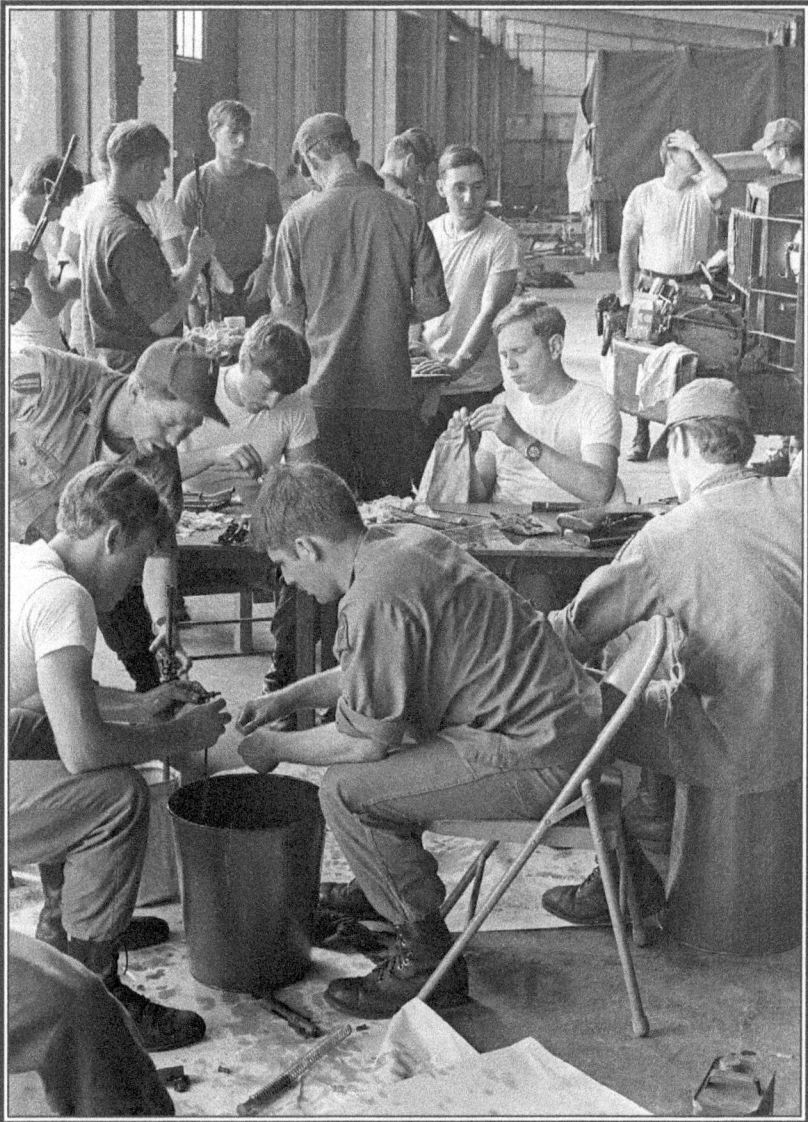

WEAPONS CLEANING AT RAMP BEFORE AN IG
(PFC WEVER TOP LEFT, AREY TOP CENTER, LOVELY BELOW AREY,
NORMAN "SCOTTY' SCOTT LEANING OVER AT LEFT CENTER)

American-style hamburgers were all the rage, though they usually had little resemblance to the real thing.

The third group that hung together, The Straights, had no use for alcohol or drugs and whiled away their free time with nightly trips to the base movie theater (the same theater where German troops were forced to watch Nazi propaganda films), or they made numerous weekend trips to the RheinMain PX (Post Exchange) to buy the latest Hi-Fi equipment and heavy metal albums. This allowed them a few hours to forget where they were, behind concertina-wire fences just

PAUL BALCAVAGE PRINTING WORDS LETTER BY LETTER ON A PHOTO TYPESETTING MACHINE TO THEN BE BURNISHED TO MYLAR SHEETS WITH BEES WAX (Frank Dulfer Photo)

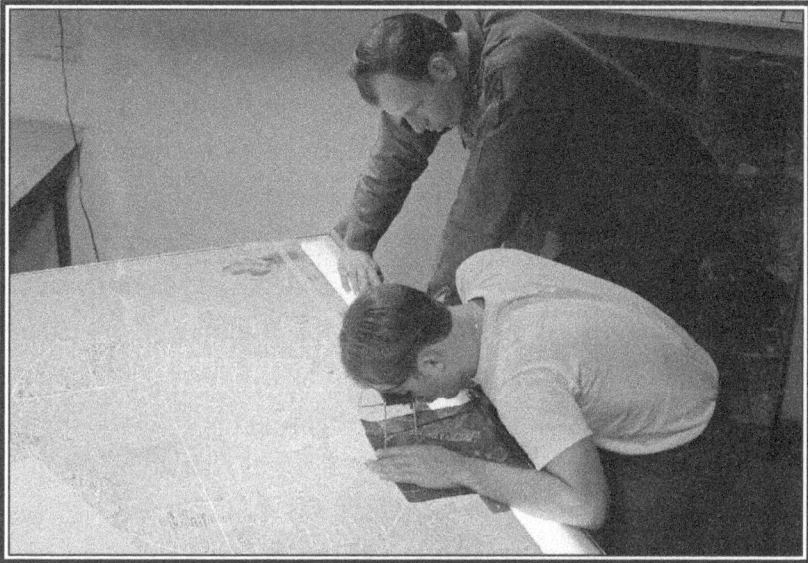

SGT BARNS AND JOHN WOODBURN WORKING
ON THE LAMPERTHEIM MAP (Frank Dulfer Photo)

like those at the military stockade. Outside that wire was a foreign country with people who spoke a foreign language. It intimidated some, like SP4 Wilkie Ross, one of many who chose to be a "barracks rat." Transferred here from the 63rd Engineer Company at Ft. Brag, North Carolina, he was suffering from what sociologists call "culture shock," afraid of what might be out there, stayed in and built a first-class stereo system at tax-free prices, while others got out and enjoyed the people and places of Germany. Some bought 35mm cameras and took photographs, some traveled, and others imbibed in the many varieties of German beer at local Gasthauses (an inn or tavern).

CRAZY, STONED, AND DRUNK

Some enlisted men were so distraught with life at Tompkins that they concocted ways to get out of the Army before their ETS (Expiration of Term of Service) date. The worst case was Private Leonard "Looney Tunes" McMurray from Headquarters Company (some called him "Wackjob") who attempted suicide on a routine basis to make the Lifers (career military men) believe he was mentally unstable in the hope they'd give him a Section 8 discharge, something between an honorable and dishonorable. Instead, they gave him routine trips to the Frankfurt military hospital where he was resuscitated, then sent to the stockade for a few months, and then, to his chagrin, hauled back to his unit. And then there was the very-small-in-stature Larry DeCamp who went AWOL (Absent Without Official Leave) when it fancied him, often not returning after a weekend pass. From time to time he'd return on his own a few days later, other times it was

FOR SOME, TOMPKINS BARRACKS FELT LIKE
A DUNGEON WITH NO WAY OUT

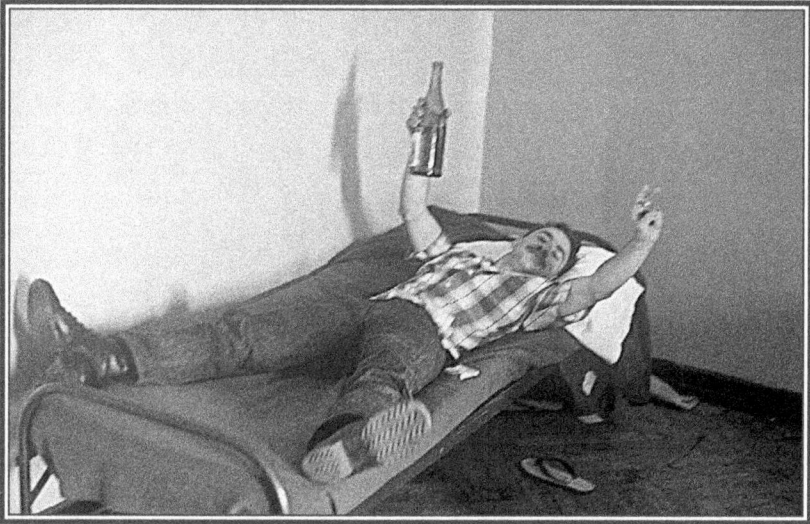

JIM "BEETLE" BAILEY WITH CIGARETTE AND BOTTLE OF <u>VINO</u>
(George Taylor Photo)

the military police that tracked him down and that would land him in the stockade. And I must mention another soldier with a few "bats in the belfray." Every free night of the week when he wasn't pulling extra duty, the "chimney smoking," Private Second Class Jim "Beetle" Bailey—who never washed his underwear, only bought new—jumped the <u>strassenbahn</u> (streetcar) to Heidelberg to make use of Germany's legalized prostitution. There were numerous government-inspected houses in Heidelberg. "Susie's" (not coincidently, a WWII name for a GI's sweetheart) was located just across from the military's AAFES (Army and Airforce Exchange Service) car concessionaire. According to PFC Floyd Wever, one of the guys in our platoon, "either place you went you got screwed." At this bordello, you could climb several floors to find the best—but most expensive—German whores. "Please come in GI, I have good favor for you." Or in Beetle's case you could choose a more expeditious—but intense—visit to one of the fine ladies driving around in their car wearing no clothes below the waist, better for you to assess the worth of their merchandise. A "knob job" was Beetle's favorite form of entertainment and he spent a considerable part of his meager paycheck on the activity. He was as Picklo said, "a real piece of work." If he wasn't in Heidelberg, he was laying on his bunk with a bottle of "Vino" (a cheap Italian Vermouth).

THE ATTIC

The barracks had a little-known fourth floor in the attic created by the steep slate roof. Stocked with burning incense, a lava lamp, black-light posters (the PX had just started selling them), and bean-bag chairs, the attic's "Dope Den"—cordoned off at one end of the building—became the living-room getaway from army life. The officers and many of the enlisted men had no idea they were up there "living it up," stoned out of their ever-lovin' minds. Always gone from their rooms, the Heads were assumed to be either at the movies or the EM club. PFC Michael Church from Headquarters Company (having a deep voice and football-player stature it seemed odd watching him write poetry), PFC Paul Balcavage, a blond wearing large-rimmed dark glasses who was always grinning and chuckling, was from a Pennsylvania mining town who volunteered for the Army even though his lottery number was 314, SP4 Kent (a slight-of-build black-haired kid with a pock-marked face), Jim McKay, of course, and the slovenly, but good-natured, Mark Hughes were some of the many who found a life up there, their motto, "never trip alone when you can do it with friends."

McKay, Church, Hughes, and Kent (and others), were in AIT at Ft. Belvoir with me, but when they got to Tompkins Barracks in December '71, they were assigned to Battalion Headquarters as there were no open slots in A-Company. (Somebody screwed up.) Even with 81D20 and 81D30 MOS's, even with promises by the higher-ups they would soon be transferred to carto, headquarters is where they stayed. They became clerk typists, runners, processed paperwork, and pulled regular after-hours CQ (Charge of Quarters) duty. That was quite disheartening to them and maybe that's what led to so many in headquarters company enjoying their evenings in the smoke-filled Dope Den.

The short, stocky, and docile Mark Hughes was a likeable high-school dropout that, encouraged by his parents to join the army hoping it could "straighten him out" (and allow him to get his G.E.D.), had an impressionable mind who suddenly became a born-again Christian after hanging out with a group of strange German teens in Heidelberg. Always wearing sloppy, wrinkled fatigues and a peace sign on his dog-tag chain made of wire soldered together, Hughes had finally found himself—and his influential peers, the Heads. He hung out with them and discussed religion—the religion you got from smoking pot.

MARK HUGHES—TOO IMPRESSIONABLE FOR THIS MAN'S ARMY

NO ONE WAS NORMAL

Troops came to work with hangovers and Hashish highs, but it really didn't matter much, the jobs we were assigned seemed to be just "make work," like digging holes and filling them back up. Picklo had been right. The <u>Lampertheim</u> map, as one example, was there when I came, and it was there when I left three years later, a map requested by some Colonel (long since rotated back to the states) that mapped the area we used for FTXs (Field Training Exercises). It was just a forest with a shooting range and a few dirt roads and it was rumored that he was planning to turn it into a golf course. Then there was the bus-route map requested by some general for his wife because she kept getting lost on the Economy. That map wound its way slowly, very slowly, through the system to finally get printed <u>after</u> she had returned to the states, never resolving her issues with riding the never-on-schedule, green military shuttle busses provided for G.I.'s in Germany. I suspect she would have painted the busses some other color, maybe pink, if she had had the pull.

Then there was John "Woody" Woodburn, a short sandy-haired kid, who had the biggest grin you ever saw. He drank only "Coke" and always wore a leather sun visor with the name "Maggie" stamped on the visor. Many thought it was the song "Maggie" sung by Rod Stewart, but it turned out to be another favorite of his: his high school

JOHN WOODBURN AND "MAGGIE"

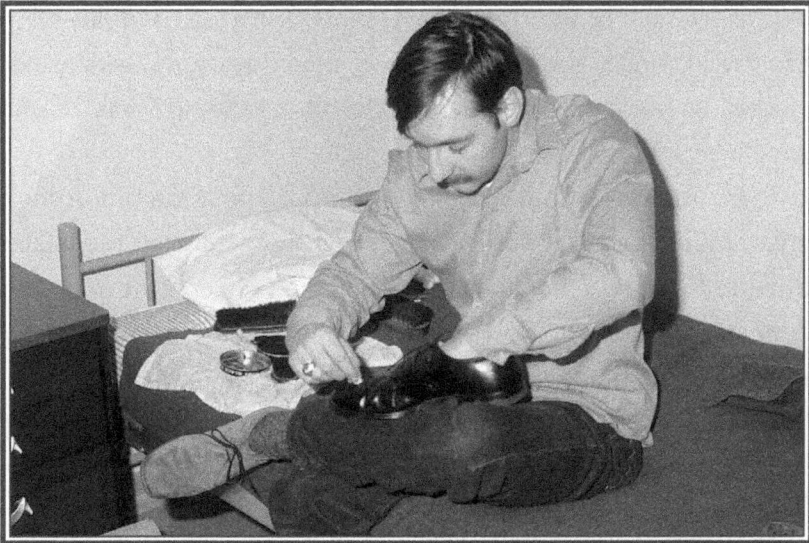

POSSUM SHIT SPIT-POLISHING HIS SHOES (Frank Dulfer Photo)

sweetheart, Maggie Wolf! But then again, if lovesick, maybe it was both: "<u>Wakeup Maggie, I've got something to say to you...you stole my heart and that's what really hurt.</u>" He also liked Jim Croche and the Moody Blues of "Tuesday Morning" and "Nights in White Satin" fame. Woody came to me one day and asked if I could approve one of the scribed lines representing roads he had added to the <u>Lampertheim</u> map. The road was not on the aerial photographs, but with it included on the map, he said, "The crisscrossing roads would read as a mighty good 'FTA' (F— The Army) and wouldn't chap the Army's ass!" In other words, they'd never catch it, but <u>we'd</u> know. Woody cracked a sly grin. Woody had volunteered for the army in hopes of a fine career, but now, because of the mismanaged Mickey Mouse unit we were in, he felt he had been betrayed. This was not the Army his military father had talked so fondly about. (His father, a master sergeant, spent WWII in Mannheim, Germany running a supply depot.) He was just marking time, counting his days to calling out "short," and he was considerably more than a year from his ETS. He was like in the lame-duck years of a presidency. He played tag-football on weekends with some of the other jocks, and was a damn good wide receiver.

And then there was Kenneth Arey, a pale-looking kid with stringy, grease-soaked hair and a slight build, who came from the mountains of Appalachia, and would have been completely content if he had been assigned permanent KP (Kitchen Police) duty peeling potatoes all day and scrubbing heavy pots and pans all evening with steel-wool that would turn his hands red and raw. I'm sure he would be happy cleaning out grease traps and mopping and waxing the red quarry-tile floors until he could see in them his opossum face. Yes, we lovingly called him "Possum Shit." With crooked teeth in his Cheshire grin, he joyfully scurried around like Army was heaven on earth, and for him, it probably was. He was not the smartest kid on the block, at least it wasn't apparent on the surface, but he was a hard worker, honest and trustworthy, faithful to a fault. It wouldn't surprise me if

A CHIPPER KENNETH "POSSUM SHIT" AREY

he became a nuclear physicist. On the other hand, he was the only soldier in our mapping platoon that never could comprehend the half-tone dots gag. You see, the FNG's (F—g New Guys) in the platoon would be asked to go to the Repro platoon in B Company and pick up a box of half-tone dots, and while over there, he would be sent from one NCO to another, until one of the men gave him a box full of black and white dots from a hole punch. He'd bring the box back, and the whole platoon would be laughing their asses off. One of the "Old Timers" would finally explain to him that half-tone dots was the screen on a printed photograph that created the illusion of shades of gray even though only black ink was used. Well, Possum spent a lot of time looking through a loop at photographs trying to figure out how the big black and white punch-outs he brought back from Repro were used to create a photograph! Possum and Woody had the same job, scratching roads and symbols on orange peel-coat, but Woody was meticulous at his job whilst Possum Shit scribbled lines in much the same way he must have walked the ridges of Appalachia.

And, oh yes, there was "Damnit" Hammit. I don't remember his real first name— "Dumber than a Chicken" Hammit maybe—was one of those guys who was always screwing up, hence the handle. He was as gullible as the businessman who bought the Eiffel Tower because a conman said the government was selling it for scrap metal. Gullible kind of like Ken Arey, but even Possum Shit wouldn't have fallen for this gag. On one fine spring morning, SP5 Glenn "Tommy Turtle" O'Neill (one of the guys in carto) and some of the other guys, got Damnit to go out to the truck bay at the ramp and change the winter air for summer air in the truck tires. And so, the air compressor went to humming. Damnit went to filling the tires before he asked, "O'Neill, you sure about this, all these trucks, I sure could use some help?"

TOM "AIRBORNE" GILBERT BACK FROM VIETNAM

Tommy Turtle replied, trying hard not to split a gut, "Everyone else has other duties, Hammit. Do your part."

It took Damnit the whole afternoon, what with a dozen or so trucks, some with duel wheels.

THE AIRBORNE RANGER

One of the second-termers (or maybe it was his third re-enlistment) in our platoon (for some reason, many retreads were assigned to our unit) was SP5 Tom "Airborne" Gilbert, a gung-ho Airborne Ranger, who wore starched fatigues and custom-made, patent-leather combat boots every day of the year, including to New Year's Eve parties. He was married to a pretty redhead and lived off post and thought he was better than everyone else because he had the "cojones" to jump out of a perfectly good airplane. He looked down on the "Legs" whom he felt were too chicken to do the same. We wondered what he was doing here and not in Nam (It turns out he had been). But he didn't have the knack for scribing tools either, not an ounce of artistic talent or a steady hand. He told me he had written on his enlistment application that he was a "painter." The army didn't know he meant "house painter" and thus assigned him to this unit, one requiring at least some artistic abilities. He carried a silver flask of hard liquor in his shirt pocket at all times to keep him warm and feisty. He barked orders with slurred speech and you could often smell the liquor on his breath. They eventually promoted him to an E-6 so he wouldn't have to draw anymore, a cost benefit to the army because his work was always requiring constant revision. I, being an editor, had to use a lot of red pencil on his work, and red pencils were in short supply.

NEW BATTALION COMMANDER

Our Engineer Battalion was assigned a new commander in February of 1972. I had only been there a few months. An elaborate change of command ceremony transferred the 656th to Lieutenant Colonel Richard E. Williamson.

"At ease men."

In the heated Tompkins gymnasium—snow was on the ground outside—three large company formations witnessed the event. Many "dignitaries" came to the event in their pressed Class-A uniforms with a plethora of colorful ribbons. Even the Burgermeister (Mayor) of Schwetzingen was present. The new commander stood at attention, the former, LTC Brown, snickering and whispering something to the new man after he was handed the unit colors. Finally, Williamson stood before us to speak:

"As I take command of the 656th Engineer Battalion I wish to commend the unit for its fine record. All of you who have served with this unit can be justly proud of your accomplishments and the reputation you have earned for your unit."

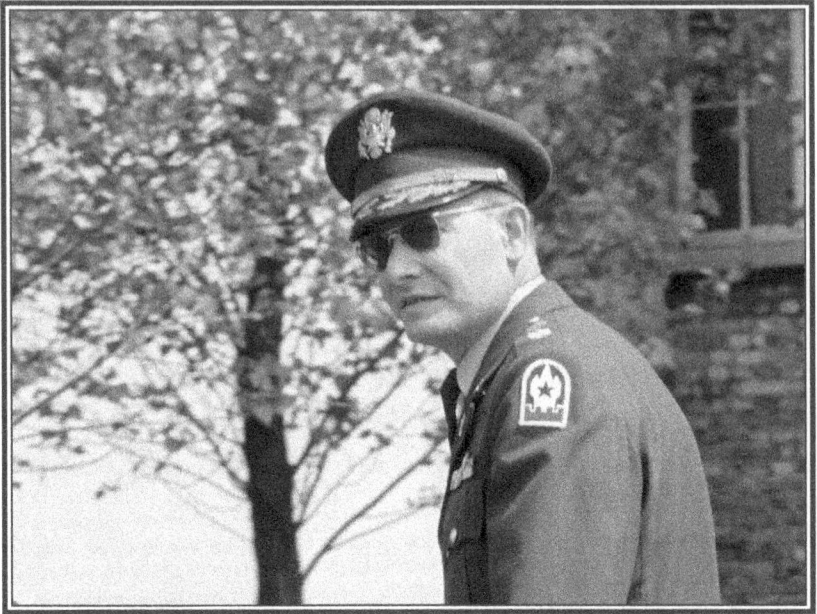

"TAKE NO PRISONERS" COLONEL WILLIAMSON

I barfed. The Colonel continued:

"I can assure you that fiscal year 1973 will be a big year for all of us and I'm sure it will present many new challenges. I'm equally sure that all of you will be up to those challenges and contribute greatly to this unit's mission..."

I barfed again. What was our mission I wondered?

"...Remember, this is your battalion and it is the members—that's you—who make it the great unit that it is."

Oh please. Well, we did have clean latrines and white rocks.

"I'm certainly looking forward to serving with you and being a part of your organization."

At that he shook a few hands and left the podium. The 33rd Army Band struck up a rousing military medley as we quietly marched back to our work areas.

ALERT-DRIVER DUTY

Everyone had additional duty assignments, like pulling guard duty, manning the phone in the clerks office after hours, sitting as a door guard, waxing floors, cleaning latrines, scrubbing the washboard hallways with a toothbrush, mowing the grass, washing vehicles, or digging out grass from between cobblestones with a butter knife, but in less than six months, I was put on the Staff Duty-Driver Roster and assigned the "cush" job of Alert Driver and was removed from most other extra-duty rosters. Pineapple gave it to me as a "benny" for my good work, but ready to take the responsibility away if I faltered. "Big Al" Picklo and "Flash" Lilburn had the job for a long time, of course, always finding ways to get out of extra duties so they could stay in their room to savor a hot cappuccino. Glenn O'Neill, a fellow Texan of short stature from Bryan (home of my alma mater), was also assigned the light duty. He was a conscientious guy who loved

GLENN O'NEILL AND HIS ASSIGNED 3/4-TON

country music and loved working on his old, faded-black Volkswagen Beetle he had bought while in Germany. Dressing sharp and squared away, but loving to have grease on his hands, he was assigned driver of the company commander's 3/4-ton and took it on himself to keep it in tip-top shape. He even made a large nameplate to put on the front grill of the truck with the words "DRIVER: GLENN O'NEILL" and bookended it with a Texas "Lone Star" flag and the "Red, White and Blue." He was proud of his home state and he was proud of the Army. His motto, "Through rain, sleet, or snow, truck on." O'Neill was a Canadian citizen adopted by an American couple, but that didn't stop our government from sending him a draft notice. Testing by the army recruiter showed he had mechanical aptitude and thus the recruiter suggested he could be a helicopter mechanic. "You could become airmobile in a Huey; wouldn't you like that, Glenn?" The recruiter then added, "But you can <u>avoid</u> Nam altogether if you

O'NEILL REPAINTING A HEADQUARTERS SIGN
IN PREPARATION FOR AN IG, BEING VERY CAREFUL
NOT TO GET PAINT ON HIS STARCHED FATIGUES

O'NEILL IN HIS 3/4 TON COMMAND VEHICLE
–"THROUGH RAIN, SLEET, OR SNOW, TRUCK ON"–

THE TASK OF AN ALERT DRIVER:
NAVIGATE A MILITARY VEHICLE THROUGH NARROW STREETS
TO FIND AN ADDRESS LATE AT NIGHT

sign up for a three-year hitch. Now there's a deal!" Sound familiar? He was a mechanical draftsman at the time and figured drafting was drafting—and being drafted to draft wasn't altogether so bad—and signed up for 81 Charlie.

Some of the members of our platoon were married and lived off the base "on the Economy" and if we received a call to move out, someone had to take the staff duty vehicle, a 3/4-ton, and pickup those soldiers. Our entire battalion was given just two hours to mobilize a multitude of trucks, equipment, and troops. The great part of the job was that being on call for a 24-hour period maybe twice a week just meant staying in the barracks and not going to the movies or EM club; I just had to be prepared to make the run at a moments notice. I wasn't assigned any extra duties like sitting guard at the door or cleaning the latrine. The problem was that I didn't—thanks to the laid-back Big Al and Flash—get enough rehearsals to know what route to take through the winding cobblestone streets of the surrounding villages to find our off-post troops. And when the order to move out was called (it always seemed to happen at night, a cold, foggy night) I found myself driving alone without a map looking for street names and buildings that all looked the same under very few street lights. I had to jump out at each apartment to bang on the door and then try to get them to move faster as I had to take them with me if they didn't have their own way to get back to the post. It made for a stressful two hours, and if any of the troops on your route didn't make it in, it was on you. On one of my few rehearsal trips with Big Al one afternoon, I saw my Nazi fire-chief buddy, Gunter Schmidt conversing with Sergeant Billy Wallow beside a canvas covered deuce loaded with wooden crates stenciled with black military lettering. I didn't make much of it, just wondered what they were doing together. It would take on a whole new meaning later.

STAFF SERGEANT FOSKEY

A unit's reenlistment NCO would do anything to get a man to re-enlist (almost as bad as the hometown recruiter), not just a nice lump sum for another year of distinguished service and maybe a monthly pay increase but, well, they would sweeten the pot with anything that might get you signed up for their new "Modern Volunteer Army." Staff Sergeant Foskey, our reenlistment NCO—a black dude assigned to Headquarters Company—was putting these ads in our Topo Topics unit newsletter, laid out like ads for real estate:

"MOS Producing School: Tired of your present job? Too routine? Same old thing, day in, day out? Pick your school: computers, ships, aircraft or any of 400 other jobs! Just let me know and I'll send you there."

"Conus Station of Choice: Tired of touring Europe? Fed up with Brat Wurst and Sauerkraut? Get choice, not chance. Why wait and be sent some place you don't want."

"Overseas Area: Want a change of scenery? Can't speak the Deutsch? Name a country: England, Italy, Japan, Okinawa, Korea, Thailand! Only one year in the command required."

"Republic of Vietnam: This is it! Land of sandy beaches, swaying palm trees and almond-eyed girls. This may be your last chance, so you better hurry. Qualifications? Just be eligible for reenlistment. Don't wait around; see me now before it's too late."

"Special Forces: For you who are more than normal men and have that something extra. Here's a rugged experience for you outdoor types. Not only the glamour and excitement of Airborne, but much, much more. Only limited vacancies available so you better grab this deal quick!"

Yes, these ads were for real. And if you really didn't want to go anywhere, Foskey had that covered too:

"Present Duty Assignment: Stay with your friends. Why move around? You know your unit needs every man on the job. Your job helps make the unit. Stay with a great unit with a great future."

Give me a break! It made me retch.

THE UNIT NEWSLETTER

We had a unit newsletter called Topo Topics that was published about once a month. In an 8-1/2 x 11 inch letter-size format with eight pages, the newsletter typically included official activities at the post, including the photos of troops promoted or graduating from various leadership-training classes. Repro would print the paper between map printing jobs and it was distributed to all members of the battalion and a few copies went up the chain of command. Even The Overseas Weekly and the Stars and Stripes were sent a copy. When the editor, SP4 Fred Demers, rotated out, they needed someone to replace him, and guess who they came to? Yes, little old me— something extra for me to

TOPO TOPICS

NEW CO SAYS HI PAGE 3
9 DAY FTX PHOTO SPECIAL pages 4-7
CHANGE OF COMMAND-ETC page 3

TOPO TOPICS

VOL.8. NO.12   SCHWETZINGEN, GERMANY   SEPT 1972

do in my spare time—but I agreed, and took on the job which turned out to have a staff of one, me, and any "reporters" I could shake out of the trees to write something. With a little begging (the persuasive form of leadership) I surprisingly got a wealth of contributors to write stories and take photographs. They gave me office space in the headquarters building to write up the articles on a manual typewriter and lay out the paste-up mechanicals. I used the <u>Kasern's</u> darkroom to print the black & white photos. Master Sergeant "Top" Tadakuma, SSG Young, SSG Eddy, SSG Mahan, Lt. Sneed, Captain Porr, PFC Kilman, O'Connell (our cartoonist), PFC Frank "Cockbite" Dulfer, and others were regular contributors. Cockbite was my best reporter. A bushy-mustached go-getter from Hoboken, New Jersey, he wrote poetry, news articles, and shot and developed his own photography. Dulfer got his handle because he went around calling <u>everyone else</u> "cockbite." He had extraordinary skills. Bic lighters were a new thing in the 1970's and Cockbite got hold of one and found it

MY LARGE FORMAT TOPO TOPICS

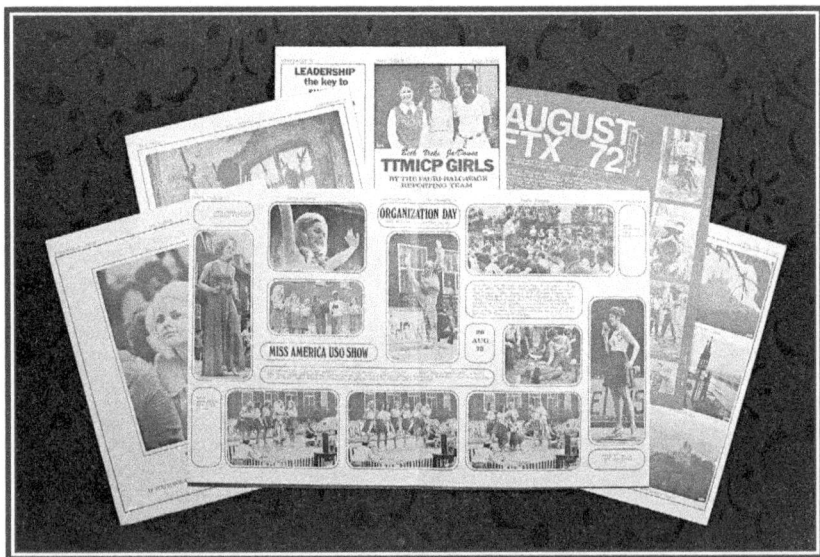

a hoot to light up the armpits of fellow soldiers wearing T-shirts and stretched out over their drafting tables. Frank pulled silly, frat-house shenanigans and acted as if he was retarded (though some questioned whether it was acting). He behaved in a loony, goofy way, and spoke with sarcastic jibes (more like comical irony). With a stiff, contorted upper lip, he would tilt his head and say in a retarded voice, "I-know-you!" We thought maybe the army was having a hard time meeting its quota. Late at night in his barracks room he would work on a plastic model of a military tank. What did it mean, no one knew (maybe he was sniffing the glue). He was kind of a dorky dufus, but lovable kind of guy (if you didn't hang around him for too long a stretch). He could put his entire fist in his oral sphincter, hold it there, and still take a swig from a bottle of beer. I called him "Widemouth" and after that he tried adding a German hamburger to his oral repertoire. He had that strong New Jersey accent sounding as if his mouth was full of marbles—maybe it actually was, he had the mouth for them.

Cockbite said he was born the sixth child of a poor Dutch family. He said, "I grew up with splinters in my ass. My father kicked it often with his wooden shoes." He said he was not a studious kid and barely made it through grammar school and high school (said he was on the high school swim team where he swam like a rock, but in kindergarten he actually graduated "Summa Cum Crayon." He managed to waste two semesters of college, so with very poor attendance, he quickly won a ticket to ride in an O.D.-green military vehicle. We figured Cockbite—who was probably voted class clown in high school—would probably still win if a vote was taken at The Ramp.

For Topo Topics, Captain Posy Lough, Information Officer in Battalion Headquarters, was assigned to oversee my work. As a lean, thirty-year old athlete who had competed in the 1968 Olympics in Mexico in the Modern Pentathlon event, he was often seen running

CAPTAIN POSY LOUGH

around the quad in his red-white-and-blue Olympic sweats, a big white "USA" lettered on his chest. He took the time to edit my work and contributed his own articles.

The official "Armed Forces Newspaper Guide (DA PAM 360-533) said, "A Service newspaper plays a vital role. Like its commercial counterpart, the Service paper is a direct reflection of the people who produce it and the command it serves. It also reveals the skill, initiative and devotion of the men and women who create reader interest through good news writing and editing." With my capable reporters, I felt this paper was going to prove that, and I strived to make it so.

I tried for a monthly distribution cycle, but that didn't work out and a quarterly issue was the best I could put out. To live up to "The Newspapers Role," I changed the format, made the paper much larger, 11 by 14 inches, and dropped most of

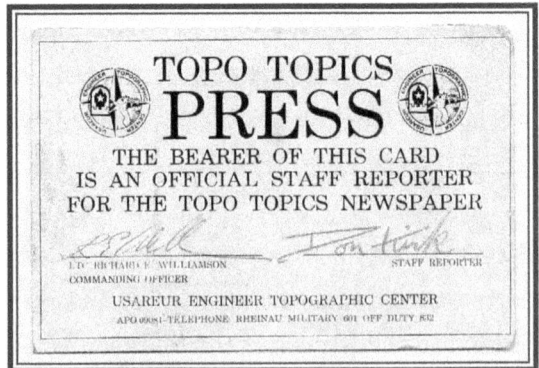

TOPO TOPICS
PRESS
THE BEARER OF THIS CARD
IS AN OFFICIAL STAFF REPORTER
FOR THE TOPO TOPICS NEWSPAPER

LTC RICHARD E. WILLIAMSON
COMMANDING OFFICER

STAFF REPORTER

USAREUR ENGINEER TOPOGRAPHIC CENTER
APO 09081 TELEPHONE RHEINAU MILITARY 601 OFF DUTY 832

the boring, stale official news and instead included travel stories, letters to the editor (often EM complaints), recreational activities, and instructional articles like tips on how to play better billiards. Yes, the Battalion had a recreation room with a pool table and even a ninepin bowling alley left over from Rommel's command. The new format

PAGE EIGHTEEN   TOPO TOPICS   SEPTEMBER 72

Pocket Billiards

Billiards is a fascinating and thoroughly demanding game that can be as exacting as chess and as rewarding as climbing the Matterhorn. The qualities which produce astronauts and jet pilots are also characteristic of the good billiard player. Both activities require a spirit of competition, the will to excell and to win, providing the thrill of executing a maneuver and of hitting a target, and put a premium on the ability to foresee difficulties, on the exercise of good judgment and on the ability to perform under duress with maximum of self-control. On the physical side, both jet pilots and billiard players need good general health, good muscular coordination, good eyesight, and a good sense of equilibrium. With the winter coming on everyone will be moving inside, many of them to rest their fingers on that green felt. So, we present here the first in a series of "trade secrets" that you may have forgotten. If practiced, it will improve your game.

Most people forget that the balls are round! The player must understand the principle of the CONTACT POINT and the POINT OF AIM. Because of the curvature of the balls, the side of the object ball nearest you and the farther side of the cue ball do not contact as you might suspect by sighting through the center of the cue ball and aiming at a point on one side or the other of the first object ball.

IN figure ONE, a line drawn from the center of the pocket through the center of ball "b" and continuing in a straight line indicates the spot on ball "a" to CONTACT with the cue ball.

In figure TWO, you can see what not to do. Generally, in lining up a shot and looking at it from down the table through the cue ball and into the object ball, the front curvature of the object ball and the forward curvature of the cue ball are overlooked, and the player shoots by aiming through the center of the cue ball at a desired spot on the object ball. This is no go.

Figure THREE, shows the right way to do it. Make allowance for the curvature of the outer edges so that the contact points of the cue ball and the object ball meet. Got it?

Study the illustrations and practice and you'll have it....right in the pocket where it belongs!

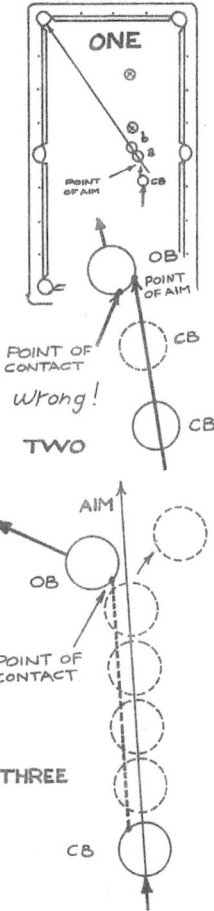

SHADA'S GRIDIRON

It's that time of year when the people start packing the stadiums to watch their college team in action.

This year the race for NO. ONE will be much closer and more exciting than ever. Every Big Eight team says they'll be ready for the National Champions: the Nebraska Cornhuskers. If everything goes right for the Big Red one, they should have the championship for the third year in a row. No other team has ever done this before.

Here is how the season will probably stack up.

1) Nebraska	6)	Tennessee
2) Oklahoma	7)	Southern Cal.
3) Michigan	8)	Washington
4) Ohio State	9)	Texas
5) Alabama	10)	UCLA

PROMOTIONS

The following enlisted men were promoted to their present rank this month:

SSG Johnson	SP5 Odinga
SSG Eddy	SP5 Fisher
SSG Bauer	

PFC Dulfer of B Co. was the soldier of the fourth quarter, FY 72. SP4 Drummond of HHC was the Soldier of the Month of August 72.

"Problems worthy of attack prove their worth by hitting back."
-Piet Hein-

ENTERTAINMENT IN A MILITARY PUBLICATION
A BIG CONTENT CHANGE FOR TOPO TOPICS

and selection of articles drew cheers from the troops—they actually were reading the thing—and battalion headquarters seemed happy. Even Repro enjoyed printing the paper, but it was soon to be one more thing to turn me adamantly against the military.

GUARD DUTY

It was my turn to pull 24-hour battalion-level guard duty, and dressed in my newest, best-pressed fatigues (and that wasn't saying much, even my best pair looked wrinkled) and scuffed, but polished combat boots, I collected my cartridge belt and M16A1, serial No. 4075237, from the arms room, surrendered my laminated weapons receipt and reported to the post MP headquarters billeting room. Rows of bunk beds lined the walls of a small sultry room near the front gate

MY WEAPONS CARD

of Tompkins. Men were sleeping here and there, fully dressed in fatigues, laying on top of a green wool blanket, their spit-shined boots hanging off the ends of the beds. Some were snoring and some were staring at the ceiling unable to sleep because of the constant commotion of duty personnel coming and going at all hours. 24-hour shifts were the norm, on and off duty at two-hour intervals. It really meant no sleep in that 24-hours unless you were good at catnapping. SP4 McKay, the Dope Head who was always trying to make up for his slight stature, had been transferred from RML (Repro Map Library) and given a black armband with "MP" printed on it in white. He was also given a loaded pistol. The work at RML hadn't been his cup of tea and he finagled a transfer. He loved playing with guns (played with a pair of <u>Dale Evans</u> cap guns in his youth), and besides, he had an easier access to his drug-using MP buddies and the Hashish dealers. An MP on duty at the gate at night could "trade" with the Germans without drawing attention to themselves.

"You buddied with me tonight?" I asked him.

"No Kirk, I've been pulled from the guard shack to pick up an Article 32 from the stockade and take him to Frankfurt for a preliminary hearing for a General Courts Martial." He fingered his holstered pistol as he said this, and spoke in a condescending way; he was now part of the "elite" and it didn't matter now if he had to look up at everyone, his gun was the equalizer.

"You know where they're sending me?" I asked.

"The duty roster puts you with PFC Hughes at the ammo dump. Been some attempted break-ins lately."

"Is that right?"

"That's right. You better be on your toes."—He looked me over— "I think I need to loan you my ironing board."

"Never used an iron in my life," I replied, "don't intend to start now. Got one for high school graduation, never used it in college."

"It shows."

"I'm not trying to brown nose anyone," I replied as I tilted my nose high and looked at his.

"What a trip man, <u>deja vue</u>!"

"What?"

"Just a flashback." He turned smartly and marched down the isle, his boots blinding me, the click of his heels irritating me to the core.

My shift began with night duty that sent Mark Hughes and myself to guard an old (inactive?) ammunitions dump a few miles down the road. On the inside of the concertina-topped chain-link fence was a dirt jeep road and we were assigned to walk the perimeter in two-hour shifts. They locked us inside the fence and gave us a sign and countersign and told us to follow the General Orders if anyone tried to enter, including anyone claiming to be an officer. It was dark, freezing, a foot of snow covered the ground, and wolves howled from the woods beyond (or so we imagined). We walked separately in opposite directions and were told to vary our pace so anyone watching us couldn't time our laps. We carried our M-16's over our shoulder, but had no shells in them and none in our cartridge pouches (they were used for candy bars). The brass figured it wasn't safe for us to carry ammunition seeing as how there were so many stoned GI's running about. Two hours was a long time talking to oneself and staring into the shadows looking for trouble. I tried to remember my three General Orders. I will guard everything within the limits of my post and quit my post only when properly relieved. I will obey my special orders and and...oh hell, I can't ever remember them. What's the use? Oh, the fourth, I remember that one, the Fourth General order, sir, to walk my post from flank to flank and take no shit from any rank. That's what it said, don't trust anyone claiming to be an officer.

When I met Hughes on each lap, we'd stop for a moment to bitch about something. I would've borrowed a match like the German guards in WWII movies, but I didn't smoke. Instead we traded candy bars and wondered why the black-plastic rifle stock of our M16 was labeled "MADE BY MATTEL." Was this rifle just a toy? The Colt rifle was actually made of an aluminum alloy and a tough glass-reinforced plastic known as "Armalite," where the letters "AR" came from as in AR-15. (It did not mean "Assault Rife.") It had a 30-round magazine using 5.56mm center-fire cartridges. I walked on, in a half stupor, repeating to myself: "This is my rifle, this is my gun, this is

TROOPS ON THE WAY TO GUARD DUTY STATIONS

for fighting, this is for fun." I grabbed my crotch. It itched.

Every two hours we were relieved by another two guards and were driven back to the post for two more hours of sleep. On this schedule, you would think we could get a good twelve hours of sleep. Ha, no way, that two-hours-on, two-hours-off crap meant two hours at the duty station and another half hour or more spent getting up and traveling each way.

When I got back to the guardhouse, the word got around that an Article 32 had made an escape from the stockade and was loose on the Economy and his name was our very own AWOL expert, Larry DeCamp, from B Company. Apparently he had made his break during the exchange from the stockade to McKay and a supervising lieutenant. Luckily, no one was shot.

"Hey, McKay, how's your prisoner?"

"That's <u>Spec Four</u> McKay to you."

"I guess they'll charge you with an Article 96, releasing a prisoner without proper authority."

"I didn't release him, he—"

"Article 92, dereliction of duty?"

"You been reading the UCMJ, Kirk?"

"On the sergeant's desk. You know all the articles, right?"

"You should stick with your map-making crap."

McKay, his feathers ruffled, went away.

On my next trip to the munitions dump an officer approached on the outside of the gate:

"Here, soldier, I'm Capt'n Range."

"What's the password sir?" I asked.

"Don't give me that. See these silver bars? I out rank you. Now open up!"

"Password, sir?"

"I'll report you to headquarters command."

"You do that," I replied, standing my ground.

"You're asking for a courts marshal, soldier, and that'll be in your 201 for life. Just try to get a job."

"I understand, sir."

"Then open up."

"Can't do that, sir." I dropped my M16 from my shoulder and presented it across my chest. The officer took a step back.

"What's your name, Specialist?"

"Spec Four Kirk."

"Good show Specialist, carry on."

I took a step back in surprise, shouldered my rifle, and walked on down the fence line. Apparently it had been a test. I took a deep sigh of relief and happily repeated my forth General Order: "Walk my post from flank to flank and take no shit from any rank."

MAIN GATE OF TOMPKINS BARRACKS
–STONED MP ON DUTY?–

The next morning, tired and groggy, and twelve more hours to go on my shift, I was sent to the military stockade and assigned to walk a parapet wall inside the security fence overlooking the exercise yard. This time I was given a clip of cartridges (placed with the rest of my candy bars), and was authorized to shoot anyone trying to escape. Yeah, right, I wasn't authorized to shoot someone like maybe a terrorist group, like the German Baader-Meinhof Gang, trying to get at our munitions, but it was okay to shoot one of my fellow grunts. It was true that some of the prisoners were murderers and rapists, but most were there for dereliction of duty or AWOL. Do you kill a man for that? Absolutely you do. Besides, this was Germany, former home of the Third Reich.

PROMOTION TO SPECIALIST GRADE 5
Tokushia told me I had been put in for a promotion and my yearly evaluation by Chief Maxwell was very good. "As soon as the

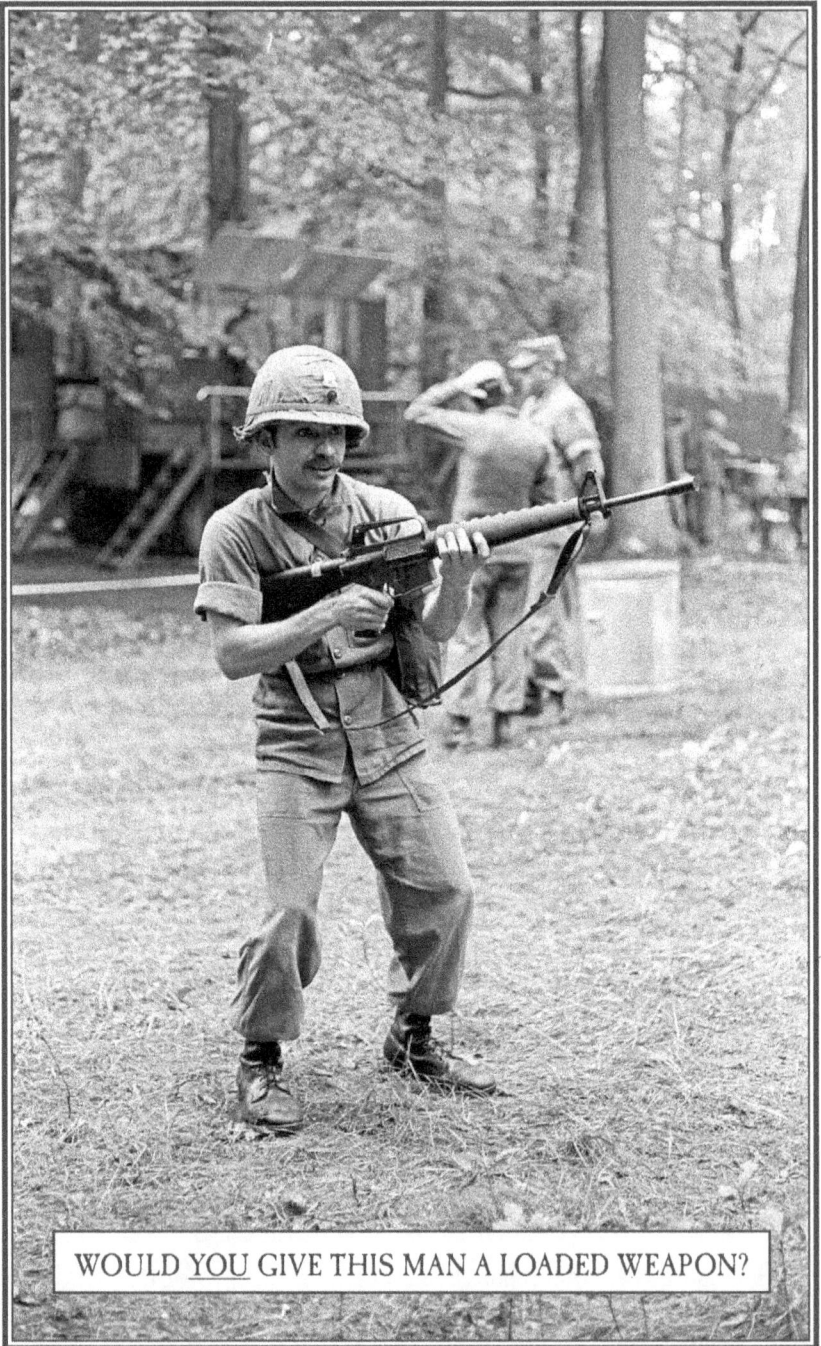

WOULD <u>YOU</u> GIVE THIS MAN A LOADED WEAPON?

promotion board comes up, we'll get you in," he promised. Even our Staff Sergeant, Junius Hayes, had written in my most recent Enlisted Efficiency Report, "SP4 Kirk is a hard working compiler that shows a willingness in understanding each and every task assigned. SP4 Kirk has demonstrated a potential for leadership and dedication to duty equaled by very few of his contemporaries." What constituted "contemporaries" I wondered? But the idea of getting promoted was a stressful, unwelcome, concept to me. I think I had a fear of success, that maybe I couldn't handle the job. And then again, did I really want the job? SP5 was a non-command position, but it was a supervisory job instead of actually doing the work and I was an artist not a manager. I surely didn't want to be a squad leader and sing Jodys. I preferred sitting quietly at a drafting table lit by a bare light bulb. Well, time went by and I never heard anything more and forgot about it. Then one morning they told me the board was meeting again; I was to get my uniform sharp and read the newspaper because I'd be asked about current events.

"What? I don't get the paper."

"Be sure and read the sports section," replied Chief Maxwell.

"Sports? I could care less about sports," I said. "What did football or tennis or <u>Fußball</u> have to do with being a good little soldier?"

"The army wants well-rounded soldiers," said Maxwell.

"Does that include knowledge about architecture, bridge building, philosophy, psychiatry, nuclear physics?"

"The board's tomorrow at one o'clock." Max turned back to his oak WWII desk stacked high with oodles of paperwork.

I tried to hunt down a newspaper; had no idea where it could be purchased at Tompkins. I eventually found it at the Service Club, skimmed through it, and went to bed. But the next morning I was told the promotion board had been postponed. So much for that. If I had gone to and "passed" the board, I would still have been put on a long list to await an opening, a "slot" as it was called, and it wouldn't be until I reached the top of the list that I <u>might</u> get that promotion—surely about the time of my scheduled separation and I figured, that's when they'd dangle the SP5 pay as a reason to re-enlist. No thanks.

FIELD TRAINING EXERCISES

The phone at Battalion Headquarters rang at 1:00 in the morning. An NCO on night duty picked it up.

"All units of the Engineer Topographic Center are to move out promptly at 3:00 am. Orders are from USAREUR command. Call Headquarters to verify."

And that was the beginning of another Field Training Exercise—we had several each year—or this could actually be the real deal: going off to war. We never really knew which until we got to our destination.

The duty NCO of A Company shook my shoulder until I knew where I was—unfortunately still at Tompkins. I tried to turn over and go back to my escapist dreams.

"Kirk, get your ass out of bed, here take these." He dropped a set of keys in my hand.

"What's this?"

"The duty roster says you're the staff duty driver. We're moving out in one-and-a-half hours."

It finally hit me like an Airborne Ranger falling without a parachute. I sobered quickly, jumped up, and searched for my pants. I could hear an unusual amount of noise in the hall. <u>God, I'm late,</u> I thought, <u>Fuel! Was there gasoline in the three-quarter, hell, where was it parked? The NCO would know, but where was he just now? Boy, I needed those rehearsals.</u> Dressed, I clambered down the hall to the Company Commander's office and already I could see that off-post personnel were wandering in. Soon, there would be a beehive of activity (a bunch of soldiers running around in circles like chickens without their heads) and I'd be racing around on cobblestone streets in the black of night with sleepiness in my eyes. I wouldn't have time to organize myself (make sure I had all my personal belongings like shaving gear) before we moved out. My duffle with fatigues and socks was already packed in a trailer. I just grabbed the list of personnel I was to notify (those without telephones) or pick up (those without transportation), and drove out the gate of Tompkins. I turned left to head for Schwetzingen, or no, I need to go right to Hockenheim first, hum, or should I?... I raced through the quiet streets, the sound of my little diesel truck bouncing off the walls of three-story half-timber houses. I pushed the doorbell of Sergeant McCrory's apartment, and pushed again. No one answered. Willie McCrory was a personable,

WHITFIELD, McCRORY, AND EASTER—MARRIED AND OFF POST
THEY'D HAVE TO BE NOTIFIED OR BROUGHT IN

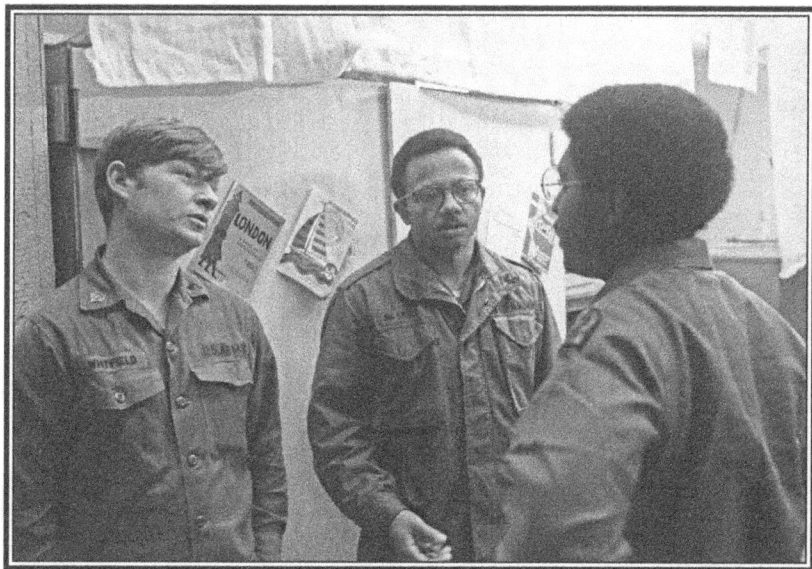

soft-spoken, married black man with a high I.Q. who spent much of his free time as a scout leader. He had enlisted dope-head Creech, a PFC at our Ramp, to assist him with the scouts and Creech frequently asked the question, "Do you know the difference between the Boy Scouts and the Army?" When no one had the answer, he'd reply, "The Boy Scouts have <u>adult</u> leadership." I stepped back to see if a light had come on in one of the upstairs windows. Nothing. Dark as the Congo. <u>Christ!</u> I banged on the door again. Had he already received the message to come in? Another one of our men staying in the same apartment complex might have woken him up and brought him in, but how would I know? He could at least have left me a note on the door telling me he had gotten the message to come in.

No answer.

I drove on. Street intersections split off in numerous directions. Was I on the correct street? <u>Here it is, Sergeant Eddy's pad</u>. I rang

THE NARROW STREETS OF SCHWETZINGEN

the bell. A light went on upstairs and Eddy stuck his head out his bedroom window.

"What do you want?" he called out in the manner of a man whose warm and wonderful sleep had been abruptly disturbed.

"It's me, Spec. Four Kirk. The battalion received a call at one a.m. to move out. Get your clothes on; we're to move out at three. Do you need a ride?"

"No Kirk. What time is it?"

"Two fifteen."

"Christ, where have you been?"

"Trying to find you, and I've still got more stops to make."

"Then get on with it."

"Yes, sir."

"Sir, Hell! I work for a living." He closed and locked his casement window.

Two more stops and I still didn't have anyone riding with me and time was running out; I too had to get back by 3:00, and now I was lost. I looked around and came to the realization that I had no idea where I was, what with the winding streets, the various towns grown together, and no sun to give me a sense of direction. I was sure they'd be gone by the time I got back.

I finally drove into Tompkins Barracks just as a procession of trucks was driving out. Glenn O'Neill came running up to me.

"Move over, that's my truck. I'm the assigned driver now."

I slid over. "They've already had formation?"

"You're late, Kirk, it's four o'clock. They've been looking for—"

"Four o'clock! It looks as if they're late too."

O'Neill picked up Captain Arthur R. Shean—our company commander—and his clerk, and we headed out. Shean was an intelligent, straight-up, by-the-book officer from West Point who took his job

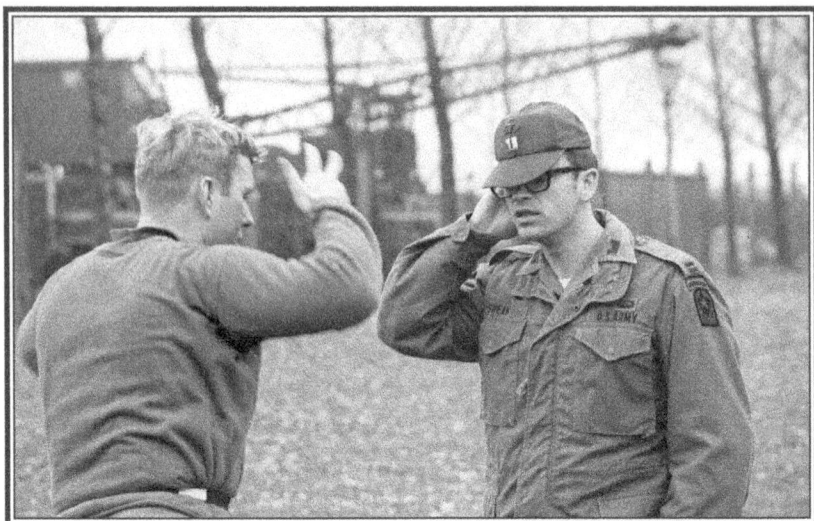

"WAS THAT A SALUTE LIEUTENANT, OR ARE YOU
SCRATCHING OUT THE LICE?" ASKED CAPTAIN SHEAN.
"I <u>COULD</u> USE A SHOWER, SIR."

seriously and I would expect him to get General's stars someday. He
wore black-rimmed military issue glasses with a heavy subscription
and his tan Class-As were always creased perfectly.

FTX AT LAMPERTHEIM

Generators were being dropped and our 5-ton expandable vans
placed according to someone's master plan. We had driven only a
few miles to the Lampertheim woods—and we did it without the
<u>Lampertheim</u> map. It looked like it was just going to be an FTX, no
real deal this time. It was still dark and a chilly breeze found its way to
my bones. Flashlights whipped around like searchlights at the grand
opening of a new auto dealership. The mess tent was the first to go
up next to the portable kitchen, a truck that looked like a tin chuck
wagon with stairs and a ramp on one side. As dawn filtered through
the tall, dark pine trees, the troops lined up at the foot of the stairs.

The cook raised the plywood canopy over the serving windows and we were ladled something white and slimy from big stainless steel containers with "G.I." embossed on the side.

"When is the Army going to emboss a "G.I." on my forehead?" I asked, "I'm Government Issue."

"Huh, what?"

"The 'G.I.' on the can?"

"Oh, Kirk, that means 'Galvanized Iron.' They were labeled that in World War II."

"World War II?"

"Yeah, these are World War II vintage."

"Thirty years of S.O.S.?"

"You bet."

"Any toast?"

"Plumb out."

Well, at least the stuff was steaming hot and beat those cold,

MOBILE MESS KITCHEN—A METAL CHUCKWAGON

dry, stale C-rations. Rows of tables were set up in the mess tent. I sat down next to O'Neill.

"How long we here for?" I asked.

"I heard fourteen days."

"Crap, I didn't even get to bring my toothbrush."

Platoon Sergeant "Pineapple" Tokuhisa came up to us.

"Come on boys, finish up, we've work to do."

We jumped.

We set stakes and raised several more field tents and then set up rows of cots and diesel-fuel stoves; the higher-ranking NCOs would get first-class accommodations. We put the leveling jacks down on our vans and cranked out their sides. Motor Pool fired up the generators and ran large black electrical cables to our trucks. We had to be operational—back to mapmaking (working on that damn Lampertheim map)—as soon as possible. This was a field training

LOTS OF S.O.S. AND STEAMING COFFEE FOR BREAKFAST
–THE TOMPKINS MESS HALL IN A DEUCE–

SETTING UP A "JENNY"–ELECTRIC POWER FOR THE VANS

exercise, a test of our speed and efficiency. A perimeter guard was set up and foxholes were dug. Some of us would have to spend the night in those holes. When the common areas were ready, the enlisted men began to set up their pup tents. Some men cut a trench around their tents to drain water away in case it should rain. Others gathered limbs and stacked them around the tent. One tent was surrounded with some scrap pieces of concertina wire.

"What's this for?" I asked.

Norman "Scotty" Scott replied, "Wild boars."

"Wild boars?"

"Big three-hundred-pound pigs with stiff black fur and sharp tusks that curl out of their vicious mouths. They'll be coming in here tonight, tearing through our camp rummaging for food."

"You're kidding."

"Nope."

With Scotty's fifteen years of FTX experience, I figured he knew something. Pineapple came up to us as Scotty was describing these night creatures of the forest.

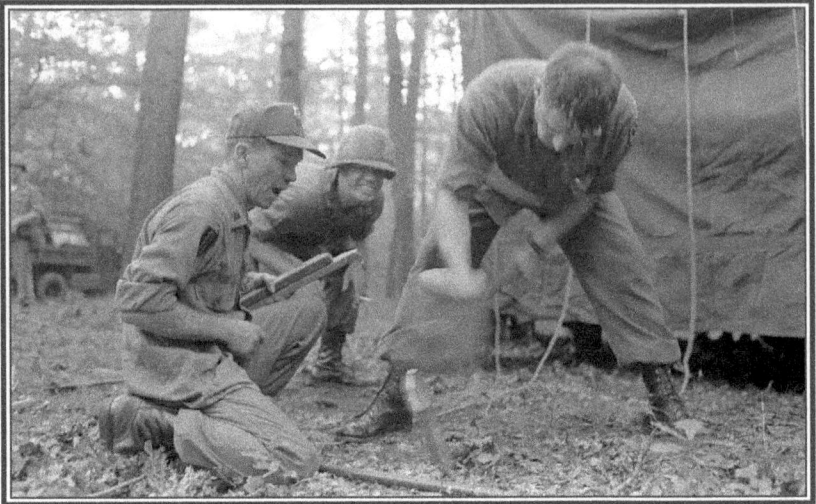

SCOTTY DIRECTING PLACEMENT OF TENT PEGS

"You two are pulling perimeter guard tonight, hugging each other in a foxhole. Eddy is the NCO in charge; he'll assign you a first-class hole in the ground for tonight."

Still sleepy, confused, and groggy, I wondered when I would actually get to sleep.

I set up our M-18A1 Claymore Antipersonnel Mine in front of our foxhole, ran the connecting wire to our detonator, and hunkered down in the foxhole with Scotty and our M-16s. We were given our General Orders and told a roving NCO would check on us periodically. We were told to watch out for the boars, that they were quite dangerous, and were told not to let any of them pass. I wondered if I should ask the boars for the password.

Night fell early in the forest and the temperature began to drop. Scotty pulled out a flask of whiskey from his ammo pouch and offered me a swig. I passed, at least for now. We swapped stories until about 2:00 am when it began to rain. We pulled our ponchos out, put them

LAYING OUT SLEEPING BAGS IN A PUP TENT

I'M READY TO PLAY ARMY MAN
(From the collection of the author)

on, and pulled the hoods over our heads. Water began to run into our foxhole and the cold dampness of the ground penetrated our very souls. I climbed out of the foxhole and drug some tree limbs over and tried to stack them over our hole to create a roof structure. One of us would have to remove our poncho and use it for the roof. We drew straws, I lost, but the roof was a big improvement to our comfort. We scooped mud up around the perimeter of the hole to divert the trickling streams of water. The rain intensified and we heard grunting noises just beyond the Claymore.

"That's them," said Scotty.

"The Claymore will get 'em," I said.

"Did you face it in the right direction?"

"Huh?"

"Convex side away from you, it says 'FRONT TOWARD ENEMY'."

"Um, I'm not sure."

TENTS AND COTS FOR THE NCO'S—FIRST CLASS!

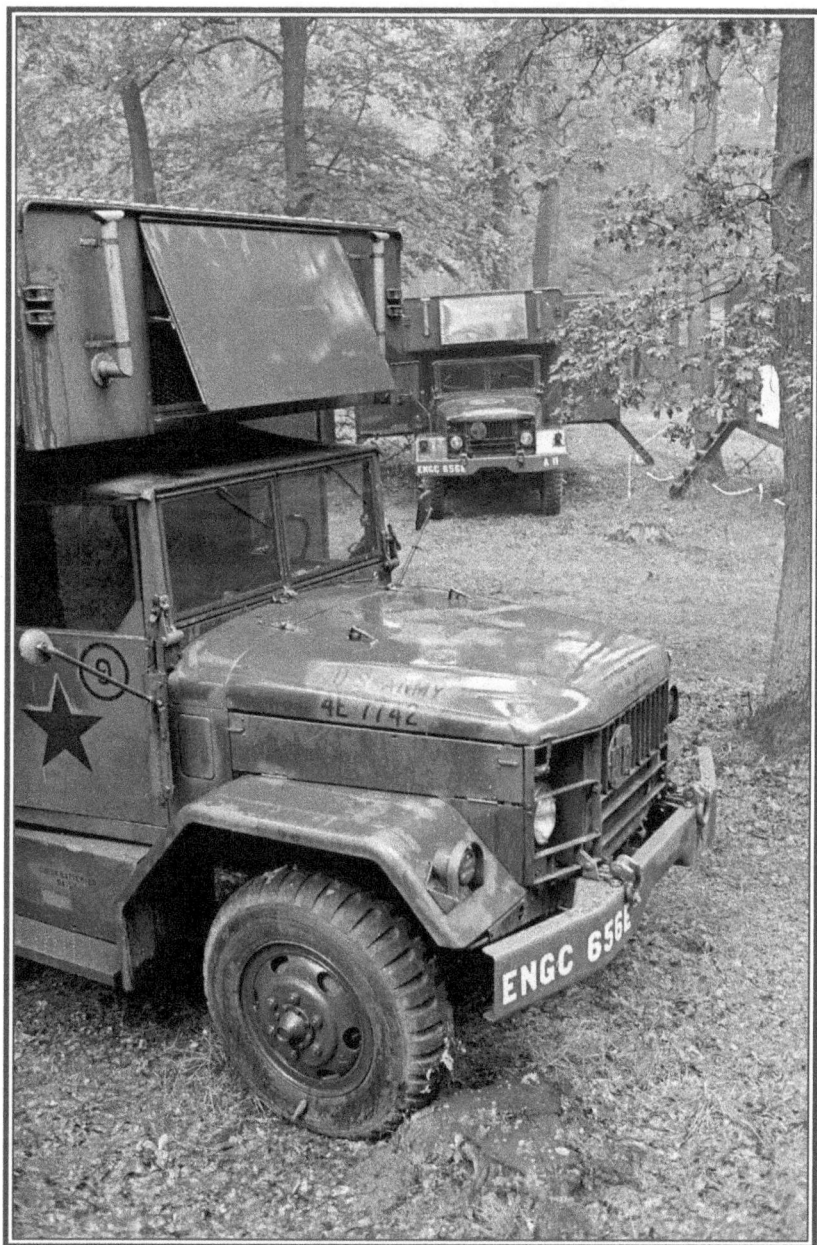

THIS 5-TON, EXPANDABLE VAN
GREAT FOR OFF-ROAD TRAVEL

"You're not sure! You want to blow us all up?"

I crawled out of the foxhole toward the Claymore, toward the noise of crunching leaves. I saw that the Claymore was placed correctly. Back in the foxhole I went, wetter still, my ass as soggy as bran in milk. Scotty was laughing.

"What are you laughing about?"

"That Claymore, it's a dummy. You didn't think they would issue real ones did you?"

"Then how do we stop the pigs?"

He laughed again and offered me a drink. I took a swig this time. I thought, the pigs must be a put on too.

Sergeant Eddy came by to check on us once or twice, and I told him I heard rummaging noises in the woods.

I never saw a boar that night, but the next morning as we returned to camp for breakfast, we found the mess tent hanging askew, some tent stakes pulled up, tent poles down, tables turned over, and trash cans dumped.

"What happened?" I asked.

"Some S-O-Bs fell asleep on guard duty," replied Sergeant Wallow in his grease-stained apron. "A heard of wild boar ransacked the mess."

"No shit!"

"Crap it is! I'll get the sons uh bitches who fell asleep. That's an article one thirteen!"

Scotty and I looked at each other. What was an Article 113? Did we fall asleep? We couldn't say for sure. But, if anything drew the pigs to our Mess, it had to be Wallow's apron.

The cold rain continued to fall in fits and starts as we were driven

QUALIFYING ON THE FIRING RANGE

LOADING AMMO AND GRADING TARGETS

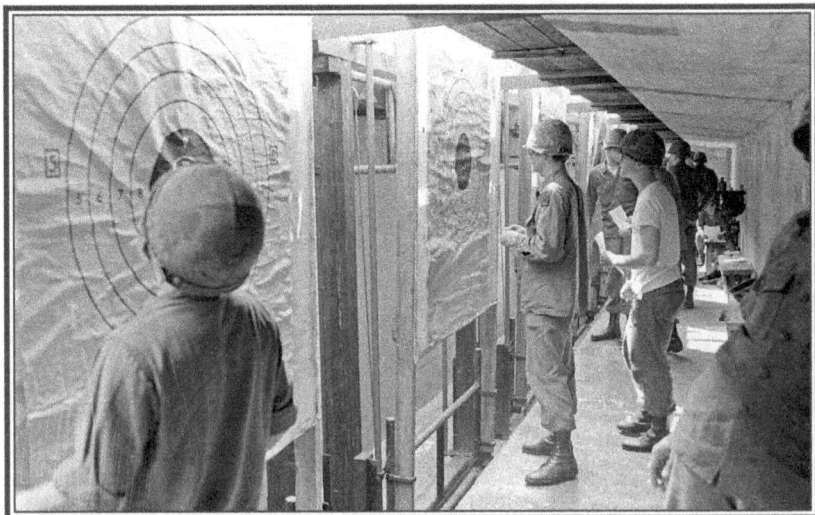

to the firing range in the back of open deuces. We first went to the zeroing range to adjust our sights. We laid our rifles on wooden frames with a cutout for our weapons and shot at targets to set the sights. We then moved to the seventy-five-meter range, picked up more loaded cartridge magazines and lined up on a sandy, clay-packed field, and either in a standing, kneeling, or lying position, locked and loaded and waited for the command to fire. It was an annual requirement to re-qualify with our assigned weapons. We shot targets on several other ranges, all the while sweating profusely in our wet ponchos as we lay in muddy puddles of water and brushed gritty sand from our M16s. But they kept on working; I was proud of that weapon and wouldn't be afraid to carry it into battle (actual combat veterans might say different). We also had a competition to see who was the most accurate shooter. Even under these lousy, cold, wet conditions, I succeeded in staying near the top, but Floyd "Bean" Wever and a headquarters dude kept me out of the gold and the silver.

Our work schedule in the vans ran continuously all 24 hours with twelve hour shifts, but we all had reorientation classes, weapons training, and extra duties leaving but a few hours dedicated to sleep. We were never so glad to be working in the vans because in there we had heaters. Every morning, we'd roll out of our warm sleeping bags and rush over to the mess tent where a diesel-fuel stove burned—doing a fantastic job, if you could get past the odor of the fumes—and we could, because boo-koo rain continued to pound on the canvas. We sloshed through sticky mud that was beginning to worry some of the officers. Would they be able to get their battalion out of the forest? Our bivouac was becoming one hell of a bog. Later that morning, our battalion commander, Lt. Col. Richard Williamson, gave us the order to load up and move out; we were moving to higher ground. We had only been there about 48 hours, I hadn't any sleep, and now

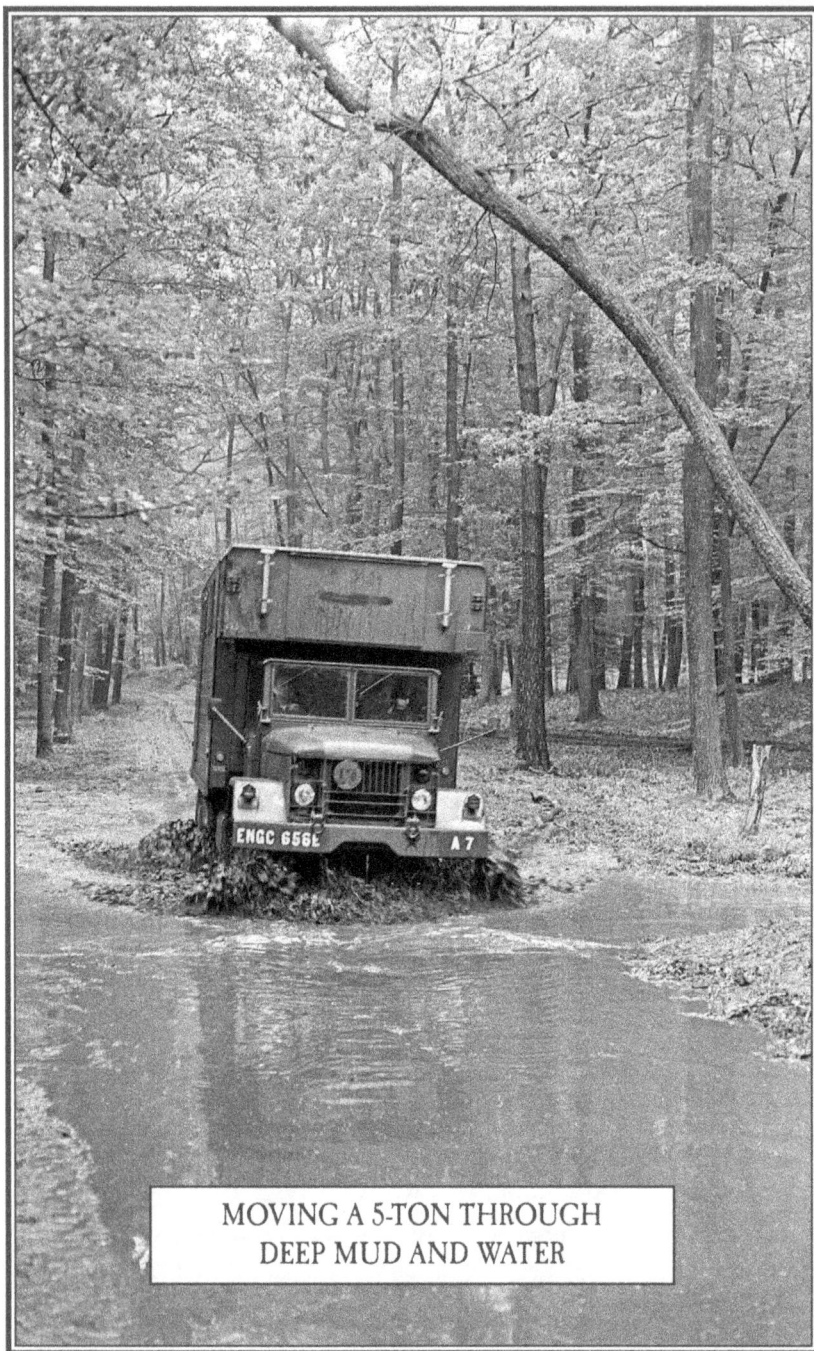

MOVING A 5-TON THROUGH
DEEP MUD AND WATER

everything had to be torn down and packed up. The slit latrine and foxholes had to be filled in, mapping projects put away, printing jobs suspended, trash collected, and trailers hooked up. I was handed the keys to a five-ton van and told to drive her out. The road looked like a canal, but the vans pushed diligently through the two to three-foot deep water and mud. I was told to keep her in low gear and not to stop. The engine's exhaust pipe ran vertically up over the hood so the high water wouldn't choke the engine. The heavy, duel-wheeled, four-wheel-drive vehicles kept moving. I couldn't believe it. These babies were ready for war—at least the last one anyway.

We drove about twenty miles and set up camp in a farm field. It wasn't long before we noticed this awful odor all around us. The air stunk; all our clothes stunk. We had bivouacked in a turnip field, a field fertilized with fresh, biting cow manure. And that wasn't the worst of it. With our trenching tools and tent stakes, we had disturbed ground-nesting sweet bees and they swarmed like Monarch butterflies in a field of milkweed. We tried to bury the nests with shovels of sand, but to no avail, they would just bore themselves through it and swarm again. We tried RAID aerosol sprays and failing that, we set kerosene lanterns on the mounds and tried to just stay clear of them because Colonel Williamson wasn't going to move us again. The colonel stood there in his poncho and fatigue cap, smoking his beloved pipe, the bowl turned down to keep out the rain. I wondered what advance guard picked out this site (not that we had much choice, a deal had to be struck with some German farmer).

We continued to have trouble with the bees, especially when they turned up in our tents. Picklo and Lilburn set a large wooden mallet (used for hammering in tent stakes) on the ground in their tent (they, of course, managed a large four-man tent reserved for the officers) and placed a drop of honey on the face of it. They waited until one

AN UNIDENTIFIED LIEUTENANT (OR AN ALIEN?) WEARING HIS "GAS" MASK (PSG Tokuhisha Photo)

by one, bees tried out the cuisine and then they clobbered each one with a second mallet. Sergeant Eddy wanted to clear the camping area entirely of bees, so he requisitioned a canister of CS gas and figured that might run them off. The gas would also run <u>us</u> off we didn't have our gas masks at the ready. We were scheduled for our annual biological warfare training anyway, and a decision was made after several soldiers were stung, to get our CS training right here and now. Eddy released several canisters of gas and we reached for our gas masks (kept in a bag we had to carry over our shoulders at all times). I removed my piss pot (helmet liner), pulled the mask over my head, and blew hard to expel any gas trapped in the mask. A fog of white smoke engulfed the encampment. I watched as "Airborne" Gilbert wrenched off his mask and began to run, scratching and rubbing at his eyes and face. I had to laugh. The CS reacted with the moisture on his skin and caused a burning sensation, a flood of tears, a runny nose, a blistered throat and nose—and restricted breathing. Quite

WHO'S IDEA WAS THIS? WHERE'S SERGEANT EDDY?
(PSG Tokuhisha Photo)

91

a painful experience. I guessed Mr. Airborne hadn't trained with a gas mask in jump school—not required when jumping through city smog? I was feeling very lucky; my mask was working just fine. If it hadn't worked, I would have been throwing up and feeling I was about to die. The CS gas—the same tear gas used for riot control—wouldn't kill you, but it sure made you wish it had.

The torrential rain had slackened to a drizzle and we got on with our photomapping operations and a multitude of other duties. At supper-time we were all issued two bottles of beer, and no more than two, to help us sleep (I couldn't understand why we weren't also issued Mary Jane—our Dope Heads would've liked that). That third night, I finally got some shuteye.

The next day we set up a barbed-wire fence around one of the vans and a 24-hour guard was put on the gate. S-3 had brought real classified documents out to the field to work on. S-3 was the unit I was to work in if I ever received the top-secret clearance I had been "put in for" six months earlier. I had already heard from my parents and

WEAPONS RE-ORIENTATION CLASSES IN THE FIELD

PSG TOKUHISA INSTRUCTING ME ON HOW TO CLEAN TIRES
(John T. Young Photo)

neighbors back home that the FBI had been there to question them. That was a sobering thought, and what were they asking?

Rumor continued to circle around the camp as to how long we would have to stay out. Ten days was the latest guess, less than the original fourteen. We were operating under simulated combat conditions, and perimeter guards had to be kept up. For a little "fun," the survey platoon was assigned to be "aggressors" and try to break through our defenses. Second Louie Sneed was assigned to lead them, and with smoke grenades, blank ammunition, and grenade simulators, they mounted an attack. I was glad I wasn't still hunkered down in a foxhole. Sentries were given blank ammunition and warned to keep their gas masks at the ready. If a soldier was caught off guard, "bang," he was declared dead and a white cross of tape was slapped on his chest. I suppose it was the forerunner to paintball games. Inside the perimeter, several platoons were ordered to fall into formation

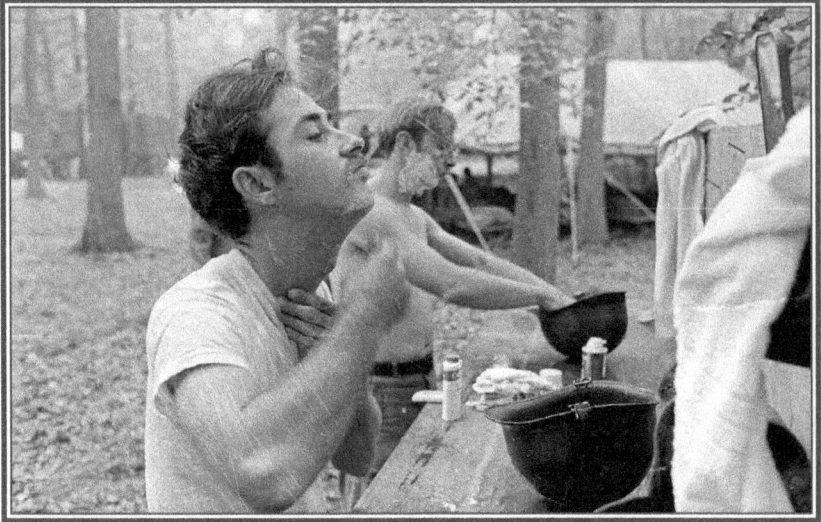

SHAVING IN THE FIELD USING A HELMET LINER FOR A SINK
–SP4 O'NEILL ALWAYS WORKING TO KEEP UP A "STRACK" APPEARANCE–

and march beyond our perimeter on a simulated maneuver. While traipsing through the woods, they were hit with CS gas and the men scrambled to get their masks on. The NCOs were apparently having a ball. We didn't think it was funny at all.

Our off-duty pastimes, if we weren't sleeping, consisted of playing poker or going to one of the field tents set up with a 16mm projector and screen to watch old black & white movies with Laurel & Hardy and The Three Stooges. Me, I was taking Tri-X black & white pictures with my 35mm Nikkormat for our unit newsletter, the Topo Topics. They were the only photos I took of my military experiences (I chose instead to shoot the architecture and scenery of Central Europe and continued to deny the Army's existence).

Wilkie Ross, while pulling perimeter guard at some remote location, found he was amongst a bunch of wild blackberry bushes and feeling he had hit the mother lode, devoured them like a kid in a candy store; they sure trumped C-rations. But the delicious juicy fruit

OFF-DUTY CARD GAMES A POPULAR PASSTIME
–CW2 MAXWELL IN BACK, PSG TOKUSHIA ON RIGHT (John T. Young Photo)–

left him running to the latrine for the rest of the exercise.

On the ninth day, we were told to pack up, run police calls, and head home. We had to leave the place the way we found it. Yeah right. Deep tire tracks in a farmer's muddy turnip field, him busting a gut knowing full well that he had the plethora of bees on his land and had, the day before, spread fresh, wholesome animal fertilizer.

One of our squad leaders, Sgt. Decker, had a run of bad luck on that last day. He lost a finger while hitching up a generator. With heavy equipment, it was a dangerous task and as they tried to hook up the trailer to a 5-ton, his middle finger was sliced off and no one thought to pick it up and send it along when they rushed him to the hospital. By the time someone had found it and carried it to the hospital, it was too late to reattach. On his return to the Ramp, "Stumpy" proudly held up the fingers of his left hand, one was missing. That reminded me of Gunter Schmidt's finger, but, in his case, it was the British Army that had tortured him. Would Decker get a

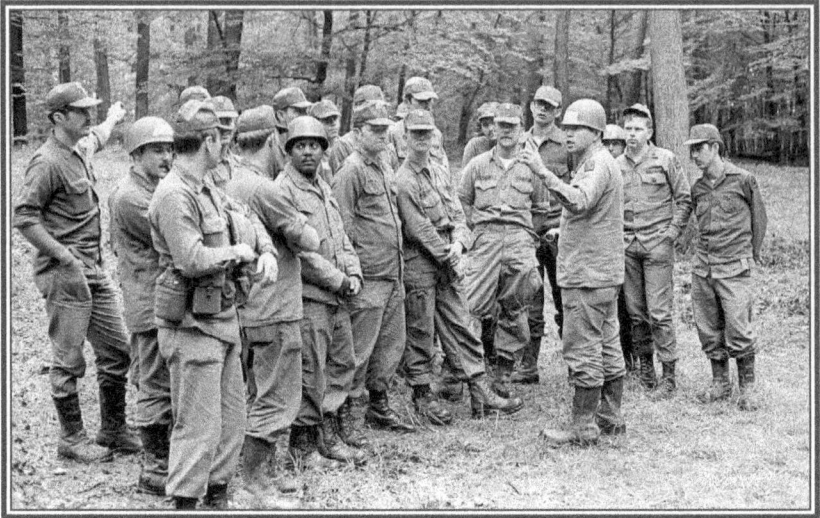

PSG TOKUHISA DOLING OUT DUTY ASSIGNMENTS
(THE TALL PICKLO ON FAR LEFT, THE SHORT O'NEILL FAR RIGHT)

USAREUR COMMANDERS INSPECT THE FTX
–CW2 MAXWELL SHAKING HANDS WITH A USAREUR COMMANDER–
(John T. Young Photo)

GET THOSE SIDE DOORS LOCKED!
(SP5 WHITFIELD–O'NEILL IN BACKGROUND)

purple heart? Would the FTX be reported as a success? Did we prove we could still produce maps while maintaining a state of combat readiness in the field—even when we failed to turn away hungary hordes of wild bores and wild honey bees? From the enlisted man's perspective, it was just a very bad drippy and dank boy-scout camping trip. The officers probably felt the same.

THE BRIDGE DEMOLITION DERBY

At times our military convoys were out there on the <u>Autobahn</u> where there was no speed limit and we could "blow out the carbs" of our Deuce-and-a Half's and five tons. Our command jeep would lead

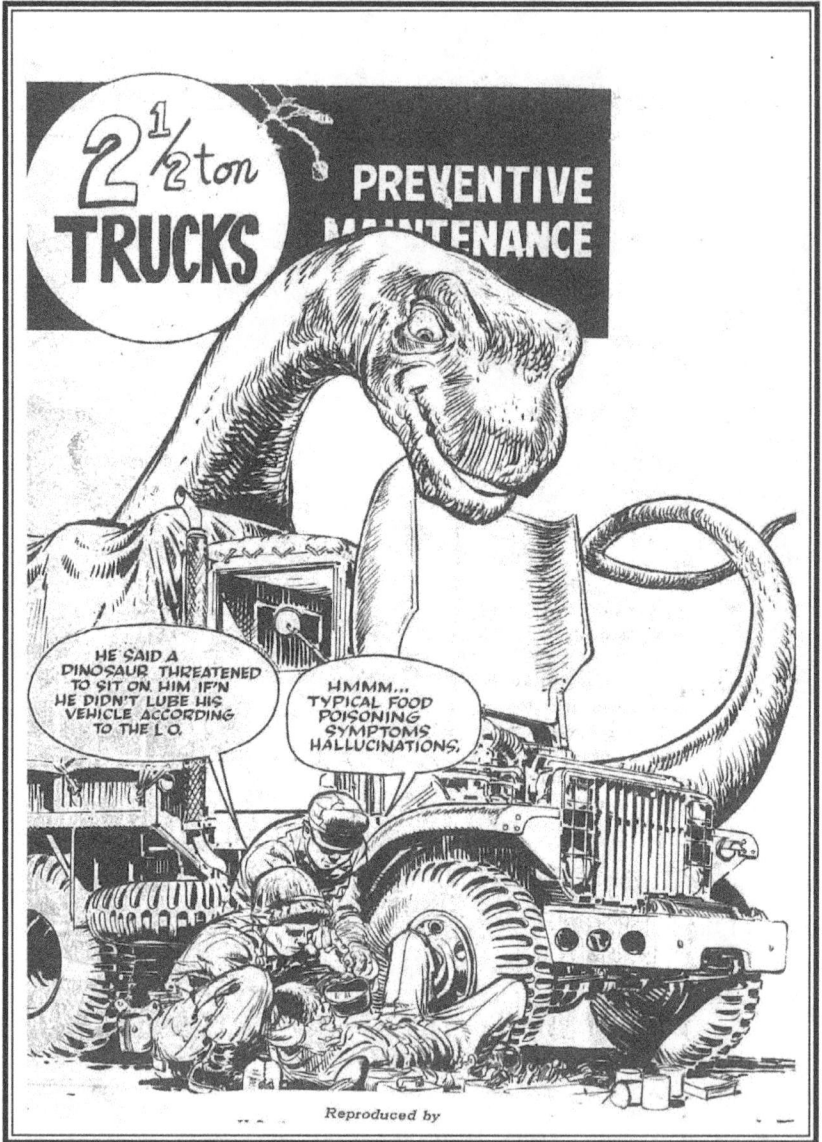

ARMY MAINTENANCE MANUALS WERE PRODUCED
IN A COMIC-BOOK FORMAT
SO THAT, MAYBE, THE G.I. WOULD ACTUALLY READ THEM!

ATTRACTIVE, WELL-ENDOWED LADIES WERE INCLUDED
TO SPICE UP THE READING MATERIAL

the way. Running at full throttle, black smoke billowing out of our stacks, the German Mercedes-Benzs would flash their headlights as they whizzed by us in the left lane like a flash of impatient lightening.

Part of pulling maintenance on the vehicles was to drive them around once a month. Nearly everyone had an assigned vehicle he was responsible for and once a month we would drive out of the barracks and convoy to a little town called Seckenheim just to keep the oil and grease moving around. Frank "Cockbite" Dulfer, the class clown, would yell out the window as we laced our way through those narrow streets: "To arms, to arms, the Russians are coming!" Farmers turning their dung piles would stop and take a step back to protect their feet and watch us go by. To them the American GI was a pain in the ass, but also brought in revenue—at the Gasthauses. (I don't know how they felt about the idea that we were providing protection against a Russian invasion.) There was a small overpass about halfway to Seckenheim that the M292 carto vans would just barely fit through. On one of those trips "Flash" Lilburn didn't get the sides of his van closed and locked properly so when it came his turn to go through the underpass, one side slid out and he wedged that big old elephant into the overpass. A big wrecker from the motor pool had to be called out to dislodge the van. After that we took a different route to Seckenheim, proof that the Army can learn from its mistakes.

NEW UNIT DESIGNATION

"Following reassignments directed. No travel involved." That's what our new battalion orders read. All our names and social security numbers were listed. Order dated "2 November 1972. Special order No. 307." We were "relieved from duty" at the 656th Engineer Battalion and were to report immediately to the "649th Engineer Battalion." Well, where was that? Turns out, right here at Tompkins;

656th UNIT CREST
"THE EARTH ON PAPER"

649th UNIT CREST
"THROUGH MAPS WE SERVE"

we didn't have to move a centimeter! Just our unit designation had changed. We were no longer in the 656th Engineer Battalion; we were to be "re-designated" as the 649th, and had to design a new unit crest as soon as possible and paint the new numbers on our vehicles. We were told the 656th had officially ceased to exist. (I later found out congress had published a list of decommissioned units in military downsizing efforts near the end of the war. In other words, the public was told the Army was smaller, leaner, and their troops were coming home. We weren't, of course, smaller and leaner; our battalion stayed there, in the same place, there in Schwetzingen, with the exact same mission and number of personnel. (Years later, I learned

U.S. ARMY ENGINEER
COMMAND, EUROPE

101

to nauseous disillusionment, that our government made a habit of lying to the public for political gain or to cover up bureaucratic botch-ups.)

(In April of '72, our Engineer Topographic Center was re-assigned to the United States Army Engineer Command, Europe and a new patch replaced our colorful blue and gold USAREUR patch.)

THE BERLIN WALL

Assigned to go to Frankfurt and do the labeling on a big war map at the TOC (Tactical Operations Center) for a Germany-wide USAREUR NATO force deployment exercise known as REFORGER IV: CERTAIN SHEILD (REturn of FORces to GERmany), I got to hang out with the generals, so to speak. I watched as the Generals of the Red and Blue Armies pushed the symbols for their armored and infantry battalions across the board to other parts of Germany. It was the biggest game of Risk I'd ever seen

1895 CHURCH RUINS WITH MODERN 1961 ADDITION

because the playing pieces were full scale; the field commanders had to actually move their men and armored tanks on the ground, down Autobahns, through narrow village streets, and across farmer's fields in as short a time as possible. The Germans hated these disruptive and expensive exercises, and every year, the American government had to make restitutions for destroyed crops and broken cobblestone streets.

For the privilege of making labels for the big map, I was given the additional reward of a trip to West Berlin. From there, a busload of us GIs took a trip to the east, East Berlin that is—on the other side of the wall. We drove passed a huge pile of stone rubble on the Kurfürstendamm, the city's main drag. It was a church left there in ruins as a reminder of the horrible destruction caused by the war. Two modern polygonal glass buildings, shaped like a lipstick case and powder compact, flanked the ruins and served as the new church and bell tower. The rest of West Berlin had been completely rebuilt

THE BERLIN "WALL" AND KILL ZONE BEYOND

so little of the old Berlin remained. The bus ran along the Berlin Wall that separated the East from the West, parts of it just the brick fronts of abandoned buildings. Behind them was a no-man's zone—a kill zone with tank traps, concertina wire, and foreboding guard towers with sullen soldiers, never a smile on their faces (their duty to watch for, and shoot down, any refugees trying to leave East Berlin). With their crow's-nest view of the West—a West teeming with life and lively commerce completely contrary to the East's life style—was it any wonder that the other assigned duty of these border guards was to watch for any comrades that might try to run the gauntlet and shoot them down in cold blood (For this reason they weren't allowed to meet the other guards much less make friends with them). Barbed wire memorials were set up along the sidewalk to denote the places where East Germans had attempted to breach the wall and escape to the West—and didn't make it.

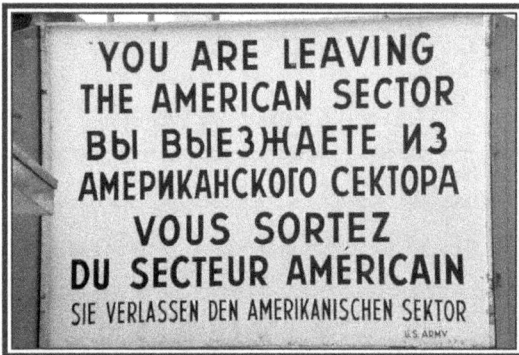

YOU ARE LEAVING
THE AMERICAN SECTOR
ВЫ ВЫЕЗЖАЕТЕ ИЗ
АМЕРИКАНСКОГО СЕКТОРА
VOUS SORTEZ
DU SECTEUR AMÉRICAIN
SIE VERLASSEN DEN AMERIKANISCHEN SEKTOR
U.S. ARMY

We came to Check Point Charlie, the bridge from the American sector of Berlin to the Communist East. Russian and American soldiers stood at opposite ends with locked and loaded rifles. A white, foreboding plywood sign printed in three languages, Russian, German and English, read: YOU ARE LEAVING THE AMERICAN SECTOR. It was sobering. The American guards boarded our bus, checked all our military IDs, and then we drove on over the bridge to visit the East Berlin soldiers. They boarded our bus and stared carefully at each of us and our IDs. They then asked

LOOKING OVER THE WALL INTO EAST GERMANY
–THE BERLIN WALL WAS 26.5 MILES LONG–

if we had any cameras with us. None of us said a word. Face to face with them, the deadly serious look on their faces, I felt like I was in the middle of a spy movie and was wondering if I'd ever see America again. Once past that checkpoint, we drove to the center of East Berlin and parked. We had four hours to wander the streets on our own. Yeah, right. We left the bus in wolf packs and walked the main drag, careful not to venture down a side street. We were wearing our Class-A uniforms as required. The East Berliners moved like primitive robots and appeared lifeless. Clothed in drab overcoats, fury hats, and gray scarves, they passed each other without acknowledgment, without normal human facial expressions. They appeared to be very unhappy beings. The buildings were still in ruins, shrapnel scarring the few surviving facades (only the facades facing the Wall—those visible to Westerners—had been repaired). An exclusive high-end retailer displayed in their street window, a claw-foot bathtub and a stack of real bars of soap. Who knows how many rubles a single bar of soap cost, a year's wages, maybe more. And East Berliners had to stand in line for hours to get one rationed roll of toilet paper that felt more like sandpaper than tissue. I was very glad to get back to the West and I could see why the military promoted this trip to the East, to show a few of us just how good we had it in America. Maybe this East Berliner's life was what we were stationed in Europe to prevent.

THE NUDE BEACH

"Big Al" Picklo and "Tommy Turtle" O'Neill also made a TDY (Temporary Duty) trip on the duty train to Berlin and crossed over to the East as I had done. But it was while working on the Grunewald Forest Map (a NATO training area) for the Berlin Brigade that Cockbite and others led by SSG Junious "Sonny" Hayes (the man Cockbite called "Cloudy") that they had a story to tell. After doing some field checking with the survey platoon, they drove through

EAST GERMAN SOLDIERS LEANING ON TANK TRAPS

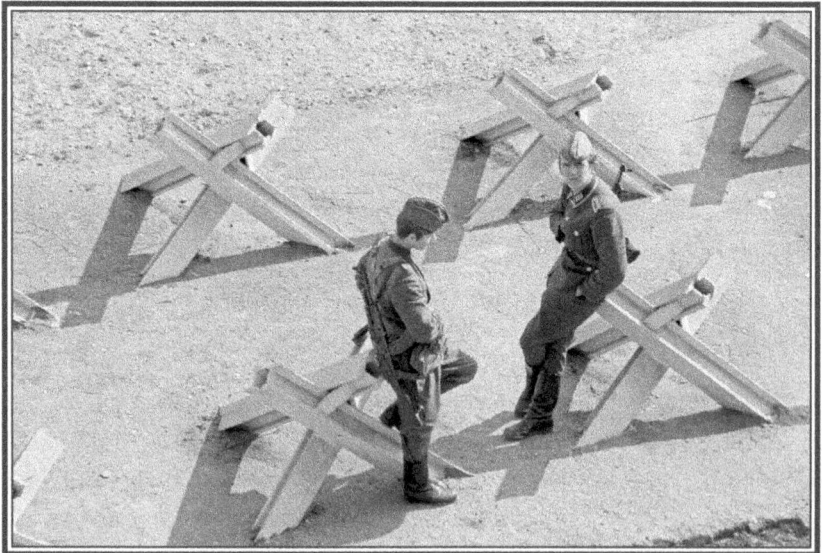

Check Point Charlie. While there, face-to-face with the "Russian Horde," they came across a nude beach smack-dab in the middle of a city park. Nudists, real nudists in East Berlin! "We had been told there was a 'free-from-clothing' beach over there," said Dulfer, "but we didn't expect to come across it. But here they were, Germans bare-ass naked. That would have been enough for us young GI's, but a full-bearded German in his birthday suit came up to our jeep to converse with us Americans, his <u>cojones</u> dangling there in front of our faces. We tried to avert our eyes, instead looking for any pretty young white-skinned <u>fräuleins</u>, but no such luck. Why is it that it's the ugliest of the human race that wants to bear all?"

"American cigarette?" asked the sun-wrinkled German.

Paul Balcavage pulled a pack from his Class-A pants pocket and offered him a cancer stick.

"<u>Danke</u>. American cigarettes <u>schmekken</u>. Good, no?"

"Good, yes," nodded Paul.

FORMER BUILDING FACADES DEFINE THE "WALL"

RUSSIAN SOLDIER IN EAST BERLIN

With a cigarette they were apparently instant friends. Cockbite kept the conversation going, "Any of you men military?"

"KGB."

Our eyes widened, he laughed, "Joke. F—, no one like KGB. Shit."

The vulgar words of any language were the first to be learned. The survey crew forced a set of Cheshire grins.

Their driver then started the jeep. "We need to go boys," and to the German he waved, "Willkommen, auf wiedersehen!"

"After all, we were visitors behind the iron curtain."

ANOTHER CARBON COPY FOR MY 201 FILE

Our Battalion Commander, LTC Williamson sent me a Letter of Commendation for my work at the just completed REFORGER IV where all I actually did was print out labels and arrows for a big wall map of Western Europe. I reprint some of it here as it was so typical of the letters many of us got for our "outstanding service." "It is with great pleasure that I commend you for the outstanding performance of duty while in support of Reforger IV...Your wholehearted devotion to duty and intense desire to accomplish the completion of assigned topographic products is most commendable. Working long hours under difficult conditions, your innovative methods and products brought high compliments from the chief umpire and personnel of the VII Corps staff...The professionalism you demonstrated was in the best tradition of the topographic Corps and reflects great credit upon yourself, your unit, and the United States Army. A copy of this letter will be placed in your 201 file." I wondered how many letters Williamson signed like this each week. Maybe it would have meant something to me if I had gotten a metal with this "commendation." Maybe not. I didn't really want to be here.

A CASE AGAINST OLIVE DRAB

I found men in my company re-enlisting at an alarming rate and wondered what could be causing such a lemming-like stampede over the cliffs of Liferdom; the reenlistment NCO's enticing ads in Topo Topics couldn't be all there was too it. It was true that the army was offering a $6,000 to $10,000 three-year re-enlistment bonus, and Staff Sergeant Foskey was committed to, and even enjoyed, his job (he was a smooth talker and could have made good money on the outside as a car salesman), but nothing explained this exodus from a life of freedom. Finally, John "Woody" Woodburn, who showered at least twice a day and flossed his teeth incessantly, but cogitated about life while doing so, came up with an interesting theory after observing the behavior of some of the men in the barracks, men like Wilkie Ross, a highly intellectual sort, who was slow to remove his fatigues after he got off duty and was dropping hints about re-enlisting. I wrote this treatise based on Woody's theorem and passed it around the battalion to warn prospective Lifers. I print it here for your perusal:

AN OVERDOSE OF O.D.
By SP4 Kirk, 1973

Olive Drab, a bland, non-descriptive color, (used extensively throughout the army) may well be the culprit to the U.S. Army's unending barrage of problems. A theory, originally purported by Dr. John B. Woodburn, has gained support in the lower echelon's scientific community that could very-well explain the high attrition rate of army-enlisted personnel. Briefly, the theory states, "Olive Drab paint when used on any mechanical or electrical device, such as a motor vehicle, will cause that device to malfunction." The theory

OVERDOSE OF O.D.

by Don Kirk

Olive Drab, a bland, non-descriptive color, may well be the culprit to the U.S. Army's unending barrage of problems.

A theory, originally purported by Dr. John B. Woodburn, has gained support in the lower echelon's scientific community that could very well explain the high attrition rate of army enlisted personnel. Briefly, the theory states that "olive drab paint when used on any mechanical or electrical device, such as a motor vehicle, will cause that device to malfunction". The theory also suggests that continued contact with the paint can cause (as yet unproven) harmful effects to human beings. But let's analyze and develope this theory further so that we might better grasp its full implications.

Statistical research seems to indicate that O.D. paint is of such a chemical make-up (probably caused by the untested mixing of various colors) that it acts much as a cumulative poison like strychnine, resulting in damage to the human body. Over a period of time the O.D. dyes in fatigues, for example, will penetrate the skin, be carried by the blood stream to the brain, and there slowly destroy the brain cells. Studies show that not all the cells are effected, but instead, the O.D. deteriorates only those areas of the brain that carry on value fuctions such as innovative creativity, pride, and aggressiveness.

The cumulative effect of this O.D. seepage into the body means that at some point (and this will vary according to body weight and psychological strength) the limit will be reached where the brain cells have deteriorated beyond repair, resulting in the victims succumbing to the babble of the reenlistment NCO. Then of course, all is lost.

The only solution to this army community disease is a preventive maintenance program that 1) insures that all enlisted men wear their fatigues and greens ONLY during duty hours and 2) that EM either be allowed to "pull" the very minimum of extra duties or else wear civilian clothes while on extra duty. The importance of this preventive maintenance cannot be overly emphasized. Every minute counts. One minute too much could mean a life(r). As soon as a man gets off duty he should immediately change into the more comfortable civilized attire, even before the trip home or to the billets (a possible loss of as much as thirty minutes PER DAY). If a man's separation date can be reached before the body's tolerance level to olive drab, he is home free.

P.S. This was typed with an army typewriter.

AN OVERDOSE OF OLIVE DRAB (THE ORIGINAL TYPED LETTER)

also suggests that continued contact with the paint can cause (as yet unproven) harmful effects to human beings. But lets analyze and develop this theory further so that we might better grasp its full implications.

Statistical research seems to indicate that Olive Drab paint is of such a chemical make-up (probably caused by the untested mixing of various colors) that it acts much as a cumulative poison, like strychnine, resulting in damage to the human body. Over a period of time the O.D. dyes in fatigues, for example, will be absorbed by the skin, be carried by the blood stream to the brain, and once there slowly destroy brain cells. Studies show that not all the cells are affected, but instead, the O.D. deteriorates only those areas of the brain that carry on "value" functions such as innovation, creativity, pride, and aggressiveness.

The cumulative effect of this O.D. seepage into the body means that at some point (and this will vary according to body weight and mental strength) the limit will be reached where the brain cells have deteriorated beyond repair, resulting in the victims succumbing to the babble of the reenlistment NCO. Then, of course, all is lost.

The only solution to this disease of the army community is a preventive maintenance program that 1) insures that all enlisted men wear their fatigues and greens ONLY during duty hours and 2) that enlisted men either be allowed to "pull" the very minimum of extra duties or else wear civilian clothes while on extra duty. The importance of this preventive maintenance cannot be overly emphasized. Every minute counts. One minute too much could mean a "Lifer" (one who makes a career of the military). As soon as a man gets off duty he should immediately change into the more comfortable civilian attire even before the trip home or to the billets (a possible loss of as much as thirty minutes PER DAY). If a man's separation date can be reached before the body's tolerance level to Olive Drab, he is home free.

Realizing the dangers these young GIs might be in, I made it a priority to try and stop them from possibly making the worst decision of their lives. I found out who was Short (less than 90 days left) and I made trips to their rooms to council them. I explained to them what wearing Olive Drab fatigues was doing to them and told them what life would be like in the military. I was an army brat myself, and a year in this Mickey-Mouse battalion gave me some wisdom these new guys didn't have. Now, mind you, I didn't push them into what might be a wrong decision knowing some of them might actually enjoy the army's way of life; I figured the color green—Olive Drab green—<u>could</u> be for some people.

SP4 KIRK
–I SO LOVED SPIT SHINING BOOTS–
(Frank Dulfer Photo)

It wasn't long before Staff Sergeant Foskey came knocking on my billets-room door.

"SP4 Kirk, may I sit." Foskey removed his cock-bite cap and grabbed his perfectly straight, seamed-and-starched pant legs and pulled up on them as he sat carefully down on my bed.

"Of course," I replied. I hadn't actually met him, only heard of his unflappable reputation as a man who succeeds meritoriously at his job. He was a well-groomed, sharply dressed, black man with a likeable-enough personality; I guessed that was why he was good at his job. You could talk to him about your problems like he was your chaplain.

"Kirk, your name's been coming up a lot lately."

"How so?"

"Some of the men I thought were going to re-enlist in this man's army have changed their minds. They decided not to take the $6,000 bonus, not even the $10,000 I've offered them for five years additional service to our country."

"That's good to hear," I said, "I mean, it's good to know a little horse trading even in the army can get you a bigger pay check."

"You're not trying to keep them from re-enlisting are you?"

"No," I said, "just offer them some pros and cons. They have to make their own decision."

"I see. I'd like to hear some of those advantages and disadvantages to reenlisting."

With that, Sergeant Foskey sat uncomfortably on my sagging bed for over an hour as we discussed those "primary factors of unfavorability," and I talked about the problems with the system, that it wasn't the people in the army that were the problem, it was the system itself, this top down, vertical structure that stifled creativity and limited improvements in its management. He said we had to have a clear chain of command in wartime. I asked why the crap always flowed down the chain and never dribbled back up. He said he couldn't answer that. Higher ups never seemed to want advice and ideas from down below. I know; I tried to send dozens of letters with suggestions up that greased chain.

After that first meeting, we ran into each other at Headquarters or at the mess and continued to have discussions about the problems with the military, and before long, he was trying to get _me_ to re-enlist, saying they needed good men like myself. I returned the favor and tried to get _him_ to get out of the Army, saying they needed good men like him on the outside to sell used cars. We each continued to keep score, how many men I saved, how many men he conned into re-enlisting. To me, re-enlisting was like making a deal with the devil.

I didn't tell Foskey in so few words, but trying to turn me into a military man was like trying to put a square peg in a round hole. A uniform was not, and would never be, something I could bear.

NICKNAMES

Everyone seemed to acquire a nickname. If you had a nickname, no matter how crude, you were probably liked. If you didn't have a nickname, well, maybe you weren't such a cool cat. There was always someone in the unit who was the instigator of the new handles. Frank "Cockbite" Dulfer coined his fair share—like "Possum Shit" Arey—, but the high-spirited Sp4 Rich Taylor (known only as "The Kid") was the chief architect of most of the nicknames. Like it or not, his name for you would stick, like fresh cow dung. He dubbed his roommate, SP4 Childress, a blond ridge runner from Virginia, with "Chilibean" and PFC Floyd Wever, a tall, skinny-as-a-toothpick character with long flowing hair and a sunny disposition was called "Bean," a truncated version of "Beanpole." Bean built plastic airplane models in his room, and was a voracious consumer of Boone's Farm Apple Wine. He'd buy a case at the PX every payday. NCO James "Grit" Whitfield probably got his handle because he was from Georgia where one eats "grits" for breakfast (southerners never got an even break). Whitfield was a very nice, confident, and even-tempered squad leader, not always the case for some of our supposed leaders of men. PFC Oliver, a quiet, round-faced kid, was branded with "Ollie" after the Ollie of <u>Laurel and Hardy</u> fame: "Another fine mess you got us into!" William "Bill" Fauri, who wrote an article for Topo Topics, had scruffy blond hair, wore octagon-shaped glasses, and because of his quite-unassuming intelligence, reminded us of Hardy Krüger who played "Heinrich Dorfmann," the genius German airplane designer in, "Flight of the Phoenix." He was the aloof man who said he could build a flyable plane from the wreckage of their crashed plane so they could get out of the desert and back to civilization. The pilot, Jimmy Stewart, puts everyone to work only to find out Krüger is just a model airplane designer. We thought Bill was like that, very smart, just not in an obvious way. And then there was "Arab" Shada, a tall, skinny as a toothpick, Lebanese Nebraskan who could talk about nothing else except the University of Nebraska <u>Cornhuskers</u> football team. "The Big Red One" was in the running for their third championship in a row and he insisted upon keeping us all apprised of each week's scores, even to the point of recording his predictions in <u>Topo Topics</u>. Walking in formation, his head would bob above all the others. PFC Frost was a very short, five-foot, uppity, northeastern Jewish boy with a heavy mustache and "shadow" on his face; he always needed a shave even right after shaving. He was always at odds with Arab. When they got assigned a room together we knew there would be missiles fired. Arguments over Jerusalem's history would raise the roof.

Tompkins was a boiling pot of mixed personalities and cultural identities. "The Kid" Taylor, for example, worked out frequently, saying he was getting in shape to survive the end of the world. He said he was expecting some kind of thermonuclear holocaust and wanted to be prepared. He said the Islamic world would try to conquer all and kill all the infidels. He had already purchased a cabin in the woods somewhere in the States—he wouldn't say where—and was studying solar-energy technology and vegetable gardening. He was also collecting medieval weapons like the crossbow and mace. He was definitely headed off the deep end—and then again, maybe not?

WILKIE & VANDERDYKE

When Wilkie Ross first arrived at Tompkins, he was billeted with Headquarters Company on the third floor until space could be found for him on the second floor. He was assigned a room with the Battalion's Mail Clerk, PFC Vanderdyke, and Adan "Hiney" Hinojosa from Kingsville, Texas. Hinojosa, a quiet and reserved Hispanic who wore blue shirts with silver snaps, managed the armory located in the basement of our building. He handed out our M16's when we needed them and carefully inspected our rifles when they were returned. If they didn't pass muster, he wouldn't accept them. Vanderdyke was just the opposite, a typical Tompkins Barracks malcontent who complained about everything, the food, the duties, the job. But what pissed off Vanderdyke the most: The troops would drop by his mail room asking the same question, "Is there any mail for me?"

"Like yeah, man, who ta F— are you? I'm not gettin' paid ta know everyone's name?"

And when Vanderdyke's roommate Wilkie went to pick up his mail:

"Who ta hell is 'ME'? Do I have to know every swingin' dick in this F—n' battalion?"

If those letters from stateside hadn't been so important, Wilkie would have replied, "No, that's alright, Vanderdyke, you can keep my F—g mail. Shove it up your ass, you bellyaching a-hole."

"You understand," said Wilkie, "he wanted identification from me and I was his own damn roommate!" Vanderdyke did turn out to be an okay guy and soon Wilkie found his mail tucked under his pillow every evening when he came in from the Ramp.

Vanderdyke would smoke his bowl of weed—coughing after every hit—in Wilkie's room while playing his guitar every evening and that's when Wilkie began to spend all his free time at the movie theater or going on long jogs in the nearby woods. It was a godsend, he said, when he got moved down to the second floor and into a room with me and Kenneth Arey.

SMOKING AT THE RAMP

There were many cigarette smokers in our company, including Chief Maxwell, and the foul habit was condoned while working in the vans and the interior office areas of the Ramp. But I was allergic to many airborne particles and, as I later found out, had a deviated septum that obstructed my right nostril causing mucus to build thick and ugly. Running in cold weather—a daily PT exercise—made me throw up. I went to the military doctor in Heidelberg, and instead of identifying and treating the malady, he just gave me a permission slip

CHIEF MAXWELL MOCKING ME

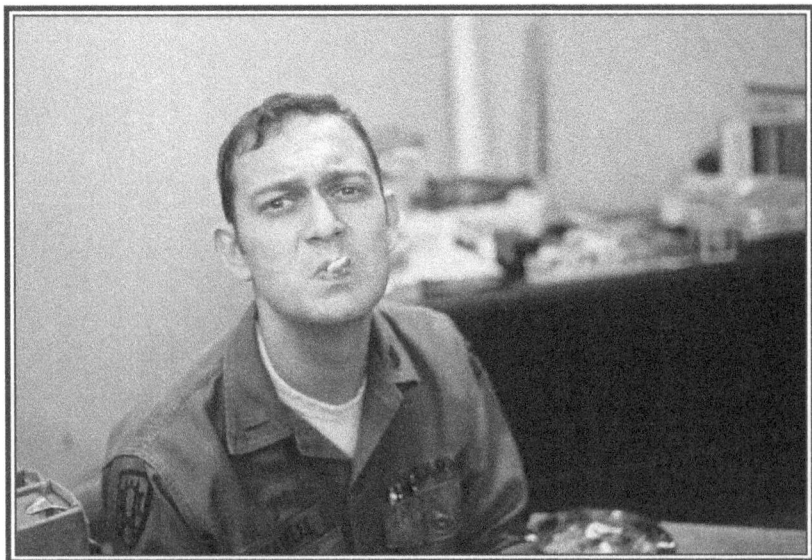

authorizing me not to run on cold mornings. That didn't help me at the Ramp when I was assigned to be an editor in the room where both "Big Al" Picklo and "Flash" Lilburn worked and smoked, so I raised a stink about it, saying I couldn't work in that putrid air. I was already a paying member of N.A.N.S.A.S.H.S., the National Association of Non-Smokers Against Second-Hand Smoke, and espoused, fervently, the evils of smoking. Everyone knew my opinion of this foul-smelling cancer stick. I told them it was more than just an annoyance to us non-smokers, it caused us psychological stress. They laughed. I said the smoke drifting from the burning ends of cigarettes carried more cadmium (a metal poisonous to man) than the smoke inhaled by an inconsiderate smoker. They said I was trying to take away their rights. I said smoking increased one's heart rate, blood pressure, and carbon monoxide in the blood. They said it was their only pleasure around this god-forsaken place. I said they'd be smoking no matter where they were; that they were "F——g addicts!"

"Do you want hypertension," I asked, or bronchitis, or maybe emphysema?" I had read the NANSASHS literature numerous times. "I care less if you get sick and die," I continued, "but us non-smokers are affected by cigarette smoke in the same F——g way as you and that takes away our right to clean air."

They didn't say anything. I stood my ground, acting like some kind of wimpy ingrate, and the M.A.S.H. boys, Picklo and Lilburn, were soon told by Chief Maxwell to kindly smoke outside. So they did (The Chief went outside too) and weren't seen much in Edit after that; it was just another excuse for them not to work and I found myself finishing their assignments. They had snookered me again. When they returned to The World, other people, like Glenn O'Neill, were moved in to replace them and I made sure they weren't smokers.

MY SLOT-CAR TRACK MOUNTED IN A CABINET

THE SLOT CARS

I found a hobby store on the <u>Haupstrasse</u> of Heidelberg that sold slot cars and I designed and built a seven-foot-tall cabinet with a table hinged to fold out, painted it red and black—not red, white and blue, <u>or</u> green—and screwed down an elaborate Grand Prix track with triple overpasses and exciting chicanes. It became a popular pastime and kept my room buzzing with activity until Captain Peal, our new, quiet and unassuming company commander, informed me that it wasn't allowed in my room, that it was exceeding the new army's VOLAR regulations (VOLAR was an attempt to recruit more volunteers by allowing longer hair and mustaches and by authorizing new furniture and beds for recruits. We actually got a cherry-red, steel desk for our room and many of us, including me, grew mustaches in an effort to express our individuality). My slot-car track folded up against the wall into a nice neat cabinet only nine inches thick. No said Peal, it had to go. The quiet and unassuming Captain Peal had just been assigned to our unit—replacing the sharp, intelligent, by-the-book Captain Arthur R. Shean—and he was going to do his best to prove he could step into Shean's boots. But I had a lot of money and time invested in it so I protested—respectfully. The compromise, if you can call it that, was to take the cabinet to the Day Room on the fourth floor where everyone could use it, including Depot and Headquarters. So that's where it went. And that's were it got brutalized and all the cars lost or broken. (When I got my separation papers, I was able to retrieve the track, ship it home, and later rebuild it.)

MAKING IT HOME

We were always trying to make the rooms in our barracks more habitable. The latest stereo equipment provided a peaceful aural atmosphere and something to do, but we needed more than just a wool O.D. green blanket-covered bed, so we slipped in what comforts we could (at least until the next GI inspection). For example, Glenn "Tommy Turtle" O'Neill went to the third-floor Day Room (the company's activity room having not much more than a television set showing German TV—and a broken slot-car track) and absconded with the couch, hauled it downstairs, and squeezed it into his room. The married guys got to live off post and live a normal life, but we single guys lived the life of a Basic Trainee: bunked together, showered together, frequent room inspections requiring hospital-cornered beds, emptied and cleaned trash cans daily, and no dust anywhere. After "Flash" Lilburn left, "Cockbite" Dulfer, and O'Neill found themselves bunking with "Big Al" Picklo. It was then that they really turned the refrigerator into a profitable business. After duty hours, they began to sell their beer and goodies to others in the

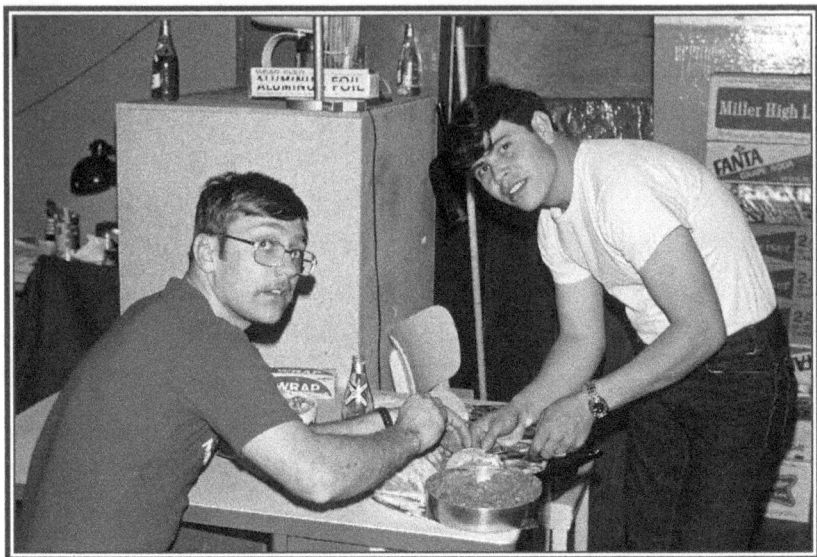

DULFER, HINOJOSA AND TEXAS CHALUPAS
(From the collection of Frank Dulfer)

barracks. It became known as "The Store." "Hiney" Hinojosa would come in to make real Mexican Chalupas and those would sell like hotcakes—they weren't the Mess Hall type.

While I was on CQ duty, I noticed smoke billowing quietly from under Picklo's door. I knocked.

"COME IN!" replied a crowd in unison. I entered.

Hinejosa was stirring ground beef in an iron skillet on Picklo's hotplate, hot oil splattering all over the place. I truly expected the fire marshal to show up.

"Hope you guys have a fire extinguisher," I said.

Picklo lifted up a bottle of red wine from the table.

O'Neill was chopping up onions and tomatoes and shredding cheese on his new red VOLAR desk.

Frank Dulfer, lying on O'Neill's couch, perked up, "Ahh, I smell Tacos!"

"Hey punto, don't call them tacos," rebuffed Hinejosa. "This is my grandpoppy's recipe for chalupas. He cooked for the hands at King Ranch. Call 'em tacos again and I'll have you cleanin' rifles."

Frank threw up his hands, "Love you man—and your chalupas too. I–know–you."

"Cost you double, Cockbite."

Hinojosa began to add other ingredients to his skillet. "Chili powder, cumin seeds, paprika, cayenne..." He then pulled from his shirt pocket a tiny jar, "And this is my secret spice—manífico!"

"They'll be manífico when I get them in my mouth," said Dulfer.

"Now for the Chalupa shells," continued Hinejosa as he slammed a small roll of dough into the skillet and after a loud performance of crackling and popping, flipped it over with his metal tongs. "Deep fried for fluffiness; crunchy on the outside, soft and chewy on the inside."

"Let me test 'em for taste," begged Dulfer.

O'Neill filled the shell with beef and makings and started to hand it to Dulfer, but pulled back and took a big mouth-watering bite for himself, "Damn! Beats Taco Bell by a kilometer. We can charge a dollar for these."

"Two dollars for Cockbite," added Hinojosa.

"Bite me," interjected Dulfer.

"Smell that aroma, "said Picklo.

"Smells a hell of a lot better than an Ozalid machine," added Dulfer."

"Cockbite!" barked O'Neill, "You just F—n' ruined it for me."

"I'm looking at the money we'll make," said Picklo. They'll be banging on our door any moment now."

"Just better not be the fire marshal," I said, "I wouldn't want to loose my honored duty as a CQ grunt."

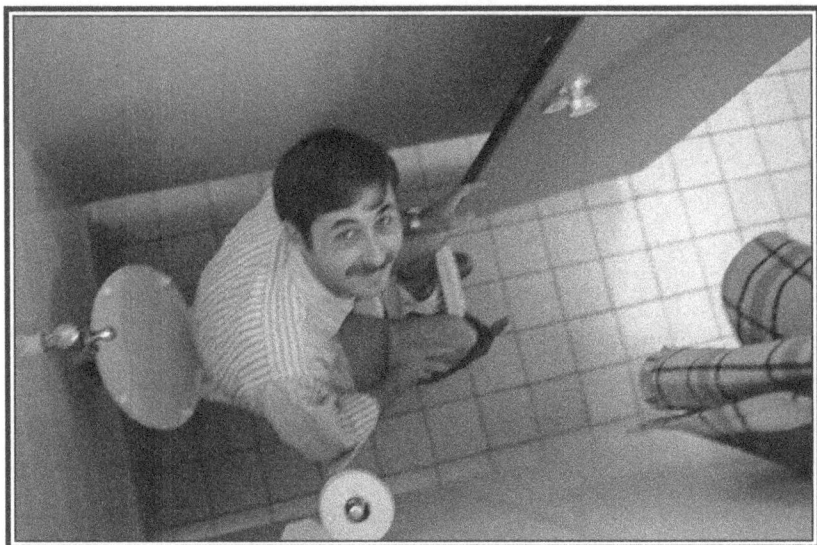

"I JUST LOVE THOSE CHALUPAS!"

"Get out of here, Kirk."

O'Neill took another bite, "Ooom, marvelous!"

Dulfer, cringing with desire, pulled out two dollars.

"These chalupas," said O'Neill, "may change my life. I may want to become a Mexican after this even if I don't have the requisite iron stomach."

Unfortunantly, the jalapeños left a lasting impression with O'Neill on the next morning's trip to the can.

Tokushia eventually made O'Neill return the couch to the Day Room. It broke his heart; who can blame him; it sure beat sitting on the bunk bed. Glenn then went to collecting <u>Mattel's</u> <u>Hot Wheels</u> which he found at a hobby store on the <u>Hauptstrasse</u>, the same place I found my slot-car racers. Old cars and hot-rods were his favorites and he would customize some by changing out wheels and, I swear, he'd try to tune up the cars. He should have requested reassignment to the motorpool. Having grease on his hands would have made him happy. Later, O'Neill found the old skeleton key to the original lock of his first room and that allowed him to lock this room from the inside. Glenn could then hide from anyone looking for him, like his squad leader, SSG Bruley, who was always coming to him to pull some "pissy detail." But, it wasn't long before SSG "Pineapple" Tokuhisa took the key away. O'Neill would have to find another way to avoid Bruley.

A NEW REGULATION

To combat the epidemic drug problem, General Michael S. Davison, Commander in Chief, USAREUR (United States ARmy EURope), declared that any door found locked in the barracks while you were inside your room would be removed. And taken from the hinges, many doors were, and stored in the basement, this happening all over Germany. But this new policy didn't hinder the Heads, they had there hashish room, the "Dope Den," in the attic.

GIs HIGH ON DRUGS WITH LOADED WEAPONS?

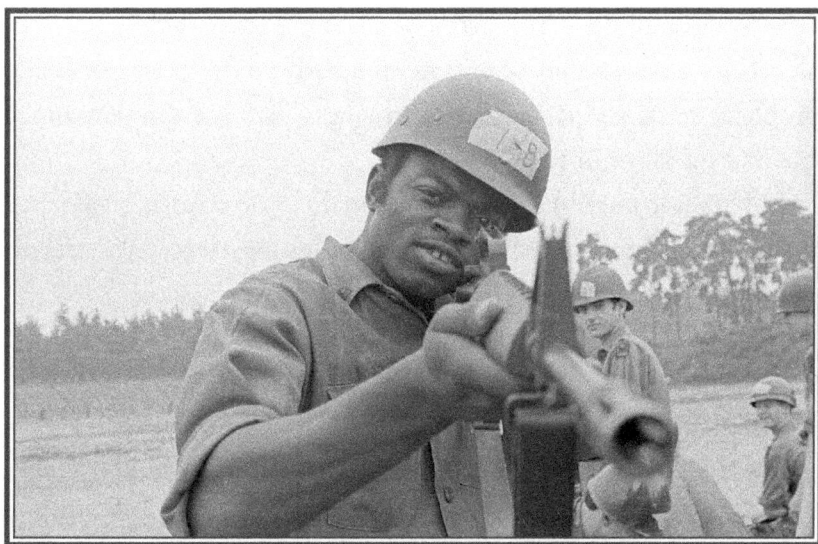

"This is good shit man!"

"Got it from a dude on the Hauptstrasse," said SP4 Kent.

Suddenly Jim McKay blurted out, "Cool, far out man, colors of a tie dye, make a real pretty American flag."

"You trippin', man?"

"Far out! The room ain't grey and green no more."

Michael Church looked up from his writing pad where he was writing the best poetry he had ever done, "Ho-hoh oh man, beautiful!" He then took a drag on the joint stuck between his fingers, "Assemble the squad on the quadrangle!"

"Huh, what, Church?"

"I've got my latest masterpiece to recite to you."

"You're shit-faced, Michael Church."

"F—in'-A, man."

Everyone ignored Church as he mumbled and fumbled and bumbled through his poem.

Mark Hughes was drawing a picture, or shall I say 'finger painting' on a piece of paper, "I'm likin' it, a Picasso."

"Yeah right, man. Tomorrow you'll say 'This is shit!'"

"I do my best stuff when I'm stoned. If you've got a personnel problem, see the Chaplain," said Hughes, This is F—in' amazin'. I can make a career of this."

"They don't need Pablos in the military," said Kent as he pinched the last of his roach and tried not to burn his mustache, "We need to Recon for some more shit, man."

"F—in' A," they all replied in unison.

O'NEILL SHORT?

Now that "Cockbit" Dulfer was a roommate of O'Neill's, Dulfer took the gloves off when it came to giving "no quarter." Cockbite was a laugh-riot even when sober and no one was immune to his ire. For example, Tommy Turtle was so short, and I don't mean time in service, that Cockbite would say to him, "O'Neill, you look like you're standing in a hole, a deep one, one that, maybe, goes half way to China."

Tommy Turtle would take it lying down, mainly because if he stood up the not-so-tall Dulfer would still tower over him.

"You need to carry around a crate to stand on, O'Neill, so I kin see you eye-to-eye."

"Who'd want to see you eye-to-eye?"

"They ought to have you cleaning the floor tiles in the hall, O'Neill, permanent duty, you wouldn't have ta get down on your knees."

"Dulfer, they ought to use your mouth to blow out the fire hoses." Glenn tried to get his own dig in, but it didn't catch fire.

"Anyone who thinks that cleaning out deuce-and-a-half battery boxes is one of the most memorable things about Germany has got to be a half-a-bubble off. You just like doing the battery boxes because you can stand upright while scrubbing them."

"I'm warning you, Dulfer!"

"Don't you have to use a ladder to clean out the cab, O'Neill?" asked "Big Al" Picklo as he savored a carefully-crafted cocktail.

"You know, Tommy Turtle, I'm thinking a story about Tompkins Barracks would make a good slapstick comedy, " added Dulfer, "I'd surely be played by Burt Reynolds—strong, handsome, genial—but I can't figure who would play your part."

"Steve McQueen could play my part," replied Glenn quickly.

"You hip and cool? You're kidding, right? They'd have to cut him off at the knees to play you."

"What do you mean? He's only five foot nine and a half!"

"And one half! You'd know his height wouldn't you?"

"A fellow short person."

"Not even in your league. To play you in the movie, we need the guy we just saw in Malatesta's Carnival of Blood, Bobo, the little runt with the high-pitched voice. He would be perfect to play you.

"They wouldn't even have to remove his shoes to get him down to your level, O'Neill," added Big Al.

"Let me see your boots, Tommy Turtle, you got high heels?" asked Dulfer, "The truth now."

"I got it," said Al, "How about Danny DeVito, the pirate in Scalawag?"

"Ha, hah, that' it!" cheered Dulfer, "He could wear your fatigues. Wouldn't have to add too much to the pant legs...well, not too much."

"I'm locking the refrigerator, right now, Dulfer, no more Weldebräu."

"I-know-you, I understand why they always put you in the front row of formation, O'Neill—so they can see you!"

"You're sick, Cockbite."

"When you fall into formation, it kinda messes up the nice symmetry of our platoon, don't-ya-agree, Big Al?"

Picklo nods.

"Why you nodding, Picklo, you've always got your hands in your pockets, even in formation?"

"Just playing pocket billiards."

"No doubt," said O'Neill.

"Don't change the subject, Tommy Turtle," interrupted Dulfer, "You're short, that's why they assign you CQ duty in the barracks when we march in front of the reviewing stand."

Picklo laughed and almost spilled his cocktail. He took the cherry and savored it. "Don't lock the refrigerator, O'Neill; get me the Bacardi and some ice."

"You want it shaken and not stirred?"

Picklo replied matter-of-factly, "In the movie, I'll be played by Sean Connery."

NO PRIVACY, MAN!

Down at the other end of the barracks hallway on our floor, I overheard—and you could hear a pin drop in that tunnel, what with the hard materials on all four surfaces—the "clean-sleeved" Depot Dudes venting to one of our black sergeants, Willie Green.

"This place, man, is becoming dreary and lifeless, they're making it like boot camp in the billets. Nobody's hip to what's happenin' man. This is our home," blasted Private Second Class Donald Waddell, a tall, slender, black man from Baltimore with an unauthorized Afro hairdo and tinted glasses, his fatigue cap setting askew way up on top of his massive Afro. Everyone looked up to Waddell, especially since he carried an impressive switchblade to claim his place as Depot "gang" leader. The officers and sergeants didn't mess with these guys and tended to let them be.

Another Dude butted in, "I think it sucks, man. No privacy, taking away your personal possessions. It's like, man, taking away your rights or something." He removed an Afro-Pick—a long-toothed, heavy wire comb—from his back pocket and ran it repeatedly through his long kinky hair.

"They've taken the doors off the room for a reason," replied the sergeant, "those personal possessions of yours are illegal."

"My water pipe cost me two-weeks pay."

"Ain't that a bitch, Waddell. Better do your smoking outside— better yet, off the post."

"You a brother, Green?"

"I hear what you're saying, Waddell, just chill man, they can't keep this up."

"What a rip-off!" Waddell spun around on his heels. "Oh, man, I'm bummed out, you can't even go to your own room no more and sleep without somebody comin' in. It's unconstitutional; I knows dat. They takes your stereo and clothes away. Just 'cause they're taking doors away, that ain't goin' ta stop drug use. There's gonna be a severe drop in morale and some swinging dick's going to get hurt. A pig will come in the room and somebody's going to get mad. I'm F—g mad now."

"Slack off Waddell, you boys chill." The sergeant was feeling the heat. But he didn't have to live in the barracks, he could toke a bowl at home all he wanted. "I'll see what I can do," he says.

"Eyes know it's da army's right to pull inspections, but dis is F—d!"

"Right on, brother." They all slapped each other's hands.

"Listen here, Willie," butted in Private Weeks, "We's stuck in thirteen-man rooms and we's at least had lockers partitioning the rooms for more privacy, but now we's got to move them all against da wall. All's we need now is butt cans and we'll feel wees is back in basic."

"If you had butt cans, Weeks, you'd just use them to dispose of the last of your joints."

"We don't leave no roaches, Sarge."

"Explains your burnt fingers."

"No," interrupts Weeks, "we uses a Roach Clip."

"The burnt fingers?"

"Lightin' my Bong."

With that, the Depot boys went through their "dap," a complicated three-minute soul-brother hand-shaking routine with each other. They palm slapped, bumped fists, snapped fingers, and clasp hands consuming at least another fifteen minutes before they finally cleared the hall. There was no way a "white dude" could learn the routine, and to do the "dap" you had to have it down pat or look stupid as hell. The dudes wanted to show they were "brothers" and everyone else was to stay out.

Coming from down the hall, blasting its way to us with glorious power and reverb, was our unofficial Vietnam anthem sung by The Animals: "We gotta get out of this place if it's the last thing we ever do..." In the end we were all brothers.

ON AND OFF THE ECONOMY

The Germans were cordial to me, quite nice actually. I took every chance I could to get off post and see Germany; I could travel to adjoining towns on the strassenbahns (streetcars) that scurried about with only a few minutes of waiting time between trains. For cities further away, like RheinMain, the standard gauge Federal Republic railway was the way to go. You could even take a bicycle with you and toot around the cobblestone streets of the many beautiful farming

THE STRASSENBAHNS MADE IT EASY TO GET AROUND

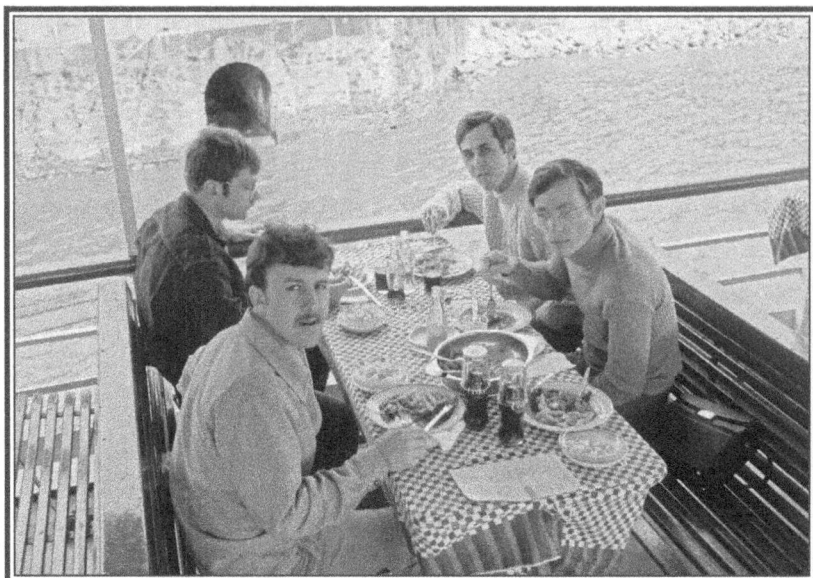

GREAT EATING ON THE RHINE RIVER
(WOODBURN, DULFER, O'NEILL, AND FAURI)

HOCKENHEIMRING–BUILT IN 1932
FORMULA ONE GERMAN GRAND PRIX

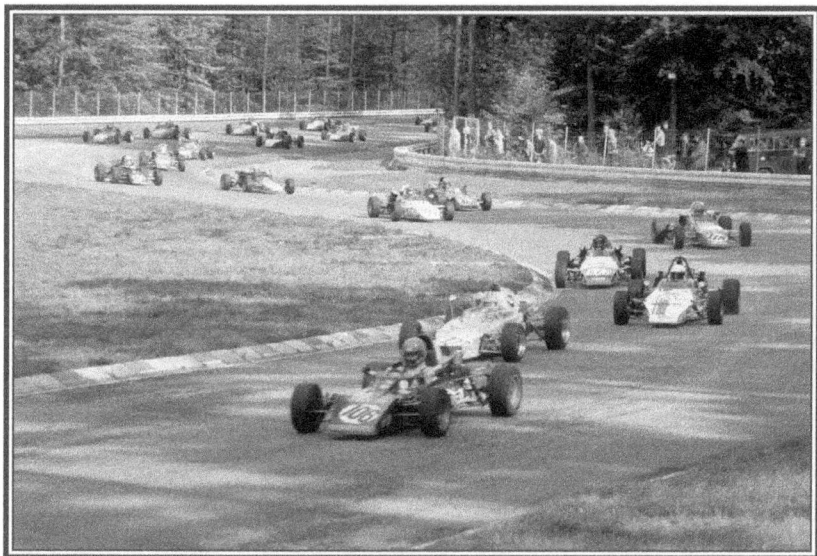

A CHICANE ON THE HOCKENHEIMRING

villages. There was no urban sprawl; instead, lots of green farmland separated the towns. I took a three-day pass when I could get it and took week-long, inexpensive tours provided by the Service Club to other countries. I got a taste of France, Switzerland, Italy, Belgium, Spain, and even England. I, along with others, took a boat trip up the Rhine River to see the mountaintop castles and Paul Balcavage and I would walk to Hockenheim to take pictures of Formula I races. You could get to most areas of the track—which wound through the woods—and stand right next to the course. To get better views, many Germans climbed into trees to watch the race. Not daring to climb down and loose their good "seat," they would unzip and pee out of the trees, not concerned with who might be standing below.

VOLKSMARCHING

Lieutenant Sneed invited a few of us—no more than a carload—to go on Volksmarching trips with him on weekends. We would travel

VOLKSMARCHING ACROSS GERMANY

to some town in Germany and hike ten or twenty Kilometers (6 or 12 miles) through the countryside and receive a medal for our efforts. "Volksmarch" means "people's walk" and on weekends families take part in organized walks through the beautiful European countryside. Each hiker (a "wanderer") received a souvenir medal illustrated with either the local village crest, a historic site, or a famous person. Scenic routes were chosen by the sponsors and the hikers came dressed in colorful jogging suits, hats, and footwear. Some jackets were covered with award patches, country flags, ribbons, etc. After thirty medals or so in my collection, Lt. Sneed offered us a special trip, one that he wanted to do, but which allowed only uniformed organizations to participate. It was the Internationale Bodensee-Wanderung, a three-day hike in three different countries—Germany, Austria, and Switzerland—for a distance of 100 Klicks(62 miles). From one campsite, we would be taken across Lake Constance to each country. One catch though. We had to have a uniform, so Sneed bought red baseball caps, and

–VOLKSMARCH MEDALS–
MORE VALUABLE TO SP4 KIRK THAN MILITARY AWARDS

white sweatshirts so we could represent America. I was wishing he had printed the organization's name as "The Tompkins Inmates." Instead, we carried our bright-red Corp of Engineers guidon with our great castle logo. We would carry our O.D.-green military backpacks, but our civilian hiking shoes all looked different so we decided to wear our black combat boots. What a mistake for me. I wore some shiny new boots I hadn't yet broken in and on the first day I got blisters so bad my feet had to be treated and taped up at the first-aid tent. I managed to complete the next two day's hike, but with a limp and searing pain. We got three good meals a day. Dulfer, Wever, SGT Eddy, SP5 Allen Jedd, and others were regulars on our marches.

DISTRAUGHT

As I said, I got off the post as often as possible, using every day of my accrued leave and all my three-day passes to wander through the streets of Heidelberg with my Nikkormat in tow, taking pictures of the architecture and the people who lived within. It was a great respite from the stuffy, gray and green world of Tompkins, a place that I compared to a prison, a place that would enrage me for years to come. It seemed like a contradiction, I was

MY VOLKSMARCHING OUTFIT
LEDERHOSEN AND SHINY MEDALS

making many trips outside "The Prison" and still felt I was trapped. It was simple, I didn't choose to be in the Army, and America was about freedom and rights of the individual wasn't it?

I sat in a corner café where I could see out the window and up and down the little cobblestone streets, watching people walking, talking, and shopping. I watched the bustle of small cars, Mercedes-Benz delivery trucks, and horse-drawn lorries as they wound their way through the narrow streets of Schwetzingen. Shops were on the street level and the owners lived above them. And along any street, behind double doors, you could find a barnyard in the middle of town. The milk cows were stabled at ground level so that in winter their rising body heat would provide warmth for the family living upstairs. A person could bicycle to work or hop a quietly-running strassenbahn between picturesque villages—villages separated by farm fields, forests, and green hills—not at all like the urban sprawl of America's single-family homes. The café was cozy, quiet, and laid back. Guests were encouraged to stay as long as they pleased, play checkers, talk, guzzle beer, and guzzle more beer. I ordered a Wienerschnitzel, the only German word for a food I knew, so that's all I ever ordered, and

TYPICAL CITY BARNYARD BEHIND CLOSED DOORS

popped one of the tavern's beer coasters into my pocket. I reflected on how the world was so much different out beyond the walls of the Tompkins compound, its concertina wire making it perfectly clear that it was a prison. How did I deduce this? The three barbed wires at the top were angled inward, just as the ones at the stockade, designed to keep people in, not out. Maybe we had on the back of our fatigue jackets, the word, "INMATE." I ordered a Heineken, a good Dutch lager, smooth to the pallet, something I could tolerate, and sipped on it. No the army was not for me. My dad was a career officer, a Bird Colonel in fact, and I'm sure he would have liked to see me stay in, but it just wasn't my predilection. I couldn't envision what work I would do in the military. I sure didn't like the idea of marching men around a quadrangle, left right, left right, platoon halt, about face, dress right dress. To me innovation was not encouraged and progress was not apparent. The U.S. Army was always ready for the last war; any changes and improvements happened only under duress, during a frickin' war. For something to do, I wrote a screenplay titled "Erika" with the hopes of shooting it with the Bolex super-8mm camera I had brought to Germany with me. I had bought the camera with the money I had made at a summer job as a "Fallout Shelter Analyst." Yes, in 1969, I was crawling through musty schoolhouse basements trying to determine if they'd qualify as protection from a nuclear blast. They never came close. It was an obvious waste of taxpayer money, but it was another government program that once started couldn't be stopped. The great locations in Germany were inexpensive "money shots" on film and would make for a great action-adventure thriller— but rounding up guys to help me make it, what with them drinking and smoking and getting put on last-minute extra-duty rosters, I gave up on that idea.

PRACTICAL JOKES

For entertainment, practical jokes popped up on occasion, especially when a FNG was assigned to the unit who just happened to be a born-again jokester, and no one was immune, but some soldiers deserved everything they got. SSG Francis Bruley, a "bumbling fool" of a squad leader, well, things were always happening to him by some unseen force. According to O'Neill, the man couldn't function without his clipboard. His plans for the day were scribbled down along with the names of his squad members and without it Bruley was "plumb flustered," didn't even know who was on his squad! "Eddy, is he in my squad?" asked Bruley. O'Neill replied, "No you dumb bunny, he's also a squad leader!" And it seems Bruley's clipboard was frequently being misplaced, by him, or some unseen force! The clipboard was apparently his brain and thus his memory bank, and nothing could be accomplished without it. Once, he found his fatigue cap nailed to his desk, and black printer's ink mysteriously appeared on his left ear. The ink just happened to be on his telephone's handset. When it came time to rotate out of the unit, a quiet cheer went up, but Bruley couldn't find the orders for his new duty station. Where was he to report? What military base? When? He didn't remember. For the first time the squad members wanted to help him and went frantically looking for it. "Just one more minute of this sergeant and I'm going to..."

Soon, one of the guys found the orders in the top drawer of Bruley's desk, of all places, and then thought, "Hold on just a darn minute. Do we give it to him, or make him jump through hoops to get another copy?"

"Hoops!" of course was the answer by all and they mounted a grand "D-Day" assault. They figured Bruley would first go to the Company Commander's office and see if a copy could be had. One of the guys made a beeline to the office with the found orders. The clerk on duty was PFC Church who also disliked Bruley and was quick to help with the D-Day plan. He pulled the company commander's copy of the orders from Burley's file, snickered a devilish grin, and with his typewriter and a dab of white correction fluid changed the Frankfurt am Main out-processing date to the very next day instead of the week away that was shown on the form.

"Here, give me the original and give this copy to Bruley."

We did and Sergeant Bruley panicked and scurried like a chicken with his head cut off as he turned in his blanket and sheets, packed up all his gear in his O.D.-green duffle bag, and filled out the necessary paperwork so he would be ready to leave the next morning. That next day, the assigned duty driver picked him up and headed for Frankfurt, but the driver got lost on the way. Burley screamed at him in a panic as the driver went down one narrow street and then another. Bruley would miss his scheduled arrival time. The duty driver was one of ours, in on the plan, and got lost on purpose. He eventually returned Burley to Tompkins Barracks and the Company Commander's office.

Bruley handed PFC Church his orders, "I missed my out processing. This F—g idiot got us lost!"

"Oh, hell," replied Church, "you've got the wrong orders, those were to be thrown away. Headquarters has delayed your out processing at Frankfurt for another week. Here's the correct orders." Church handed him the original orders. "I guess you'll have to get your bedding back out of Supply." Church said the expression on Bruley's face was priceless.

STREAKING TO BEAT THE BAND

In another practical joke, this one on me, four of us managed to get together and agreed to streak across the parade ground in the

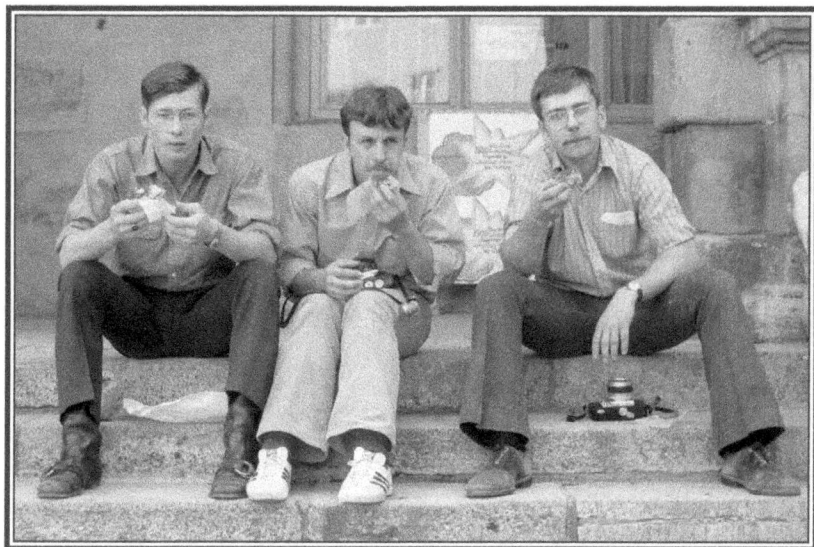

SIGHTSEEING—FAURI, WOODBURN, AND DULFER

early evening just after dark. Streaking—running naked in public—was a popular pastime in the states. Carefully planned, we placed our clothes at the back of our barracks near a window over the roof of an attached building, a window we could climb back into. Then we ran naked from our rooms down two flights of stairs and out past the door guard to the quadrangle where we ran lickety-split to the flagpole and then circled around to the back of our barracks. When we got there, we found our clothes gone and the window closed and locked. Guys were peering down at us through the second-story windows and laughing their tails off. It was cold; we had goose bumps the size of double-ought buckshot. And by now, since we were required to sign out and didn't, the CQ had probably reported us. This was not a good way to pass the time, I thought, and then realized, there were only three of us standing there shivering. The Kid was missing. He was the one that had goaded us into pulling this stunt in the first place, and now I knew...<u>he</u> had absconded with our clothes! The sec-

EATING—AERY, CHILDRESS, WOODBURN, AND MYSELF

ond-floor window opened and The Kid stuck his head out and said, "go back around to the front, the guard's in on it, he'll let you in." I didn't buy it. We tried the basement door to the MESS kitchen, it was locked and it was then that some animal started scratching and screaming in the bushes. It was Suzie, Scotty's pet raccoon (he had lowered the cage out of his window with a hook and line). We freaked out and ran buck naked back around the building, into the quadrangle, and back to the front door. We pulled open the heavy door, our privates dangling, and ran in and past the door guard and up the steps and back to our rooms. We were "The Streakers," the fastest things on two feet. The Kid had a laughing, fall-down fit, but nothing came of it, just cheers and jeers for the next week as enlisted men and officers alike got word of it. We wanted to go hide.

LaCROSSE

It was The Kid who played Lacrosse in his little barracks room, you know, slinging a rubber ball at each other with nets on sticks. I hoped he didn't insist on the rules—rules for body checking, face-offs and a goalie sitting on the sill of an open window! Did he mark the center of the field with white tape? The room was only 20 feet deep and fully furnished. "Body checking is permitted if the opponent has the ball," said The Kid when John Woodburn, who liked to play flag football, asked about the rules, "you can hit above the waist and below the shoulders. So yeah, Woody, it is a contact sport. Wanna play or not?"

There were many evenings in the barracks with nothing to do; no wonder games like this came into use.

MACHT NICKS

I took a class in German, but I lasted through just two of their lessons, all they taught was a complicated grammar scheme—and had us conjugating verbs—and Mark Hughes, Kent and I, just looked at each other with a "Huh?" Mark mumbled something like, "There's no chance in hell I'll ever get my G.E.D.," so instead of going to the class, I picked up a book of Berlitz phrases like Guten tag, Auf Wiedersehen, Wo ist der Bahnhof? and Entschuldigen, bitte (pardon me)—just in case I bumped into anyone. And I added Ich liebe dich (I love you) to my repertoire in case I met someone absolutely beautiful and irresistible, even if her legs and underarms were unshaven. But unfortunately, I pronounced my phrases far too well—I was of seventy-five percent German ancestry—and the Germans always came back to me in German spiel and I was lost, I would say Ich verstehe nicht, or Sprechen Sie nein Deutsch, and they'd shrug their shoulders and walk off. We young Americans always learned their dirty words first (Scheisse!, das Arschloch!), just as they learned ours first, and often times you could see two guys having fun throwing expletives at one another. They loved to learn the English language, but we Americans

GERMAN BIERGARTEN–EIN PROSIT!

apparently had no such desire (other than corrupting phrases like "es macht nichts" into Mox Nix (it doesn't matter). You can see why that would be a popular phrase among the GIs.

THE BREAD OF LIFE

And then there's the beer drinking lifestyle of the Germans. With a sacred four-hundred-year-old Purity Law that regulated brewing, and beers brewed in almost every hamlet, beer to them was flussiges Brot (literally meaning "liquid bread"), a vital part of their diet. GIs were happy with the cheap der Fusel (rotgut), and the EM club was the place to get it. All the soldiers knew how to order beer: Ein Bier, Bitte! And then there were the Biergartens (circus-like tents with an omm pah-pah band and rows of tables of jubilant Germans sloshing tankards of beer and screaming Prosit!—to your health!).

Sitting along miles of tables under huge tents, happy Germans and happier GI's sang In Munich Stands a Hofbräuhaus:

In Munchen steht ein Hofbrauäuhaus
Eins, zwei, g'suffa!
Da lauft so manches Fasschen aus,
Eins, zwei, g'suffa!
Da hat schon mancher brave Mann,
Eins, zwei, g'suffa!
Gezeigh, was er so verlragen kann!
Schon fruh am Morgen fing er an,
Und spat am Aben^i kam er heraus.
So schon ist's im Hofbräuhaus'
Ein Prosit, ein Prosit der Gemütlichkeit,
Ein Prosit, ein Prosit der Gemütlichkeit!

But it was only the Eins, zwei, g'suffa! that we GI's blared out as we raised our mugs and gulped another foaming swig of the tasty brew. Translated, the song mirrored our sentiments this day:

In Munich stands a beer hall
One, two, drink!
There, so many barrels run dry,
One, two, drink!
There, many a brave man has shown,
One, two, drink!
What he can guzzle down!
Early in the morning, lies begin,
And late at night, he leaves.
That's how nice it is in the Hofbrauhaus!
A toast, a toast to friendship,
A toast, a toast to friendship!

"Cockbite" Dulfer and Chief Maxwell were drinking us all under the table. Woody was a T-totaler, drinking only Coke, or what was that they were pouring in his Coca-Cola glass? But less than a litre could get me soused and dancing on the table. Luckily we had the strassenbahn to take us back to Tompkins.

There were also innumerable pubs lining the main streets of Heidelberg, the strassenbahn running from Schwetzingen (almost at our front door) and right down the middle of Haupstrasse (Main Street). GI's were lumbering from one bar to the next; in fact the streets after dark were frequently crowded with soldiers in non-regs (civilian clothes). Beer is Germany's national beverage; it is to Germans what apple pie is to Americans, so Deutschland was one big beer keg to us GIs. Me, I just collected the cardboard beer coasters with all their colorful graphic designs. "Bean" Wever collected the beer steins and

THE MILE-LONG HEIDELBERG HAUPSTRASSE
WITH NUMEROUS SHOPS AND BARS

drinking glasses elaborately decorated with the village's coat-of-arms or historic sites.

ALBERT'S

One of our favorite GI hangouts for a good meal and lots of beer was at Albert's Gasthaus located just a few miles down the railroad line to Schwetzingen and next to the Schlossgartens. It was popular among the GIs and a favorite of our Photomapping platoon. It was a great place for good food and beer. They had sandwiches called the "Heavy Duty" with an excellent bread that had a crust tougher than the sole of a combat boot. The Jaegerschnitzels (pork cutlets) and the chicken and veal Cordon Bleus swimming in a wine sauce were absolutely awesome. They had a bizarre slot machine with spinning wheels that you could, and would, feed pfennigs (1/100 of Mark) into all evening long. If you got lucky it would pay off and cover the cost of the meal, or more often than not, at least the cost of the beer (one Mark and 10 pfennigs). The conversion rate was about four Marks to a dollar.

Albert Seitz and his wife ran the Gasthaus. Albert was a relatively short stocky guy with an endearing smile and a raspy, breathy voice. He was usually behind the bar, polishing wine glasses or sanitizing beer mugs while carrying on a conversation with his patrons. His wife spoke English. She apparently learned English while living in Chicago for a time. She waited tables as did their daughter and son, Wolfgang. It was definitely a family business that cared for their patrons.

They had a large round table that was reserved for favored regulars, and it seemed that we were one of the favored. Even if the room was full of patrons and we were about to leave—the round table occupied—Albert's wife would motion us over and those at the table would grab their drinks and move to empty chairs so as to give us the table.

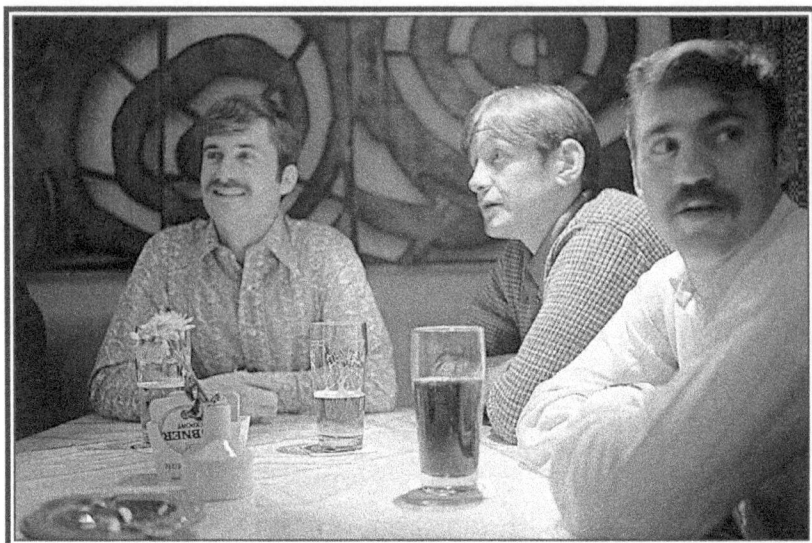

"BIG AL" PICKLO, "ODIE" ODINGA, AND "BEETLE" BAILEY

Those leaving the table would smile and nod in appreciation. We felt honored. It seemed that the Germans did indeed appreciate us being there in their country to provide them with a sense of security—as false as it might be. We felt a special friendship. After all, Germany was where many of our grandparents came from.

"Cockbite" Dulfer had been at Tompkins only a week when the Old Timers "Big Al" Picklo and "Flash" Lilburn took the FNGs (F—g New Guys) to Albert's Gasthouse for the first time. (Frank Dulfer, Paul Balcavage and Woody Woodburn were among the New Guys having just arrived together from AIT at Ft. Belvoir.) When they got to the Gasthaus, they sat in a small booth by the window and the Old Timers made sure the FNGs were sandwiched in the middle between themselves. They started off the evening with a litre of beer. Cockbite thought this was great, thought he had died and gone to heaven. It was his first litre of Weldebräu (a local beer), but it wouldn't be his last before leaving Germany. About half way

"DRINK!" THE OLD TIMERS FILL WOODY'S GLASS WITH
SOMETHING OTHER THAN COCA-COLA

through the litre Cockbite was squeezing his thighs and asked to get
out to use the Heren (the men's room). That's when he discovered
why the FNGs were in the middle. Big Al and Flash wouldn't let
them out until they had finished the litre. They eventually emptied
the pitcher—Cockbite and the others red in the face—and were finally
allowed to go to the men's room. Then the Old Timers threw in
for another litre and it was brought to the table. Oh, and wouldn't
it be a good idea for everyone to have a shot of Jägermeister with
their second pitcher? Jägermeister (Hunting Master) was a 70-proof
drink loaded with herbs and spices. A twelve–point buck was the logo
on the label. Some Germans referred to it as Leberkleister meaning
"liver glue;" I don't know why. I'm guessing it was to seal the liver so
it could handle more beer. The men stayed at Albert's until closing
and Cockbite left feeling very well indeed—happy as a lark, ready
to sing—but as luck would have it, just after his head hit the pillow,
about 1:30 AM that morning, he heard yelling in the hall and a knock

on the door, or shall I call it loud bangs. Dulfer was experiencing his first FTX "Alert." Startled by the commotion and still inebriated, he went to take a cold shower to wake up, but when he finally showed up for formation our platoon sergeant "Pineapple" Tokuhisha had a few words:

"Where've you been, Dulfer? Everyone else is here."

"Taking a shower, sir."

"Taking a shower? What ta hell do you think this is, a formation for a Saturday night dance?"

"No sir."

"If you call me 'sir' again—get your swinging dick out there!"

"Yes, sir."

"Dulfer, Dulfer..." he repeated himself, "I don't ever want to see you taking a shower when we have an Alert. Got that?"

"Yes, sergeant."

"You sleep with your boots on if you have too, be out here lickety-split because there's a damn lot of work to get done in order to roll out of here in just two hours."

"Yes, sergeant."

Dulfer never took a shower again during an alert.

REENLISTING A DRUNK

Understandably, many of the guys became heavy drinkers while they were in the Army. "Big Ron" Attenburg was drinking more and more and the army still wanted him to re-enlistment. Staff Sergant Foskey, our reenlistment NCO, signed him up. "Big Ron" was a large, husky fellow, who's drinking had gotten so bad, he missed not one, but two re-enlistment ceremonies. On both occasions, he was so bleary-eyed drunk that he couldn't get out of bed even though he knew he'd have $10,000 deposited to his bank account if he just showed up. SSG Foskey wouldn't give up on Attenburg and on his third attempt to get Ron officially re-enlisted (Foskey must have been getting a commission), he assigned "Bean" Wever and O'Neill to make sure he stayed sober and hand deliver him to the ceremony "fit for duty." They followed him around, stopped him from going to the

PFC DULFER–DRINKING THROUGH HIS EARS (Paul Balcavage Photo)

EM club, checked his Mox Nix box and under his pillow for a hidden stash of liquor (found several bottles of course), guarded his door during the night, and made sure he was up "bright and bushy" the next morning. They got him to shave, but eating breakfast was a new thing for him and when he got ill at the mess hall, they had to skip that. They got him dressed in his Class A's and chaperoned him to the ceremony. Attenburg got his promotion and $10,000. But O'Neill pointed out, "the guy needed counseling, not more promotions." I added, "The Army accepts drinking as part of the army way, and makes alcohol tax free and easily accessible. If Attenburg had been a hashish smoker he'd been out on his keister a long time ago."

BEETLE BAILEY AND ALCOHOL

One evening Jim "Beetle" Bailey was busted for DWI in a deuce-and-a-half while driving in a housing area. Beetle and Cockbite were coming back from working a pig roast at the Battalion Commanders house. Tokushia had been cooking a pig Hawaiian style and had recruited them to help set up chairs and then clean up afterwords. They guzzled a few beers while they worked and guzzled a few more. On the road back to Tompkins late that night, loaded with chairs and tables, Beetle found himself cruising a little too fast through a housing area. Talk about a prime target, a big green military truck—headlight beams vibrating on the cobblestones and buildings—weaving down the narrow streets of Schwetzingen. Flashing lights appeared behind the truck and Cockbite told Bailey it looked like the <u>Polizei</u> were behind them.

"What? Hell, man, I'm almost home."

"Better stop, Beetle."

"I'm stopping, I'm stopping."

"Sober up quick!"

A BIRTHDAY PARTY FOR POSSUM—BEER INSTEAD OF CAKE
(FROM TOP LEFT: PICKLO, AERY, BAILEY, FAURI, BALCAVAGE
BOTTOM LEFT: ODINGA, DULFER, AND O'NEILL)
(From the collection of Paul Balcavage)

BEETLE'S DRINK OF CHOICE

"Shit, Cockbite! Our goose is cooked."

"Your goose is cooked."

Beetle checked the rear view mirror and it looked like he was about to crap in his pants. He slowed to a stop and rolled down the window. A man in a military helmet appeared, on the helmet a big white "MP"—our own Military Police. That was good, much better than the German Polizei; they probably would have thrown away the key. The MP's took Beetle and Cockbite from the cab and put them in the back of their 3/4 ton. They locked up Beetle in the Heidelberg MP station (which was just across the street from Susies), and Cockbite waited in the lobby for several hours until the Staff Duty Officer picked them up. Pineapple would not be happy.

In another case, Beetle was arrested, this time, by the German Police when he wrecked "Flash" Lilburn's POV while driving drunk (surprise, surprise). He had borrowed the car with Flash's approval, but Flash had to testify that Beetle stole the car, or else Flash would have also been arrested. Bottom line, Beetle was the GI that gave U.S. soldiers a bad name in Germany. There's always one in every pack of Marlboro's. Maybe the comic strip was written about him.

BEETLE'S FAVORITE JOKE

"Beetle" Bailey, was one of the guys at our ramp who would head into Heidelberg almost every night after work to partake in beer and loose women. He would then guzzle <u>Pepto-Bismol</u> after spending a night on the town. One day, and for days after, Beetle told a joke all over the Tompkins Barracks compound. The question was, did he learn anything from it? It went something like this:

An American soldier having a good time bar hopping on the Heidelberg <u>Haupstrasse</u> walks into a German bar and notices a very large glass jar sitting on the bar and sees that it's filled to the brim with 20-Deutschemark banknotes. The soldier guesses there must be

ANY EVENT WAS AN EXCUSE FOR A DRINKING PARTY
–WEVER, WHITFIELD, AND HINOJOSA AS A MEXICAN BANDITO–

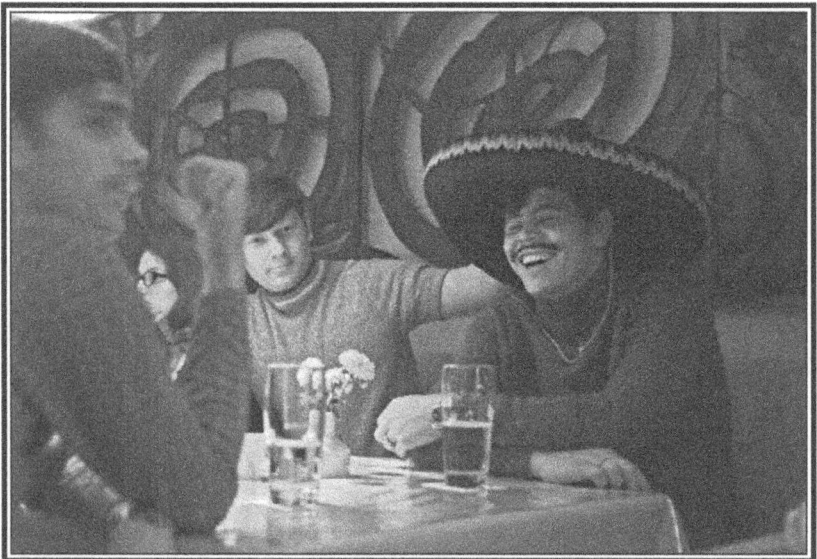

at least five-thousand Marks in it. He approaches the bartender and asks, "What's with the money in the jar?"

"Vell, you put in twenty Marks, and if you pass three tests, you get all zuh money in zuh jar and zuh keys to a brand new Volksvagen Beetle."

The man certainly isn't going to pass this up, so he asks, "What are the three tests?"

"You must pay first," says the bartender, "zoz are zuh rules."

So, after thinking it over for a while, the soldier gives the bartender a 20-Mark bill that he stuffs into the jar. "Okay," says the barkeep, "here's vhat you need to do. Erste—first, you have to drink a whole litre of tequila in sixty seconds or less, and you no can make face vile doing it." "Zweiten, zare's a pit bull chained in the back with a bad tooth. You have to remove that tooth vith your bare hands." "And dritten—there's a 90-year old lady upstairs who's never had sex. You must take care of zat problem."

The soldier is stunned! "I know I paid my twenty Marks, but I'm not an idiot! I won't do it! You'd have to be nuts to drink a litre of tequila and then do all those other things!"

"Your call," says the bartender, "but, your money stays vare it is."

As time goes on, the soldier has a few more beers and finally says, "Where's the damn tequila?"

The bartender hands him a bottle and looks at his watch. The soldier grabs the tequila with both hands and drinks it as fast as he can. His face turns beet red and tears stream down both cheeks, but he doesn't make a face and manages to finish in 58 seconds. He then staggers out the back door where he sees the pit bull chained to a pole. Soon, the people inside the bar hear loud growling, screaming, and the sounds of a horrible fight...then there's nothing but dead silence! Just when they think that the soldier surely must be dead, he staggers back into the bar. His uniform is ripped to shreds and he's

AN OUT-OF-CONTROL TRUCK ON
SCHWETZINGEN STREETS–LOTS OF FUN

bleeding from bites and gashes all over his body. He drunkenly says,
"Now, where's that old woman with the bad tooth?"

Beetle seemed to live that kind of life—on the edge.

RUNAWAY DEUCE

I was driving alone in a Deuce-and-a-half (2-1/2 ton cargo truck)
back from Heidelberg loaded with crates of supplies. Driving over an
arched, stone bridge in Schwetzingen, the truck began to gallop away
from me. Faster and faster down the lee side of the bridge, the engine
pulling me forward, people crossing the narrow cobblestone street, a
horse-drawn dung wagon poking along just up ahead. Apparently the
accelerator cable had broken. (In later vehicles, if the cable breaks,
the vehicle will slow down, but not these WWII relics.) What to do?
I stepped on the brake; the wheels only jumped, skidded and smoked.
I tried to double clutch and downshift my five-speed manual, grind-

ing the gears—the engine wined—but the deuce had no intention of slowing down. I had a bad feeling in the pit of my stomach. I could see a blown engine, cow dung and horses strewn about the street, little German ladies running in panic, a squad of Polizei interrogating me, my driver license pulled for life, and the worst of all, "Pineapple" Tokuhisha with a platoon-sergeant in-your-face deadly ire. I was cooked! How to stop this green monster? Finally, it came to me, I gathered my wits and just turned the ignition key. The diesel engine shut down and I coasted to the right side of the road. With no telephone, all I could do was get out and walk to the Barracks. I hoped my valuable load of crates would not be absconded with by a German bicycle gang bent on getting even with American GI's. But as luck would have it, the spared dung-wagon driver offered me a ride; he was going in my direction. So, what to hell, it wasn't too far; I could take shallow breaths. He did let me sit on the wagon seat next to him and not on top of the towering dung pile. That was a memorable experience, horse hoofs clopping lazily on the cobblestones.

AUDIO EQUIPMENT AND THE TARZAN SHOW

A popular activity was to travel to the PX in Rhein-Main and buy the latest and best audio equipment. We were allowed a "Mox Nix" box in our rooms to stash our personal stuff. (Mox Nix was a GI corruption of the German word " Maux nicht" meaning "It doesn't matter," and was used by GI's frequently. The wooden box was usually a hand-me-down from a GI who had rotated out, the most successful recycling system I'd ever seen. The Mox Nix box was crammed full of audio components, accessories, record albums, and audiotapes. Since these items were not taxed in the military PX, we were able to buy equipment we would never have been able to afford back in the states. I bought a TEAC 1/4-inch four-channel reel-to-reel

MY AUDIO EQUIPMENT—A COMMON SOLDIER'S PASTIME

tape recorder, a JVC Quadraphonic receiver with five-band equalizers, a DUEL turntable, a TECHNICS Phillips cassette tape deck, and four huge, heavy, mahogany cabinet CORAL speakers that I can't fathom how I got them stuffed into our small two-man room.

We used the equipment to play the latest rock-band 33-1/3 rpm vinyl's, the good ole days of free time in the barracks. We would spend hundreds of hours recording each other's albums, carefully cataloging the songs on each reel. We would carefully study the literature to decide what to buy after our next payday. To us, life was a government check every two weeks to buy stereo equipment.

One evening, refusing to be bored by barracks life and tired of listening to music, we decided to record a "Wolfman Jack" type 50's music radio show making use of my multi-track tape recorder to overlap separately recorded tracks, use reverb, sound effects, and two tape speeds to simulate a radio show called the Tommy the Tarzan Thomas Show broadcast from Hickey, Iowa. It was 1973 and already there was nostalgia for 50's music, like "The Twist" by Tommy Checkers, "Big Girls Don't Cry" by Frankie Vallie and the Four Seasons, "Chantilly Lace," and "She's Got a Ticket To Ride." Between music cuts we added comedy segments. Rich "The Kid" Taylor was the host, "Tommy Turtle" O'Neill interviewed "The Chipmunks," and "Cockbite" Dulfer was interviewed as several different phone-in-guests: Anthony "Tony" Salvador Chico Gobleeari and Jack Ett the Loser. We all wondered what Cockbite was like back in high school. I doubt that his teachers could keep him in his seat, what with thumbs in his ears, a fist in his mouth, and regular demonstrations of his ability to eat "lugars." Cockbite created an infamous comedy bit called "Who Poked Out My Left Eye in the Third Grade?" It went something like this:

"What's your name and how long have you been here at Central Valley High?" asked "Tommy the Tarzan" Taylor.

With a mouth full of marbles, Cockbite replied,

"My name is Anthony Salvadory Chico Gobleeari, but my friends call me Tony Salvadory Chico Gobleeari. And seein' as I'm your guest, you can call me Tony. I've been here four years."

"Four years? Are you a senior this year?"

"I will be a freshman this coming September.

"Oh yeah, freshman? Four years?"

" I had a little run in with my principal, yeah, with my '56 Chevy."

"What are your plans for the future?"

"Well, Jim, I tell ya, I got a lot of experience here at CV High with automobiles. I want to go into the Army and be a grease monkey and follow in the footsteps of many of my forefathers, especially my old man. I want to be maybe a first sergeant. A leader of men."

"Well, Tony, let me ask you a question and if you get the right answer you will win two free tickets to the Green Valley Drive-in."

"Oh no, Jim, let me ask you a question and if you win you get an Early Out of this man's army."

"Uh, yeah sure Anthony...but—"

A song played.

"Well, for one thing Tony, my name's "Tommy the Tarzan" Thomas.

"What? I must have the wrong station. Then, I don't know you, you gotta use my whole name, Anthony Salvadory Chico Gobleeari."

Tommy the Tarzan spun another vinyl, then another call:

"This is Jack Ett The Loser. I got a question for you?"

"Sure 'nough, Jack."

"What you win is if you don't answer you gotta play a song for me."

"Okay, Jack. What is the question?"

"Who poked out my left eye in the third grade?"

"Ohhh, man, that's a tough one. Was it Mary Ann—"

"Nope, you lose, I want to hear Loop de Loop by Johnny Thunder. Tommy the Tarzan spun his vinyl.

A cheering background crowd in our little studio (our barracks room) included the likes of "Bean" Wever, "Big Ron" Attenburg, and Ken "Arey Canary Puke-Puss" Arey. "Tommy the Tarzan" Taylor had acquired his new handle because he began running around the halls of the barracks "howling" like Tarzan swinging on a vine through the jungle.

He played "My Boyfriends Back and It's Gonna be Trouble" by the Angles and then "Smoke Gets in Your Eyes" by The Platters. Life was simpler then. Vietnam seemed to change all that. Listening to this music made us feel at home, or home-sick was more like it.

POSSUM'S DEAR JOHN

It was not uncommon for a GI to get a Dear John letter after being away from his "girl" for a period of time. "Possum Crap" Arey invited me into his room. He was clearly distraught.

"I got a letter from my girl."

Letters That Say Goodbye

Dear John,

I don't know how to say this other than come directly to the point. I don't think we should see each other anymore. I love you in a special way, but we will have to remain just friends.

Mary Jane

by douglas kirk

"I have tried to put it softly in earlier letters. Perhaps I put it too softly because you seem so sincere and involved..."

"I've been trying to write you a letter now for over a week..."

"I hope you're feeling better by the time you receive this letter..."

The European mail service developed from one of slow messenger boys to speedy pigeons, and the Dear John began to develop. More and more people began moving about, fathers improved their shooting accuracy, and soon ships sailed for the new world. As more and more lovers parted at the docks, lies became commonplace, and each ship carried its own little bundle of "goodbye letters" to the pioneers who had left the continent the month before. Unfortunate-

TOPO TOPICS DECEMBER 1972

"I didn't know you had one."

He removed a delicate pink letter out of a sweet-smelling envelope and began to read, "I have tried to put it softly in earlier letters. Perhaps I put it too softly because you seem so sincere and involved..."

"Oh hell, her letter starts with 'I'," I said.

"Huh?"

"You've been flushed?"

"Uh, huh."

He continued to read his girl's letter, "If you get to feeling really bad, try writing a poem or story. It's good for your system. I use writing as a vent for my frustrations a lot..."

"Can you believe it?" I asked.

"I can't write."

"What?"

"Never wrote a poem in my life."

"She just means get your thoughts off the breakup and do something to occupy your mind."

"She's left me."

"Sorry to hear it, but there'll be a lot of other girls when you get out, maybe even a <u>Fräulein</u> over here."

"Just look at this face, you sure about that?"

"You just need a little—well, maybe a lot—of bridgework."

He stood up and circled the room and read some more of his girl's words, "It is hard for me to tell you how I feel because I don't really know. I know I have said this before, but I truly don't know what to say anymore. I hope that we will never feel hatred toward each other. I have returned your ring to your father."

"You guys were engaged?" I asked.

"Just my high-school graduation ring."

"You graduated from High School?"

"Yeah."

"I wouldn't have guessed. Well, look at it this way, Possum, when you're old and gray, you'll still have your ring."

That was no consolation to him. He sulked around for days after that, but eventually returned to his upbeat self.

John "Woody" Woodburn was fairing better. When Woody joined the army he left all of his close high-school friends behind and that included his girlfriend, Maggie. He felt alone and out-of-place. But then he had started going to Patrick Henry Village (a married residence post) to help SP5 "Sonny" Hayes coach softball for the kids. In the process, he met a girl named "Kitty." At 4:30 every evening after work he would shed himself of his O.D.-green fatigues and peddle lickety-split on his bicycle to see her. Woody wasn't seen much around the barracks after that. What a female can do for a man even in a depressing place is immeasurable.

whose parents smoked at home than among those whose parents never smoked in the home. Some of the differences were attributed to the negative effects of the surrounding smoke.

Your Tuberculosis and Respiratory Disease Association urges nonsmokers to speak up and say "Yes, I do mind if you smoke." Defend yourself. It's a matter of life and breath. Yours. ☐

THINK twisters

Stretch your brain and look for the UNobvious in these puzzles. And don't give up before you try.

1. Three boxes are labeled

editorial

missing the point

I think the following attitude provides an insight into why the VOLAR program has been so unsuccessful. The program provides single men with longer hair and new furniture but not with the basic human needs.

Life in the Army is lonely. The single man in Germany is isolated from the life he once knew. He's denied a will of his own. His two or three year sentence starts off on the wrong foot with a Pharaoh that denies him the freedom that God has given him, and from then on he waits patiently in the corner of his cell for the lost time to pass

organization in such a state of hideous uselessness? Is it the machine or the people that make it up? Is it the changing world outside? Is this nightmare only temporary or will a ring of poison be left in the bathtub? If only there were a purpose. A common goal to actively strive for. Then it wouldn't be so lonely."

Harsh? Yes. The truth of it is immaterial, so is the rebuttal: "What's he doing to help himself?" The point is that this attitude does exist. And a very common one indeed! So what is the solution? One college educated soldier said this:"They can have my body but not my mind." Bodies aren't worth much.

—SP4 Kirk ☐

TOPO TOPICS DECEMBER 1972

MISSING THE POINT

In my second issue of <u>Topo Topics</u> I included a short editorial written by me called "Missing the Point" and what it purported was apparently a surprise to the lifers who knew me. They liked me, thought I was getting along well with the military, and they were grooming me for a life in the Army, and then this. I had several lifers ask me about it; did I really feel this way? I guess they didn't know I'd been playing a game with them, that I had no intention of re-enlisting. And this must have been the first sign that I wasn't taking this man's army seriously. Master Sergeant Tadakuma asked me about it. Pineapple asked me about it. They were sure someone else must have written it. "No, it was I," I replied, and they walked away confounded, probably revising their opinion of me. What had I said in that article? Read it for yourself:

"Life in the army is desolate. The single man in Germany is isolated from the life he once knew and he's denied a will of his own. His two- or three-year sentence starts off on the wrong foot with a Pharaoh that denies him the freedom that God has given him and from then on he waits patiently in the corner of his cell for that lost time to pass, counting the days until he can return to the Real World. Basic human needs are not even fulfilled in this cell deep in the ground with barely a single ray of hope filtering down from above, a nightmare in its own right, quiet

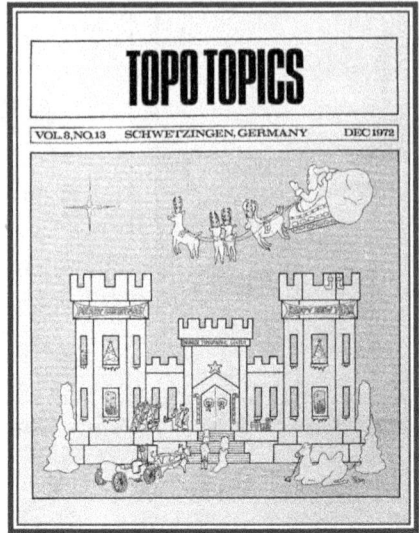

and alone, minutes slowly ticking away. For those whose life goals are not with the Army, their stretch is only a temporary delay if and only if they can manage to get back on life's road with their sense of reason and imagination fully intact. When they leave the army, they will try to forget the inefficiency, the waste, and the idiocy of a bureaucratic government originally created to 'provide for the common defense and general welfare', but mutated to a fumbling monster that consumes money and time and erodes the rights of the individual. Not really there to promote world peace as they fight on in Vietnam against the will of most American citizens. Ours is a government that plays a game of politics with the people of the world. Living in a lonely repose, with festering hostility and mushrooming anxiety as that found in a brewing thunderstorm. No home, no room that's yours, no uninterrupted dreams. No privacy, no security, no caring. We are just animals in a zoo, hibernating...every man must have a purpose,

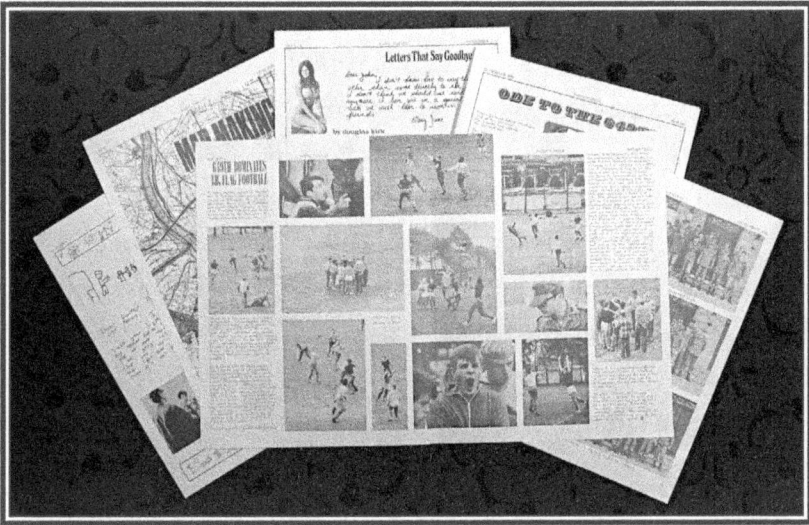

TOPO TOPICS–DECEMBER ISSUE

a worth, but no chance of that in the army...Why is this military in such a state of hideous uselessness? If only there were a purpose, then I wouldn't feel so estranged."

I wrote it because I knew many other soldiers in our battalion were feeling the same way. Was this mood, this demoralization, coming through the ranks all the way from Vietnam and affecting us all? Pineapple could not understand my disdain for the military and grappled with the concept. When I got back to the barracks I turned up the volume of my stereo system and played this song to be heard down the hall: "We Gotta Get Out of This Place" by the Animals:

> Yeah yeah yeah yeah
> We gotta get out of this place
> If its the last thing we ever do
> We gotta get out of this place
> 'Cause girl, there's a better life
> For me and you.

THE TUMBLING VOLKSWAGEN

I was hanging out one evening at the EM Club with "Possum Shit" Arey, and he took to drinking about like me, about like water and oil. It just took one drink to glaze our eyes over, but, we thought, since we were in Germany, we ought to try Schnapps, and instead of dousing it, we sipped on it and listened to a live band playing In-A-Gadda-Da-Vida by Iron Butterfly over and over again, or so it seemed, and watched the gregarious (read "horny") guys try to pick up the German girls. These girls always had a repulsive "no bath in a month" odor emanating from them and had unshaven legs and armpits. When the girls were ready to leave, they'd say they were "tipsy," and faking their drunkenness, pick your pocket as soon as you left with them. When Possum Shit and I had enough of the ear-piercing noise and stifling cigarette smoke, we staggered out of the club. Just outside was a railroad crossing with a German sitting in a signal tower, ready to close the gates when one of the very fast trains barreled through—Casey Jones would have called it "highballing"— but in fact, the seventy or eighty plus miles it was traveling was its usual speed. Because it was electrified, it moved across the landscape quite silently and would surprise anyone on its approach. Wires were strung along the right-of-way to warn people and animals to stay off the tracks. Possum and I had a two-lane road to cross to get to the front gate of Tompkins Barracks, and just to our right the road took an "S"-curve across the railroad tracks. A white Volkswagen beetle approached, but it was moving too fast and wasn't going to make the turn. Possum and I watched through bleary eyes as everything seemed to shift into slow motion. The VW's rear wheels broke loose, and it went airborne and looked like a hard-boiled egg rolling up on its pointed end, and then it dropped down again. It seemed so surreal in the night, a pool of foggy streetlights on the crossing and dark as tar beyond. The car rocked to a stop on the railroad tracks and just lay there like a hard-boiled egg sitting alone on a plate. We were stunned. It seemed like a dream—too many shots of that Schnapps?

"Christ!" screamed Possum and shook me to reality.

In the signal tower, the gatekeeper stood up and motioned for our attention. I looked back at the white VW beetle lying on its side. No one had climbed out.

"Come on!" Possum said and ran for the wreck. I followed. He looked down into the front passenger window. "I don't see anyone. There's no one here!"

"Here he is!" I said, "He's in the back seat."

Sure enough, the driver was there curled up in the back, and he appeared dazed. It was our own "Beetle" Bailey! Yes, Beetle in a beetle! We opened the passenger door and reached in and pulled him out. He was loopy and seemed unaware of his situation. Then we heard frantic banging on the tower window. The gatekeeper was screaming, about to have a cow, waving his arms frantically. I finally understood: a train was barreling down on us and we were still on the tracks. The worst scenario flashed through my mind. I could see the train hitting the beetle at eighty miles an hour, pushing the metal egg for miles until it exploded into shrapnel. I could see the gatekeeper with his first black mark in his forty-something-year career (he might even get early retirement). These gates could have been electronically controlled, tripped by the train, but this was a socialist country and everyone was given a job (the cobblestone streets were laid by hand and then re-laid and laid again). Even with modern high-speed electric trains, these traffic gates were manually operated! Unions!

"Come on!" I yelled.

THE CITY STREETS OF GERMANY WERE LAID AND RELAID
(NOT MUCH DIFFERENT THAN THE GIRLS AT SUSIES)

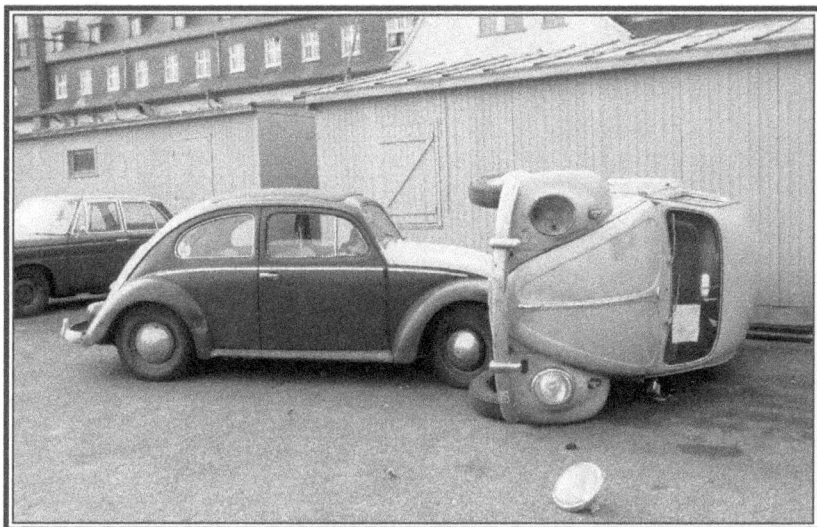

PAUL BALCAVAGE'S BLUE '59 BEETLE AND THE BEETLE THAT
MADE IT ACROSS THE TRACKS—ONLY MINOR REPAIRS NEEDED
BEFORE IT COULD BE ROLLED AGAIN

Possum and I tilted the car back on its wheels; I was amazed at the ease with which we had done it.

We pushed on the front bumper of the beetle.

"Push Ken," I said, "push!"

Possum pushed. The VW jumped easily over one rail and then over the other. I heard the rails humming and felt the ground shaking. The VW rolled away from the tracks and <u>Scheeeeew</u>; the train raced past us and was gone in a second. Einstein's train, I thought, traveling close to the speed of light.

Time slowly wound back down to Earth speed. I looked up at the gate tower; the keeper sat back down and brushed the sweat from his brow.

"That was exciting," said Possum.

"Uh-huh, right," I replied, beginning to sober up, but still existing in a half dream state.

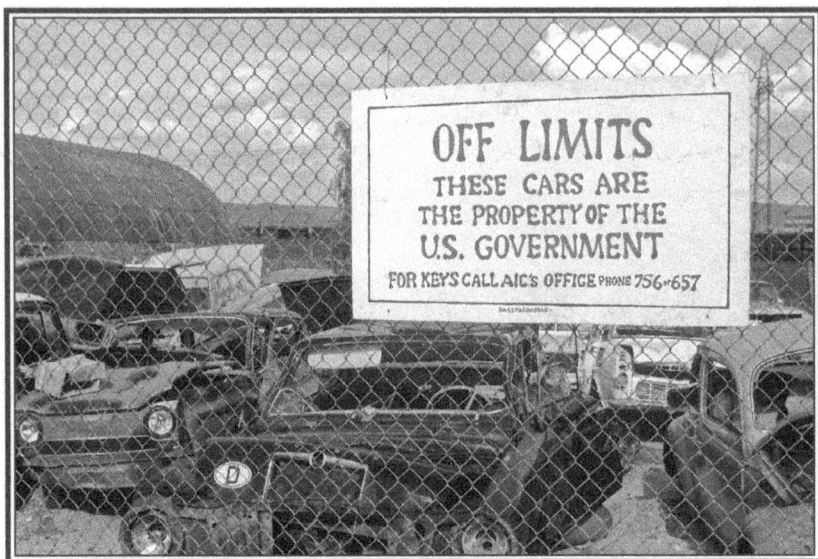

OFF LIMITS
THESE CARS ARE
THE PROPERTY OF THE
U.S. GOVERNMENT
FOR KEYS CALL AIC's OFFICE PHONE 756-657

BONEYARD FOR ABANDONED P.O.V. AUTOMOBILES
(PAINTING THIS SIGN WAS MY FIRST ASSIGNMENT AT TOMPKINS
BARRACKS BEFORE THERE WERE ANY MAPS FOR US TO WORK ON)

"Where's Beetle?" Possum asked as he looked up and down the street and into the farm fields beyond.

"I don't know," I replied. Bailey was nowhere to be seen.

"He must have wandered off."

"Who are the idiots who keep loaning Beetle a vehicle to drive?"

"See any bottles of vino in the bug?"

Was this all a dream or was Beetle going to be late for formation in the morning? Was Beetle destined for a trip to the stockade—where he might run into SP5 McKay and his itchy trigger finger?

"No more Schnapps for us," I said.

"No more."

The next day a white Volkswagen was dragged to our post junkyard and locked up. Hundreds of vehicles were there—many of them VW Beetles—left behind by GIs after rotating out or loosing their driver's license. A sign on the fence read: "OFF LIMITS—THESE CARS ARE THE PROPERTY OF THE U.S. GOVERNMENT."

After that incident, Possum Shit spent more time hanging out at the NCO Cub, drank more and more of that German Schnapps, and Army life went on like that song In-a-Gadda-da-Vida.

THE TWELVE DAYS OF CHRISTMAS

Every year we had a Christmas party, this year in the back room of a Schwetzingen Gausthaus. Most of Company A Photomapping Platoon was in attendance: Tokuhisa, Chief Maxwell, even "Airborne" Gilbert with his shiny patent-leather combat boots. The tables were adorned with open beer bottles and "dead soldiers." As the evening wore on, "Cockbite" Dulfer stood up on the table, beer in hand, and began to recite the "Twelve Days Of Christmas." Singing at the top of his nasal voice, he sang all twelve verses stopping only infrequently to take a drink or ask the soused crowd to help him remember the list as it grew longer. As Cockbite rattled on, the rest of us had plenty of time to chug a few more bottles of beer. There was merriment and frothing beers as the guys began to sing along. Finally, Cockbite reached the last verse: "On the twelve day of Christmas, my true love gave to me, twelve twid-

PFC DULFER SINGING "THE TWELVE DAYS OF CHRISTMAS"

dling twats, eleven leaping lesbians, ten torn off testicles, nine gnawed off nipples, eight gaping assholes, seven sagging scrotums, six syphilis sisters, five pubic hairs, four f——g whores, three shit-house doors, two tattered drawers, and a blowjob in the latrine." Everyone cracked up.

Cockbite was no Burl Ives, but his rendition drew hoots and laughter, bringing the house down in more ways than one. Some men lay sprawled on the floor, some threw up, others went outside for a pissing contest, literally. Get a stream over a six-foot fence that lay some distance away, that was the goal. Kenneth Kamerman from California, our unofficial bugler, a tall, clean-cut guy, who had a Hispanic girl for a wife, could drink with the best of them. According to Paul Balcavage, Kamerman had the distance record for pissing, something over twenty feet. Paul said it was an amazing feat to all who ever witnessed it.

Several of the boys made an attempt, a beer in one hand, to beat Kamerman's record, though what he did this fine Christmas Eve was all that counted. Finally it was the champs turn and he stepped up to the plate—the edge of the patio. He ceremoniously unzipped his fly and then stopped, "Balcavage, hand me another drink."

Paul gave him his. Kamerman raised it up and quickly doused the bottle, only a tiny bit dribbling down his chest. You don't waste beer, especially German bier. The stream went high and far, clearing the fence easily, eighteen, twenty, twenty two feet. Everyone cheered. Kamerman was still the hands down champion. When they got back inside, "99 Bottles of Beer" wasn't what A Company was now singing, it's what they had drank.

It seemed to me the Army should have drinking contests at the annual Armed Forces Day events, seeing as how it demonstrates important survival skills and the adroitness and ability to store recyclable water in the bladder of men in uniform.

THE BAADER-MEINHOF GANG

It was my luck to be in Germany when the notorious Baader-Meinhof Gang was terrorizing Germany and in February of '72, a bomb was detonated in West Berlin's British yacht club. The gang declared the attack was in support of the Irish Republican Army. The gang then, wearing carnival masks, robbed a bank of nearly 300,000 Deutschmarks. Wanted posters were plastered around the country on walls and poles offering 10,000 DMs for information leading to the arrest of any gang member. Then, just up the road from us at Frankfurt am Main, three pipe bombs exploded at US Army headquarters destroying the mess hall and killing a Lieutenant Colonel. He bled to death on the floor of the mess with a shard of window glass stuck in his throat. The gang then demanded the Americans stop mining

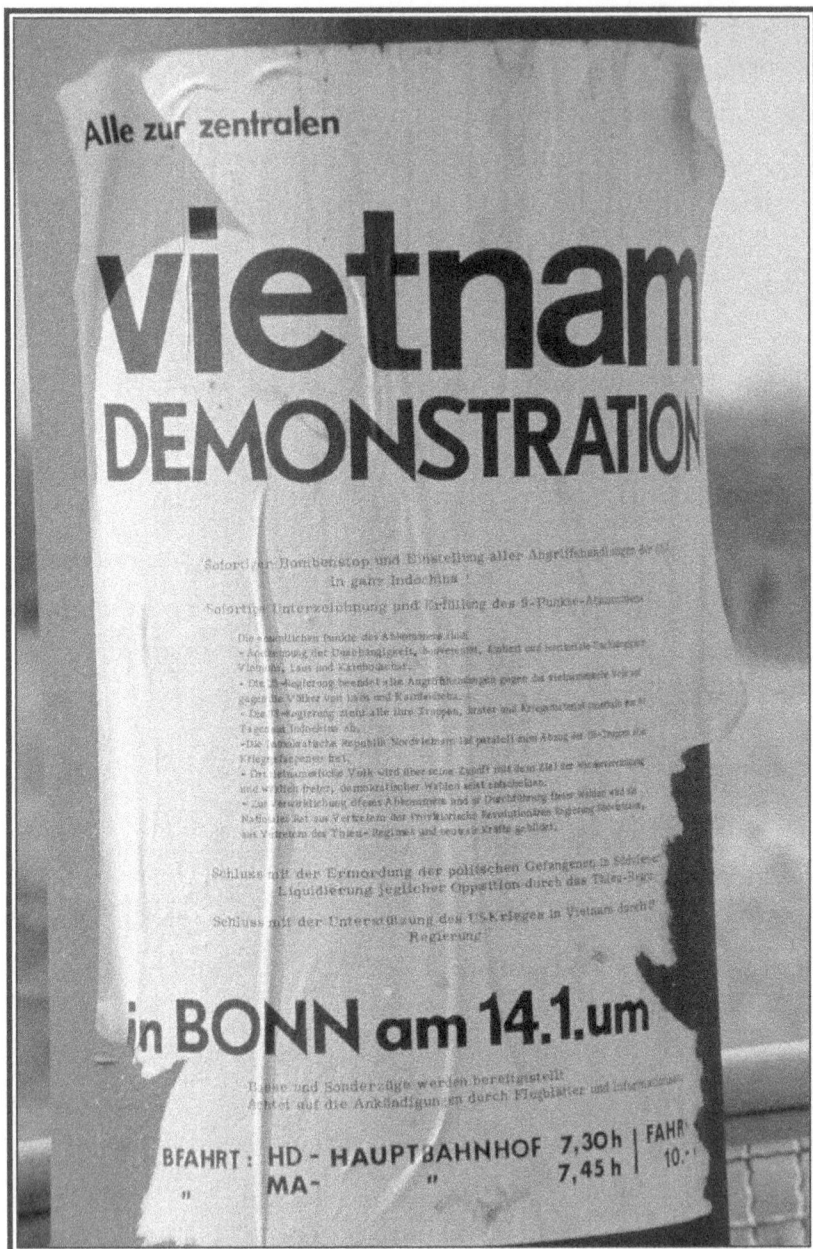

VIETNAM DEMONSTRATIONS ON THE ECONOMY
–EVEN THE GERMAN'S WERE FED UP–

the harbors of North Vietnam. Then, in Munich, a time-delay pipe bomb turned sixty cars in a government parking lot into a pile of crumpled tin cans. We watched the news on an old black and white television set in the Day Room and listened to reports on the Armed Forces Radio Network. Several more bombs were detonated around Germany before the U.S. Army realized they were also targeting American military installations, and on May 24th we got the word bombs had gone off at Campbell Barracks in Heidelberg just ten Klicks (Kilometers) from us. It was the headquarters of the United States Army in Europe (USAREUR) and the Baader-Meinhoff Gang's second attack on American forces. The terrorists had driven two cars into the compound. It was the S.O.P. (Standing Operating Procedure) for our MPs to wave through vehicles with American license plates. But the gang had simply stolen American plates and drove in without so much as a "howdy do." Each car contained a fifty-pound bomb. One car was parked next to the post clubhouse, a place frequented by soldiers and their families. When it exploded, the car parked next to it was blown sky high and the two soldiers within were blown to pieces, their bloody torsos laying on the ground with the rest of their body parts left hanging in the trees. A wall of the clubhouse collapsed, knocking over a Coca-Cola machine that crushed to death another GI.

Two days later, a letter from the gang claimed the bombings were in response to the American bombings in Vietnam. It looked as if Nam had now come to Germany. We were put on high alert and all of the American Military installations were locked down and a state of high security went up around our own Tompkins Barracks. Our movements were restricted and the EM Club was declared off limits—no more alcohol and tipsy German girls. Vehicles coming in the gates were carefully searched and a mirror on a pole was used to view the underside of a vehicle's chassis. The MP's carried live rounds in their pistols and were authorized to shoot if any vehicle refused to stop. Photos of known members of the Gang were widely distributed. A man in uniform was no longer assumed to be an American soldier. A terrorist might have a fake ID (police had earlier found an apartment laden with equipment for forging documents) so passwords were immediately employed.

About a week later, in a garage at Frankfurt, the German police found a car full of explosives. They removed the explosives, replaced them with dummies, and the garage was staked out. Hundreds of police hunkered down and waited. Eventually a Porsche (the gang always drove top-shelf automobiles) showed up and three men got out, but one of the men noticed a larger-than-normal number of "civilians" milling about and pulled his weapon and a gun battle ensued. One of the gang members was wounded and quickly apprehended, but the

WE WERE JUST KIDS THE ARMY HAD TO TURN INTO MEN

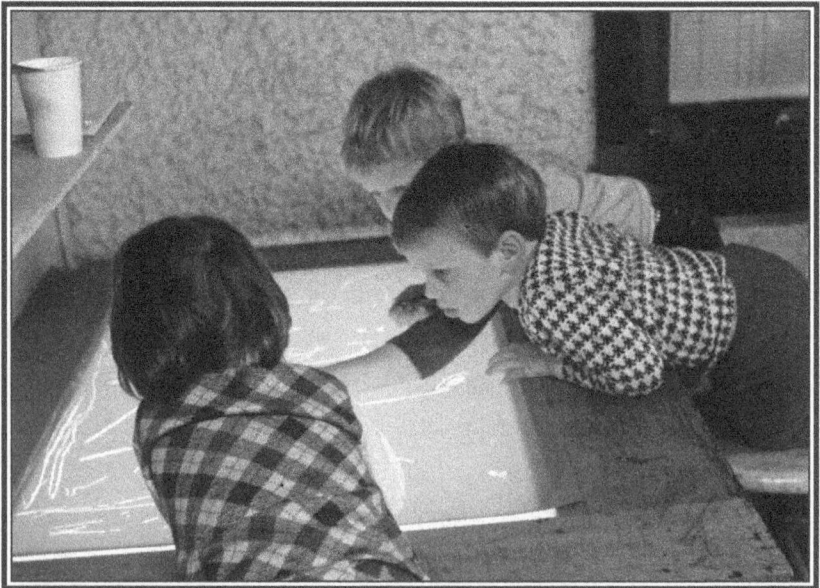

other two retreated to the back of the garage. Television crews arrived to film the siege just as tear gas was being thrown into the garage. The two other men were eventually captured alive and one of them turned out to be Andreas Baader. It was the beginning of the end of the notorious terrorist group known as the Baader-Meinhof Gang. When all known members were reportedly captured, the German people took a sigh of relief, we relaxed our security, and the Tompkins GIs went back to drinking at the EM club.

MAXWELL'S OWN DEMON

Chief Maxwell, himself a Juice Head—supposedly a recovering alcoholic and reasonably sober on the job—led a different life at home. He had tried to shake the beast, knowing it could, and probably had, affected his career in the military. But he encouraged parties at the ramp at the end of the day on some Fridays and would buy us a keg of beer to sooth our tormented souls. We figured he was just trying to be one of the boys, but drinking was an army tradition and he seemed to want to keep it going. Most new recruits were just kids out of high school and peer pressure was just as strong in the military. It's hard to believe that our wars are fought with, "wet-behind-the-ears" boys and immature college kids like myself. A lot of kids join the Army to find themselves, and the army, hoping to acquire good career soldiers, instead finds itself taking on the role of a baby sitter. The army invests considerable time and money to train their "employees" only to have most of them leave after two years. I guess armies have always been that way; what you didn't kill off, or went AWOL, you lost.

The Chief invited a few of us to a dinner and party at his apartment in Patrick Henry Village, a residence post near Eppelheim between Schwetzingen and Heidelberg that we referred to as "Lifer

Village." He had just been promoted to CW3 and wanted us to share in his jubilation. He was still an enlisted man at heart. His wife prepared a scrumptious meal served on a white tablecloth with real silver lain out beside real porcelain. We didn't know how to act; it was a far cry from Wallow's Mess Hall. Here it was no elbows on the table, a white tablecloth, and a pretty cook with a clean apron. Beer and liquor was also provided. Max must have figured he couldn't please us without including a case of Heinekens in the festivities. And well, Max, it turned out, couldn't control himself and got fall-down drunk and Frank Dulfer thought putting shaving cream all over the Chief as he lay inebriated on the floor was a cool thing to do. I had brought my 35mm Nikkormat camera at the Chief's request to take photos of this special event, but the photos ended up including those depravations of a prideful Warrant Officer. He had no idea what had happened to him that night and when I brought him the processed photos a week later, his jaw dropped and distress raced across his face. He told me he wanted the negatives, all of them. I could see the

CHIEF MAXWELL–DOWN AND OUT

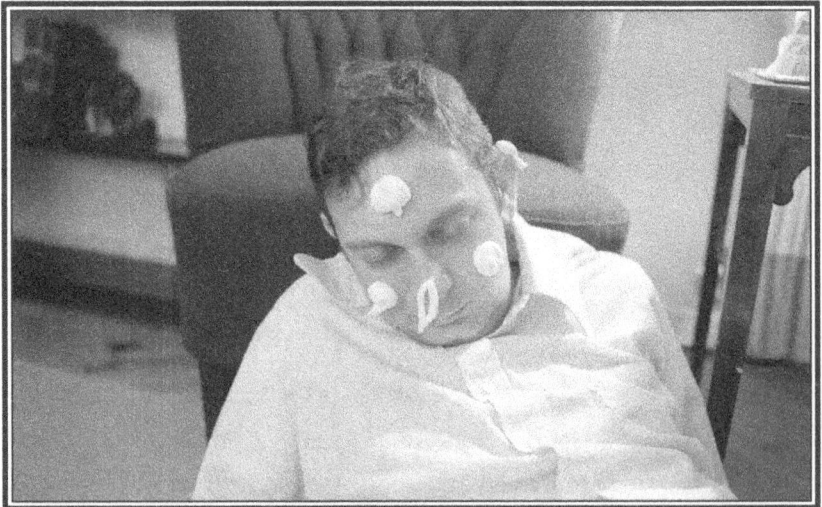

dread in his eyes and so I told him no one would see them, they were safe with me, but he insisted I give them to him, something a photographer should never do. But I didn't want him to remain concerned, so I turned—all but one—over to him.

SERGEANT MAJOR SWENSON

SGT MGR Phillip Swenson in headquarters company was another career soldier who drank way too much, and he didn't seem to be a happy man, just counting his days to retirement. He was considerably overweight and there were few men like that in this man's army. I never saw much of him, just in passing at headquarters while working on Topo Topics, but one evening SP4 O'Neill, with a beer in hand, was in my room vetting:

"The Sergeant Major shows up after hours, strolls into our barracks drunk as a skunk and gives the CQ grief over nothing and then walks into our rooms to jack up the occupants over minor infractions."

"You talking about Swenson?" I asked.

"Yeah, the fat sleaze ball. I'm missing a time on my log sheet and he's reaming my butt."

"He came into my room just yesterday," O'Neill added, "and wanted to inspect my combat boots—'can't see my face in 'em trooper!' he says. I wanted to say "you don't want to," but didn't. Then he checked for dust on top of my window casing, and this is F——g night! Can't the jackass at least wait until morning roll call?"

"Mickey Mouse," I replied.

"The whole Battalion is Mickey Mouse."

"Right on. You'd think this was basic training or something."

"The drill sergeants weren't drunk in Basic."

SCOTTY'S HELL

It was hard to imagine, Norman "Scotty" Scott already in for fifteen years and still a PFC. I guess he liked the army and figured he couldn't survive on the outside. I'm sure it was his drinking that kept him at the bottom of the promotional ladder. Scotty was a conscientious worker, and made up for his late-to-work days, so Chief Maxwell took it on himself to help Scotty get promoted to an E-4 because the army was threatening to drum him out of the service for not having sufficient rank for time in service. Maxwell gave him a glowing EER (Enlisted Efficiency Report) and enrolled him into some military schools to garnish his record with more promotion points. Maxwell, I think, was going out of his way to help because he could see his former self in Scotty. The promotion board was a success and in short order Scotty got his SP4 promotion. He was excited, even though he had that rank, and higher ranks, before, but it meant he could now stay in the army a little bit longer.

But a surprise IG that actually caught us off guard and left us all with a host of demerits, put SP4 Scott in the doghouse. You see they found his pride and joy, his racoon Suzy in a cage under his bed. Captain Peal, our "wet behind the ears" Company Commander who accompanied the IG, was red-faced by the discovery and wrenched the cage from Scotty. The Spec Four just plain freaked out—blew a gasket as it were. He had probably been a little under the bottle and wasn't able to control himself. His usual meek "Yes sirs" were laced with indignation. He broke into a mild temper tantrum and raised his voice to Captain Peal.

"You can't take her, sir!"

"No harboring of pets in the billets."

"She's family. You can't take her!"

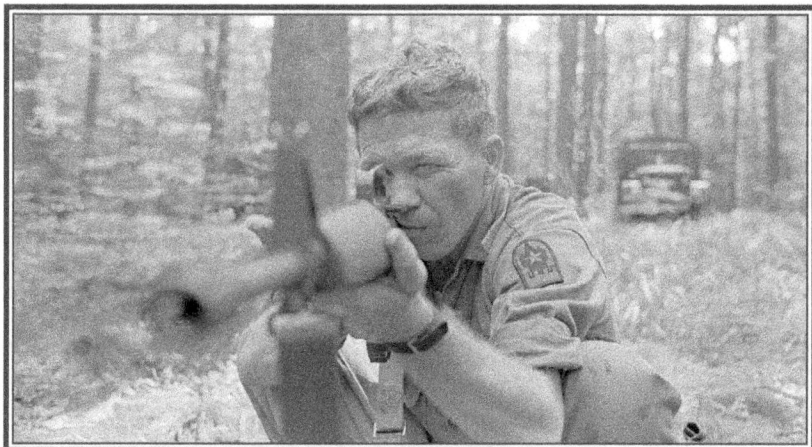

PFC NORMAN "SCOTTY" SCOTT–OVER AND OUT

"I can, Specialist Scott. I'll have none of this insubordin—"

"Not my pride and joy, please. She needs special care and loving—"

"Ease off, soldier. Step back and sit down. I'll speak to you later, Specialist."

Captain Peal left Scotty in his room fuming, and continued down the hall with the wide-eyed and astonished IG to complete their inspection. This was not a good mark for the young captain. Peal handed Suzy off to an Army veterinarian, and it wasn't long before we got the word Scotty was docked a month's pay, put on barracks restrictions, and sadly, demoted—busted back to PFC. The Chief was heart broken. This meant Scotty would also be forced to leave the Army, ASAP (As Soon As Possible). The Army was his life and his parents were, if you can believe this, in route to Germany to live in an apartment while Scotty was stationed in Germany. He—and Suzy—had planned to move off post and live with them.

Sitting on the floor, my back against the door of a one-bed barracks room, I took a swig of a fifth of gin. I was in Scotty's room and he was sitting beside me. We were shoulder to shoulder.

181

"Fifteen years and busted back to a PFC. The army has regulations on it."

"On what?" I asked.

"If you can't make rank by a certain year they drum you out."

"Kick you out of the army?"

"I've been busted way too many times," said Scotty, his head hanging low after another swig of gin, his knees high to his chest. He was in a ratty O.D. green, sleeveless T-shirt and green boxers with loose threads.

"You grew up in South Texas didn't you, on a ranch?"

"More a farm like with chickens, pigs, a few milk cows, twenty acres, prickly mesquite and scrub brush."

"Your family made a living on twenty acres?"

"We had a good fresh-water well, not to alkaline."

Scotty took another big gulp and passed me the squarish bottle. He drank gin like it was water, but I downed a light swallow and was hoping the bottle would come up empty soon.

"Fifteen years," I repeated.

"Fifteen years."

"What are you gonna do?"

"Tell you the truth, I don't know nothin' else. I've been a good soldier, done what they asked of me."

"Worked in that darkroom a long time?"

"A looong time. Just late to formation a few times, maybe more."

Scotty, seeming so sad and disillusioned, finished off the bottle and fell sideways to the floor, out cold. I rolled him aside to open the door, and left the room.

The next day Scotty continued to drink heavily as he packed his bags and processed out. His drooping head, sullen face, and sad eyes revealed to us that the life had gone out of him. Scotty had been happy at his job in the darkroom, and did it well, but the army expected everyone to be promoted to their level of incompetence. It was the only way you could sustain a bumbling bureaucratic system.

TOMPKINS THEATER

You could make a little money on the side if you worked at the post theater. Two people were needed to keep it operational with a different movie—shown several times—each week. First, a projectionist, trained by the previous projectionist (once you had the job, you really couldn't quit until you had talked someone into taking your place) and second, the manager/cashier, who took in the money, kept records, and closed up at night. "Big Al" Picklo had the manager's job when I arrived at Tompkins and SP4 Michael Lovely ran the projection room. Lovely was a tall, curiously anemic blond that didn't associate much with the rest of the guys in the barracks (though he was always looking for someone he could play tennis with, and when I was his roommate, I did). Off duty, he wore a polo shirt and pearly white slacks, looking as if he had come from some upper-crust family. He had weak ankles and was always twisting one or the other. The doctor would wrap it, hand him a walking cane, and put him on sick leave. PSG Tokuhisha had no choice but to put him on "light duty." No scrubbing bathrooms or washing trucks. Many of the guys figured it was just a scam to get out of work ("malingering," the army called it, an Article 115, feigning illness in order to avoid duty. The UCMJ (Uniform Code of Military Justice) had everything covered. Anyway, he spent his evenings in the projection room like a rat in an attic scurrying around and no one knew he was there. Two synched-up arc-light projectors were needed to project a movie. They produced a brilliant, white light by arcing a high-voltage electric current between two carbon-rod electrodes. To start them, the rods

TOMPKINS THEATER
–A PLACE TO ESCAPE WITHIN OUR COMPOUND–

were touched together and then slowly drawn apart to a point where the current arced across the gap to produce a bright blinding light at a temperature of several thousand degrees. (If the film stopped in the gate, a hole would burn through the film frame breaking it requiring the ends to be spliced together before the movie could resume.) The rods were slowly vaporized during the process and had to be adjusted regularly to maintain the arc. Adjusting the arc, switching the projectors every ten minutes, and preparing the next feature at the rewind table, kept a projectionist busy and alert.

Each movie was shipped from theater to theater in heavy steel, octagonal carrying cases with ten-minutes of film on each reel. Each segment of the movie had to be run off the shipping reels by hand and spliced together "tails to heads" onto several large projection reels. If you got one flipped, ten minutes of the movie would play upside down and backwards. You also checked for damaged or broken splices and repaired them so they wouldn't come apart during the movie. That left the projectionist with an opportunity he couldn't pass up. Some of those films, like the <u>Eiger Sanction</u> starring Clint Eastwood, or <u>The Graduate</u>, had a shot or two revealing a beautiful, scantly clad or downright nude female, often visible for only seconds on the big screen. In the scene when Eastwood is running after his Indian-girl trainer, she motivates him when he falters by turning around and exposing her breasts. Lovely would find scenes like these and cut out a frame or two, and splice the film's ends back together. Of course, it was easy to spot the nude scenes as you inspected the film because the last projectionist—and the one before him—had already removed their own frames leaving a splice you could feel with your white-gloved fingers. Unfortunately, the poor GIs at the end of the distribution chain would see nothing of those sexy scenes. Lovely would then take those nudie frames, print 8x10 black & white photos in the post darkroom and then distribute them—for a fee. Some men were just born to be businessmen. Michael "Crutches" Lovely probably went on to own a national movie-theatre franchise or major tennis venue.

A SOLDIER LOST IN THE WORLD

The small-in-stature SP4 Kim Frost came up to me in the hall one evening.

"Kirk, have you seen Mark Hughes? He's supposed to replace me in CQ. He's not in his room."

"There's one place I can try. If there, I'll send him down to you."

"Well, hurry it up, the movie starts in twenty minutes and I want to see it. Hughes should be here damn it."

I climbed to the fourth floor, then down a short hall past a dormer window, and opened a plywood door covered with a curtain. A large puff of acrid smoke enveloped me. It was the Dope Den.

Mark Hughes and Kent were sitting on the floor with their legs-crossed. I could barely see them through heavy curling smoke, sitting there around a coffee table covered with a stained table cloth on which sat lit candles, ash trays, packs of cigarettes, a roach clip, and a leather-covered bible opened to the old testament.

"Come in Kirk, join us," said Kent with blood-shot eyes.

Hughes looked up at me, "Very truly I tell you, no one can see the kingdom of God without being born again. Marvel not that I said unto thee, ye must be born again."

"Mark," I interrupted, "you're on CQ tonight."

"Tonight?"

"Yes, right now! This minute!"

Kent interrupted and reached toward Hughes, "You ain't Humphrey, my friend, don't Bogart that joint."

Hughes passed the joint to him. "I have accepted Jesus Christ as Lord and Savior in order to be saved from Hell and given eternal life with God in Heaven."

"The only vision you're having is circus clowns and Ferris wheels." Kent tried to hand me the joint, but I passed on it and he handed it back to Hughes. I had allergic rhinitis and just being in this room was closing up my nasal passages right quick like.

"I love you brother Kirk. You are beautiful. The world is beaut..."

"I didn't know it had so many colors," pontificated Kent, "Whow, man."

"You should accept God as I have," said Mark Hughes after a long drag on a short joint. "Everything will come into focus, everything will be real."

"Mark!" I insisted.

"I have four-hundred-twenty-three days and a wake up, that's real," said Kent.

"Verily, verily, I say unto thee, except a man be born again, he cannot see the kingdom of God."

"Mark," I said, "You're not gonna see it through rose-colored glasses."

"I could use some munchies," interrupted Kent, "the Mess ain't feeding us enough."

"They've go a meeting coming up soon, the whole battalion, Williamson has finally heard us," I said.

"I'll ask Sergeant Wallow Ass Crack if he'll make us some really good hash brownies?"

"That gives me an idea," said Hughes, "know anyone workin' the kitchen?"

"Hah, the whole battalion loopy as a rollercoaster!"

Dreamy, baby!"

"Pass that joint!"

I saw it was hopeless and left the room. I went to Mark's room to see if his roommate was there. Maybe he could fill in for Hughes.

His roommate, Sp4 Kilman, wasn't there—probably at the movies—and I hadn't yet changed out of my fatigues. I took his duty.

FOOD COMPLAINTS
AND BILLY WALLOW'S THEATER MEETING

Our doors were off our rooms, we were upset by a new weekend pass policy that prevented us from getting three-day passes, and our company commanders weren't taking our "not getting enough to eat" complaints seriously. Troops had always complained about their chow throughout recorded military history, and to the brass, this was no different, there couldn't really be a problem. But the uproar was sufficient enough that the battalion's Sergeant Major Swenson called our unit into Tompkins Theater—the same place we came to piss in

TOMPKINS THEATER INTERIOR
–MOVIES, MEETINGS, AND PISSING IN A BOTTLE–

a bottle on unscheduled drug checks—and invited the slovenly Mess Sergeant Billy "Ass Crack" Wallow to explain the food procurement process. I don't think he ever washed his apron, well, maybe for IG inspections...and maybe even slept with it on. He was wearing it now.

"You men," he said, "are not signing the sheet. Every time you come to mess you sign sheet. We get our allotment of food based on how many troops are eating; you not eating breakfast, especially on weekends. We don't get food allotment."

Waddell stood up, "Why should I sign for S.O.S. an' Jello cubes, we wants yams and collard greens—"

"And deep-fried chicken!" yelled another.

Wallow continued, "I'll see what we can do, Waddell, but USAREUR command writes our menu—"

"I'll give you a menu," replied Waddell. At that another dude stood up and gave Waddell a Dap handshake.

"Some of that soul food is hard to come by on the economy."

"You's can grow a garden!" yelled another.

"Enough men! He gets it," blasted Sergeant Swenson.

PFC Kent then yelled out, "Sergeant Wallow, how 'bout makin' us some Hash brownies?"

"Who said that?" barked Swenson.

The room quieted down.

"That's all men, back to your platoons."

I looked at Wallow's face. He put his hand on his chin. It seemed to me he was thinking to himself, "hum, I should try those."

That was it in this battalion-sized get together and we went back to work and continued to feel hungry. I was one of those troopers who did go to breakfast during the week and partook of mess-hall meals on weekends, and I noticed the Sarge was asking everyone to sign the meal sheet several times, not just once per meal, telling everyone, "you sign more, we get more food for you." And so we did and made nothing of it. But all of us, I think, except "Big Al" Picklo and "Flash" Lilburn, were loosing weight.

TRAVEL BY P.O.V.

It was common for GIs to buy an old beat-up car from a soldier going home, drive it, and then when he left, re-sell it to another GI. ("Big Al" Picklo bought a Chevy Corvair from a platoon leader when that soldier rotated out and it got regular use as transportation to the beer festivals. It smoked like a chimney and left an oil slick along its path. Big Al had to stop every two hours to refill the crankcase, but that didn't stop him from spending weekends sloshing grog under a German tent.)

Paul Balcavage bought a blue 1959 beetle to tool around in, and after marrying a cute girl, decided to take a honeymoon trip to Switzerland. He got "busted" at the border, his leave papers out of date. They were held up for several hours, his new bride "fit to be tied"

THE LEANING TOWER OF PIZA IN PIZA, ITALY

as the Swiss guards tried to determine if Paul was actually AWOL (many U.S. soldiers had attempted an escape to Switzerland). Paul said he learned two things on that trip: first, that his choice in a bride just might have been a mistake and second, the absolute maximum speed downhill for a '59 VW beetle is 90 MPH—the speed he drove in a effort to get back to Tompkins.

O'Neill, myself, and Adan "Hiney" Hinojosa decided to make a week-long trip in his POV (Privately-Owned Vehicle), a well-worn black VW beetle, to Spain and Italy. Hiney was chosen for this

ST. PETER'S BASILICA–VATICAN CITY
–A WALLED ENCLAVE WITHIN THE CITY OF ROME–
(JUST 110 ACRES, SMALLEST INDEPENDENT STATE IN THE WORLD)

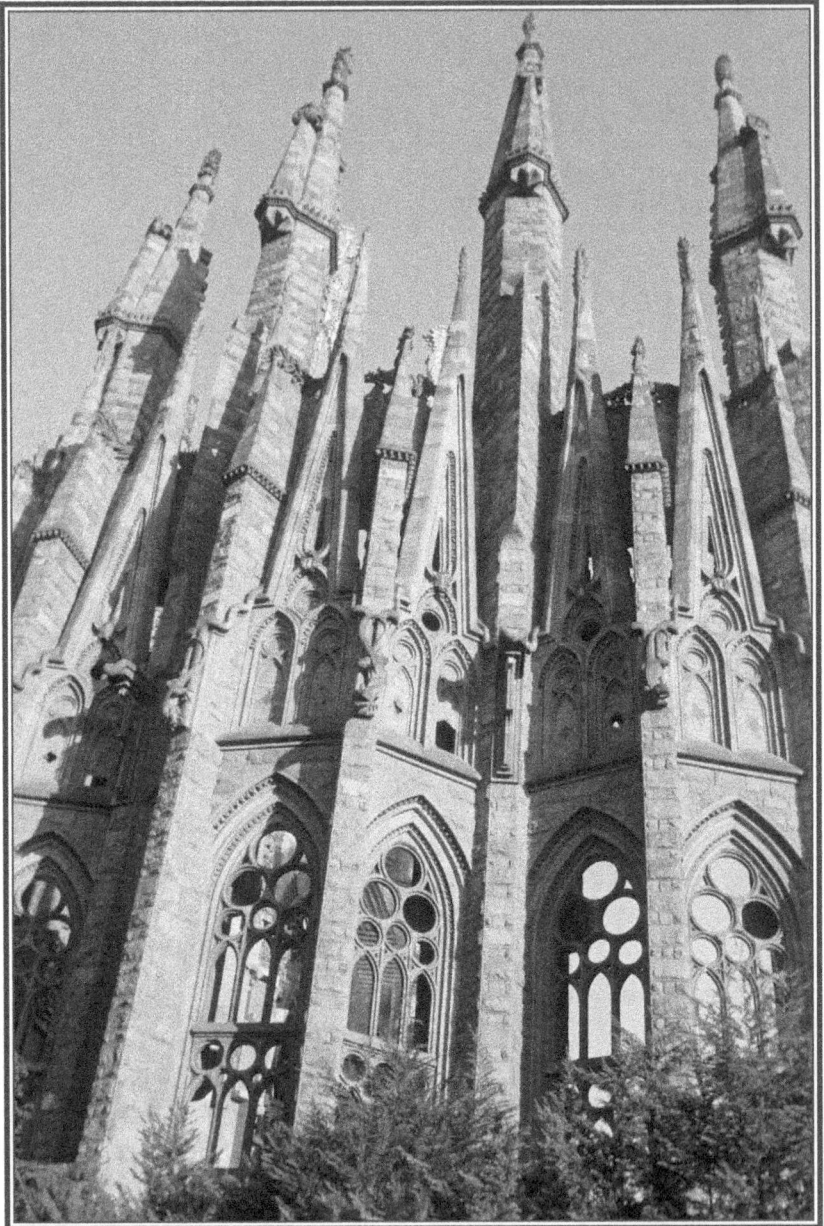

ARCHITECT ANTONI GAUDÍ'S LA SAGRADA FAMILIA CHURCH
–STILL UNFINISHED–WHERE THE WORD "GAUDY" CAME FROM
MEANING, FLASHY, GARISH, LOUD, TASTELESS, VULGAR...–

trip because he could speak Spanish, though it turned out to be "Tex-Mex" and not "the King's" Spanish. He couldn't even read the highway signs or help us, in any way, to communicate with the locals. We managed though and saw the awesome Roman Coliseum, the Vatican, and the Forum in Rome, and from there we drove to Barcelona, Spain and saw an example of Antoni Gaudí's work, the unfinished <u>La Sagrada Familia</u>, the gaudiest church I have ever seen. Now I knew the true meaning of the word "gaudi." There is nothing in the world quite like it; numerous highly-decorated spires and a façade of strange slapped-on detail cannot describe this wonder, something out of a "Willy Wonka & The Chocolate Factory" movie. Gaudí had to have been on acid.

On another trip south, this time to France, O'Neill invited me and Ken "Possum Shit" Arey. Possum, a Virginian, didn't speak French, but we didn't figure it could be any worse than a Spanish-speaking Texan in Italy. Loaded down with camping gear (we GIs had

THE COLISEUM IN ROME
–GLADIATOR GAMES STILL SURVIVE IN THE FORM OF NFL FOOTBALL–

THE FORUM IN ROME
–NO CIVILIZATION LASTS FOREVER–

ONE OF MANY TREE-LINED ROADS IN FRANCE
–PHOTO TAKEN THROUGH WINDSHIELD OF OUR VW–

plenty of that), we headed southwest and got a taste of France's tree-lined country roads leading to their biggest city, Paris, with it's Eiffel tower (we actually climbed the stairs to the top), Notre Dame de Paris, and a gray-colored gargantuan city running to the horizon in all directions. A great subway system (the Métro) made it possible for us to get where we wanted to go. And we were on our own. The French didn't seem to want to talk to us. They always replied to questions in their language (having said maybe _Dégueulasse moche Americano—_ Disgusting, ugly American) and then abruptly walked off. (Whereas German's sounded like they were going to spit when speaking, the French always sounded as if they were clearing their throat.) In much of the rest of Europe, we found that most Europeans spoke at least some English and didn't mind trying to help us, but not the French people. I thought we had liberated them in WWII.

THE SPRAWLING CITY OF PARIS
VIEWED FROM GUSTAVE EIFFEL'S TOWER

CARCASSONNE, FRANCE
–A FORTIFIED CITY THAT REVEALS HUMANITY'S FAILING–

Heading south, we found Carcassonne, a historic fortified French city of the Middle Ages completely surrounded by a high, stone outer wall with defense towers and a drawbridge. Tourists can traipse through the narrow streets and feel that they're back in the thirteenth century.

We then headed back north along Spain and France's Mediterranean coastline where the ladies sun themselves on the beach without bikinis, and where the shoreline is so steep, the towns are build on the side of cliffs. The vehicle road skirts above the towns so that one has to park their car and walk into a town having no roads, just thousands of steps up and down. The best views of the city were had by walking on the cliff-side trails between the villages. There are few towns so beautiful in Europe as these. It was a far cry from a military installation, and we had for this week of leave, totally forgotten about Tompkins.

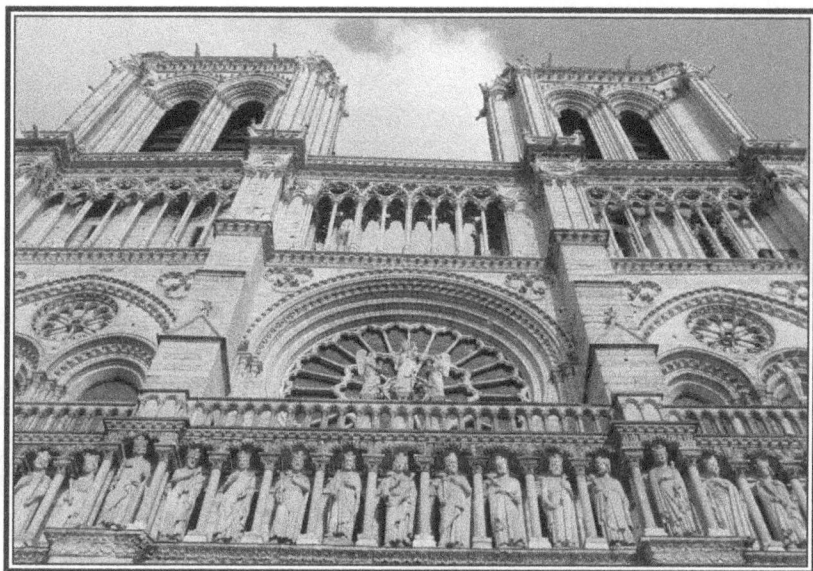

CATHEDRAL NOTRE DAME de PARIS
—BEAUTIFUL FRENCH GOTHIC ARCHITECTURE—

THE BUSY STREETS OF PARIS
—GETTING AROUND NOT EASY UNLESS USING THE METRO—

AERIAL VIEW OF THE PRINCIPALITY OF MONACO
–LOCATED ON THE FRENCH RIVERIA–

PORT HERCULE, MONACO, ON THE FRENCH RIVERA
–WITH ITS FAIR SHARE OF NUDE BEACHES–

THE NARROW STREETS OF MONACO
THE SECOND SMALLEST AND MOST DENSELY POPULATED
COUNTRY IN THE WORLD, JUST .7 SQUARE MILES!

A HILL TOWN ON THE CLIFFS OF THE MEDITERRANEAN
—NO VEHICLES, JUST STAIRS AND FOOT PATHS—

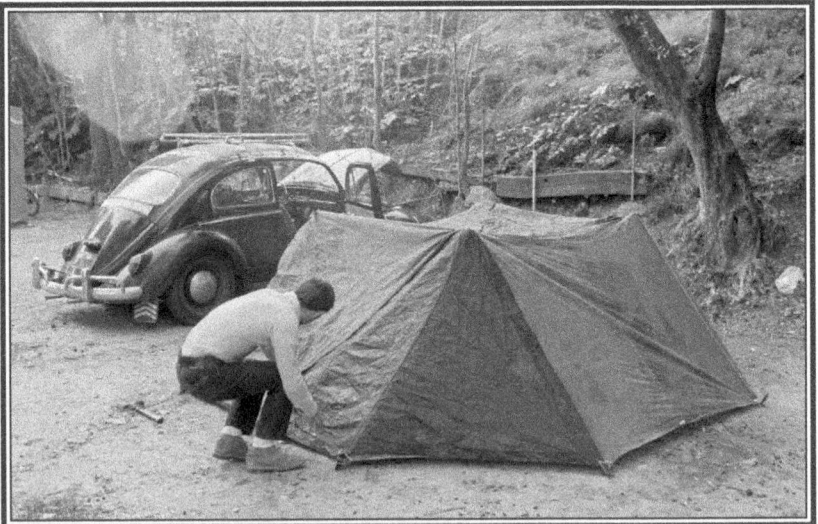

MAKING USE OF OUR MILITARY CAMPING KNOW HOW
—O'NEILL COMBINING PUP TENTS FOR A LUXURY SUITE—
THE BLACK VW BEETLE MADE THE TRIP EASILY,
NEEDING ONLY A FEW ROADSIDE OIL CHANGES—

ROADSIDE STOP TO EAT A C-RATION LUNCH
(AREY, MYSELF AND O'NEILL)
–I USED MY TRIPOD AND THE SELF-TIMER TO GET THE SHOT–

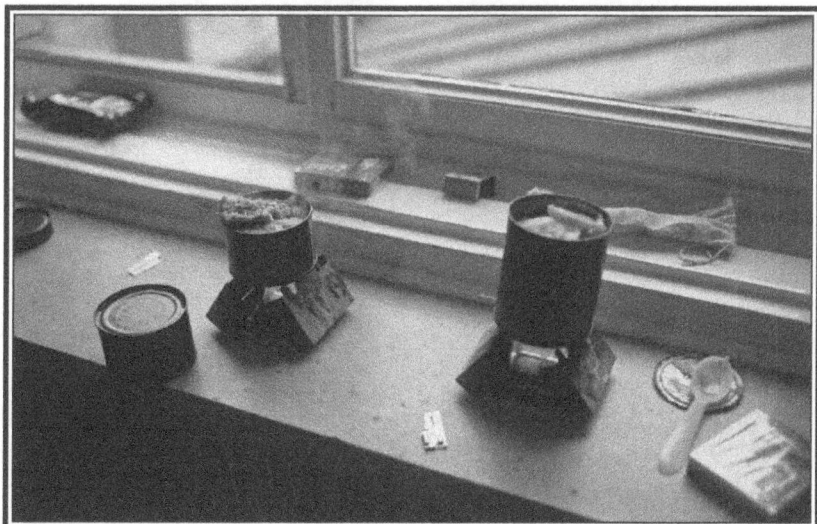

A RARE OVERNIGHT IN A GASTHAUS
COOKING C-RATIONS WITH A POCKET STOVE
–AFTER ALL WE JUST MADE $206.00 A MONTH–

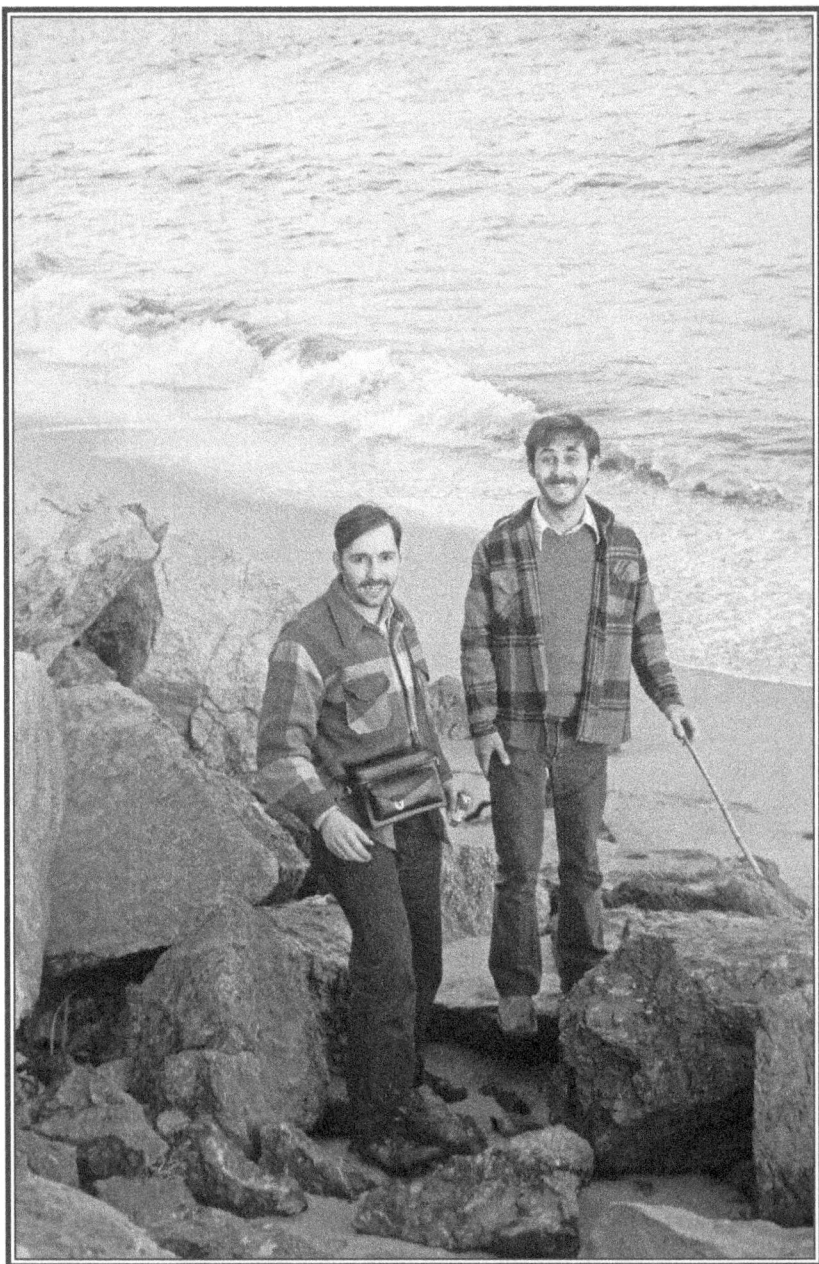

KENNETH AREY AND GLENN O'NEILL
ON AN ESCAPIST TRIP TO THE FRENCH RIVIERA

THE BACK ROADS OF BEAUTIFUL SWITZERLAND

THE STRIP SEARCH

Every country had a border crossing, some of which were easy to cross or almost non-existent, but the small country of Switzerland, known for its magnificent Alps, was another matter. The Swiss were trying their best to keep out the "riffraff" from their beautiful and pristine country, the one of "Sound of Music" fame. Our weathered and dinged-up black beetle was loaded down with camping gear and three GIs: O'Neill, Arey, and myself. A border guard circled the car and looked hard into the windows.

Suddenly, "Sortir! Please leave your motorcar."

Terrified, we got out. Two more guards then stuck their heads into the interior of the crammed-full vehicle.

"You have drugs?" one asked.

"Uh, no sir," replied Glenn.

"Not me," said Kenneth, looking as if he had been caught with his hand in the cookie jar.

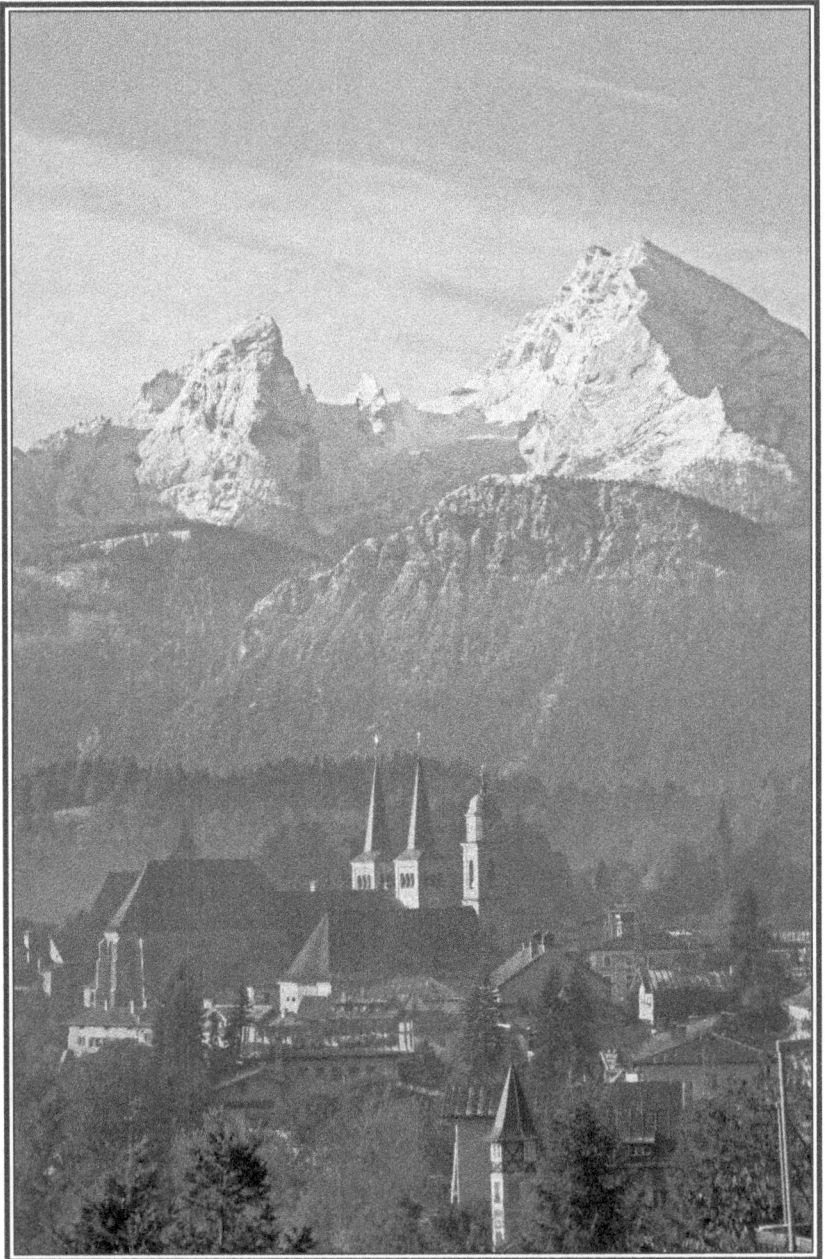

THE MAGNIFICENT ALPS
–AMERICAN SOLDIERS ON DRUGS NOT WELCOME–

Me, I shook my head firmly, but knew I had aspirin and antihistamines for my allergies. Did those count, I wondered?

Grungy G.I.'s in a beat-up Black Beetle just <u>had</u> to have drugs on them.

"Could you three please come with us?"

"Yes, sir." We were about to defecate in our pants. What had we done wrong?

We were taken to a tiny room with chairs and told to strip. We removed our clothes down to our GI skivvies. A guard looked me over and then looked through my clothes. Canary Arey dropped his boxer shorts and began to bend over.

"Arey!" blurted out O'Neill, "This is not Appalachia!"

Arey pulled his shorts back up. They looked Arey over real good. The guard motioned to us, "All, you, you, you, put clothes on."

With half our clothes in our hands, we were herded back outside. We found ourselves back at our car, and to our wide-eyed astonishment, all our gear was strewn about the vehicle as if a cyclone had hit. The VW, the only thing not overturned. Every stick of our gear was torn into, and into again, like a dog tearing into a pillow with all the stuffing strewn about.

"You can go," motioned one of the guards as he raised the gate.

We started to pack up our gear, but it wasn't what you'd call "packing," we just crammed it into our vehicle so we could skedaddle roadrunner-like.

"<u>Renderi</u>, quickly!"

Quick as a two-dollar whore we were back in our car headed down the road, watching very carefully our speedometer.

We were GI's and the Swiss knew the American army had a bad record for drug use. Our loaded-down VW was an obvious potential catch. Luckily, we were thrown back into the unknown sea of this

THE OLYMPIC STADIUM AND THE WHITE VW IN 1972
(A REVOLUTIONARY DESIGN OF LARGE SWEEPING CANOPIES OF
PLEXIGLAS STABILIZED WITH METAL CABLES.)

foreign country. Traveling Europe was fun in the 70's but there was also the fear of doing something wrong—like going down a one-way street—and getting locked up and the key thrown away.

THE 20th OLYMPIAD

On another trip, a few of us in a white VW beetle hit the autobahn headed southeast to Munich 300 Klicks away. It was August of '72 and The Olympic games were soon to commence in Munich and a large number of complementary tickets were distributed to the American forces in Germany. I got a couple of tickets to specific events as did others who said they wanted to go and we got together to exchange them like trading cards to amass our favorite events. We had to park miles from the stadium site and take a shuttle bus. Thousands of Germans, with sloshing beer steins, swarmed like marauding ants over the site. It was only the second time for the Olympics to be played in Germany since Berlin in 1936 and <u>Deutchland</u> was to "present a new, Democratic, and optimistic Germany to the World" with a motto, when interpreted, meaning "The Happy Games." Languages from all over the world could be heard. I, of course, was enthralled by the design of the stadium. The Olympics and World's Fairs were one of the few places where architects could experiment with new technologies and create real works of art. Plexiglass panels were secured over a web of steel cables, and the huge canopies hanging from tall poles looked like circus tents of <u>Saran Wrap</u>. We had tickets to a wrestling event, track & field, and a volleyball match, but it was about ten days into the event when the word got around that a terrorist group had taken Israeli athletes as hostages in the Olympic Village located near the park. We tried to find out what was going on as panic moved like a tsunami through the park. Everyone was looking for someone with a portable radio or television set and word passed

I GAVE AWAY MY GOOD TICKETS FOR VOLLEYBALL

quickly that the Olympics might be cancelled. We spent the night in two pup tents erected beside our car and ate C-Rations (canned food requiring the highly-valued P38 to open) in a parking lot many miles from the <u>Olympiapark</u>. The next day we heard that the day's athletic events were cancelled and a memorial service would be held for Israeli victims. What had happened? The Olympic flags of all the countries were to be flown at half-mast in the <u>Olympiastadion</u>. Considering the chore it would be to return to the park and the fact that our leave would end the next day (we just had a three-day pass), we decided to return to Schwetzingen, having seen only a couple of the Olympic events.

We didn't get back to the Autobahn until nightfall, and we were considered AWOL if we didn't get back by morning's formation (I didn't want McKay shooting at me). That meant driving late into the night. All we saw in our headlights that night were road signs, mostly red triangles and circles, and large signs that pointed out the exits to

THE VILLAGE OF BERCHTESGADEN IN THE BAVARIAN ALPS

AUSFAHRT, and we thought that must be a very large town. (We found out later, it was just the German word for "EXIT.") Back at Tompkins, we were told that a Palestinian terrorist group known as "Black September" had negotiated a deal for a plane to fly out of Germany, and after they and the hostages were bussed to helicopters and flown to the airport, sharpshooters tried to take out the terrorists and a gun battle ensued. Before the hostages could be rescued, they were gunned down while still strapped in the helicopter. Eleven Israelis were murdered and five terrorists killed. The disaster put a dark cloud over an Olympic event (The Happy Games) that was supposed to present to the world a new democratic and optimistic Germany, but the world blamed the death of the athletes on a botched job by the German Polizei.

Terrorism was still alive and well. I thought about Gunter Schmidt, my favorite fire chief, and his plans to revive the Nazis.

RELIGIOUS RETREAT

In the 1950's after the war, the army established a religious retreat in the alpine village of Bertchtesgaden. The village was declared a recreation center for U.S. personnel in Europe. The retreat had rooms for 100 guests and a large library of religious books. We were offered a four-day trip and I, Arey, Childress, and others took up the offer. It was a chance to see the German Alps. And a very beautiful place it was.

During the retreat, we were offered a bus ride up to Obersaltzberg located above Bertchtesgaden to see Hitler's Eagle's Nest at 1,834 meters (6,017 ft) in the hope of seeing a fantastic view of the Alps. We rode a bus up the Kehlstein road and the final leg of the trip to Hitler's summer mountain home (a gift of the Nazi Party for his 50th birthday that he reportedly rarely visited) was through a tunnel and up a gold and silver elevator through 124 meters of solid rock. But not long after we arrived there, it began to snow blizzard-like with tear-inducing biting winds. We couldn't see six feet in front of us. A large thermometer read minus six degrees Centigrade (21 degrees

BERTCHTESGADEN RETREAT–CHILDRESS IN FOREGROUND

HITLER'S "EAGLE'S NEST"–A GIFT FROM THE NAZI PARTY

Fahrenheit). Eagle's Nest employees were packing up and we were told we couldn't stay any longer, an unexpected early-season storm was approaching and they had to close up for the winter; if we didn't leave now, we'd be trapped. The sun had been shining brightly down below, and for all we knew, it was still shining. Mountains are that way; they can become treacherous and deadly at any moment. I did snap a great photo moments before the storm enveloped us.

ARAB AND THE JEW

Standing there in their barracks room, both in green wrinkled fatigues—"Arab" Shada towering over Kim Frost like Abbot over Costello—they were face to face, or shall I say face to belt buckle.

"Israel is not a country, you have no right to be there," said Shada, "You're just immigrants, a thorn in our ass."

"Me! I've never even been to Israel!" said Frost.

"All the same blood."

"Look what you guys did to us in Munich!" said Frost, "Unconscionable murder!"

"I wasn't there, Dickball!"

"You ripped up all our cemeteries," screamed Frost, "won't admit to the truth."

"What truth? That you don't belong. The prophet Mohammed came from Mecca to Israel," blasted Shada, his blood ready to boil over.

"To Jerusalem, thy city, shall we return with joy," repeated Frost, "We let you visit, you destroyed our synagogues."

"Our Mosques are Holy sites and you let them fall into ruin!"

"You're a rag-headed Desert Flea, Shada. That's all there—"

"You're a Zionist Pig!"

"A baby-diapered Camel Jockey!"

"Heeb Runt, shorter than O'Neill!

"Dune Crawler."

"What?"

"You crawl through sand dunes don't you?"

"Never seen one."

"Damn, Shada, I bet some of the players on your Cornsuckers football team are Muslim."

"Huskers! Corn<u>huskers</u>! Dare you talk that way of Nebraskans?"

"Go wipe your nose, Shada."

Suddenly the "born-again" Mark Hughes, a bible in his hand, entered the room, "Shut up Jackoffs, Jerusalem is the home of Jesus."

It seems the Arab-Israeli war would continue—with the Christians in the wings.

THE GILBERT TAYLOR FIGHT

PFC George Taylor (not Rich "The Kid" Taylor), from our platoon, was Short and had had enough of Lifer "Airborne" Gilbert who was heavy into one of his stories about his adventures in Vietnam: "We were outside Da Nang and with our guys trapped in a jungle village surrounded by VC, our platoon was going to jump from a C-130 and save the grunts."

George Taylor was just 23 days and a wake up, and figured he had nothing to loose. It was damn time to stand up to Gilbert: "I've been listening to your damn stories for two years, and I don't believe a damn thing you've said. Get off your high horse; you ain't no different than us and those stripes don't make you any better."

Gilbert coolly replied, "Airborne Rangers <u>are</u> better."

"Get over it Gilbert, past history, we've heard enough," replied Taylor, his cockles rising, "Go to the latrine and stick your Airborne wings up your airborne ass."

GEORGE TAYLOR, LOWER RIGHT, ON THE FIRING LINE
(From the collection of George Taylor)

"You know what kind of guts it takes to jump into a fire fight?"

"Stupid-ass guts," said Taylor," I'm so very sorry for you that you had to jump out of a perfectly good airplane."

"Without me, you guys on the ground..."

"Too bad a slant-eyed gook didn't use you as target practice."

And with that, Gilbert leaped at the smaller, thinner Taylor and a scuffle ensued. This was among the desks and light tables we worked at and our work got shoved off the tables and the guys began to cheer for Taylor, for they had the same sentiments as George: Gilbert was a blowhard and everyone had had enough of him.

"Burn him Taylor."

"Clock him!"

"Rip them wings off his chest!"

"Give the gooks his home address."

Just as the fight was getting really rough, Sergeant "Cloudy" Hayes came over and broke up the fight. Airborne was quieter after that, but not by much.

WHAT'S IT ALL ABOUT?

SP4 Wilkie Ross—my roommate for a time—had completed two semesters of college with straight "A's," but he said he was an "over achiever" and got burned out, so he joined the army to get away from an unhappy home of bickering parents. He thought it would make the old man happy since his father had been in the army. One day Wilkie was sent to LTC Richard Williamson's office (the Battalion Commander) where he was grilled about some of the soldiers. Williamson showed him pictures of these soldiers out on the economy handing out leaflets. They were "suspected agitators," said Williamson, "I know who they are and what they're up to. If you just give me a confirmation, just nod your head when I call out their names." Wilkie replied, sitting straight in his chair, obviously feeling like it was a Gestapo interrogation, "I haven't been here that long, I can't tell you anything." And of course Wilkie wouldn't have, even if he had known what it was all about, but what <u>was</u> it about? Strange things were going on in the barracks and not of the usual kind.

TROUBLE IS BREWING

<u>Topo Topics</u> began to run some distressing letters to the editor—GIs love to complain—but the letters, indeed, represented the opinions of many. There was a lot to do around the post (a library, snack

bar, bookstore, darkroom, auto repair shop, gymnasium, and even a nine-pin bowling alley), but most of the guys just hung around in their rooms. I, and others including SP4 Ross, was using the chain of command by writing letters to our immediate superiors about things that ought to be changed with suggestions as to how to change them. Wilkie wrote about specific inefficiencies and the wanting food portions and I, in my "persnickety" style, wrote the Army and Air Force motion picture service to complain about the bad choice of cartoons before the movies as no one in my unit seemed to like the ones they were showing. From the advice of Cockbite and Woody, I suggested they run old Roadrunner cartoons instead—beep, beep—we sorely needed a good hardy laugh. I also suggested Captain Peal have the trash dumpsters moved closer to the building's entrance so that we'd spend less time dumping our trash cans, as they had to be empty for inspections each and every day. We thought we were in basic training because it never let up. The single guy had to live with it, while the

WAS I COMPLETELY OFF MY ROCKER,
OR WAS THE PLACEMENT OF DUMPSTERS WORTH FIGHTING FOR?

6 July 1972

SP4 Donald Kirk
449-84-0351
Co A, 656th Engr Bn
APO 09081

Army and Air Force
Motion Picture Service

SUBJECT: A Suggestion Concerning The Cartoons being Shown in Europe

Dear Sirs:

THE PROBLEM: It seems to me that the cartoons that are included with many of the feature films have been selected, at least partly, in the hopes that they would appeal to a major part of the USAREUR audiences: The G.I. But, these cartoons don't even begin to come close to "Creating a laugh".

THE SUGGESTION: I have found that most people, especially those in the teens and twenties, really enjoy the old ROAD*RUNNER CARTOONS. There is a general consensus too that the early Road-Runner cartoons were much better than the recent ones, and yet it is these early ones that are now distributed, even 16mm format, to clubs, schools, and other organizations at a near nil cost.

So, considering that distributors of first-run cartoons want their product shown, is it still possible for the Motion Picture Service to put these old Road-Runner's into the circut? I believe that it is the one cartoon that is universally liked by all ages.

Thank you for listening

SP4 Donald Kirk

Included herein are a few signatures to show sincere desires to see old ROAD-RUNNER Cartoons again:

married guys were allowed to live off post and even received housing subsidies. It was definitely a Mickey Mouse unit and didn't reflect the whole army, but that was all I could see. I'll quote you a couple of the letters from that wonderful rag, Topo Topics:

Dear Editor: A married E-4 gets quite a bundle of loot to take care of his family that Joe Single never sees in his paycheck. What potential re-upper, like myself, has any incentive to stay in when he walks up and down the hall in the billets and sees a single SFC E-7 stuck in a tiny room not unlike my own? Is this the way to spend 20 years? Uncle Sugar should start treating us as men and pay for the job we do, and pay based on rank, not for the number of kids we sire. Surely, if you can trust a married PVT to keep a home on the economy, you can have the NCOs and Officers stop the daily inspections of our barracks and [stop] heaping dozens of other indignities on us.

—A second class, fed up, single soldier.

This is my first letter to an editor, and I want to say that I don't see no sense in all the CQs in the barracks. I am a SP4 and get duty too much, besides, there are going to be rip-offs if somebody wants, even if MPs are in the halls. I think we should get rid of those hallway CQs since STRATCOM don't eat here no more.   — A tired Dude.

Like man, why all the useless extra duties? Headcount, two assistant CQs, courtesy patrol, barracks NCO, and on and on...all these extra duties really cut into our production time.   —Tired of Sitting

Dear Editor, congratulations to the mess hall for their consistently good gravies of all kinds. Keep up the good work.   —SP4 Lovely

I wasn't sure what Lovely meant by that letter, but could only assume it was sarcasm and printed it. Later, I thought, this was our polo-shirted Lovely, and he was probably quite serious. I had to pay more attention to Sergeant Wallow's gravies.

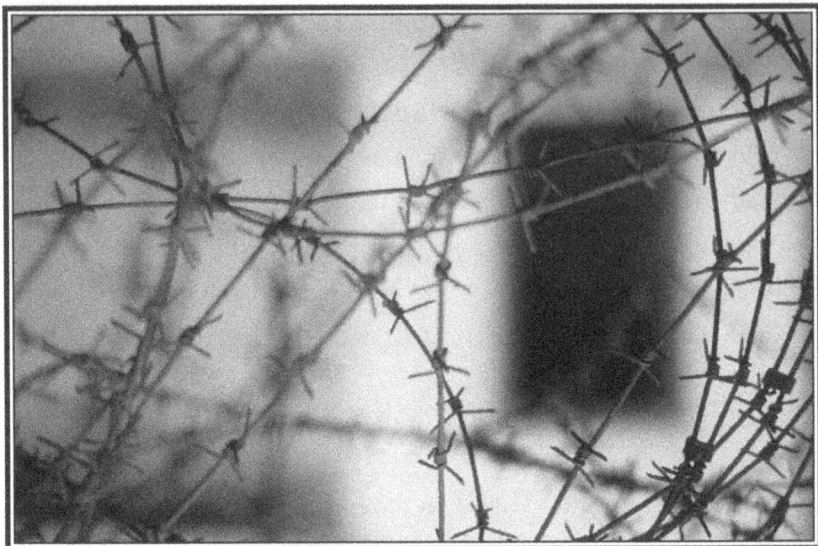

TOMPKINS BARRACKS–LIVING IN A PRISON?

OLIVER THE NARK?

We Straights thought PFC "Ollie" Oliver, a strange dude with a crooked smile and olive-shaped face, was a Dope Head because we saw him hanging around with known Headquarters drug users on the third floor even though he worked with us in A-Company. He also had a problem with body order, smelling like a farmhouse dung heap. Oliver seemed to have an aversion to water or was simply embarrassed to be in the shower with anyone else, and that was certainly something you had to get used to if you lived in the barracks. Maybe he was one of those kids who, at an early age, wouldn't even let his mom and pop see him naked and would wear all his clothes to the bathroom and then lock the door. The guys dropped hints about his need to take a good, long shower with some of that coarse sandy-textured GI soap, but he didn't catch on. No one had ever seen him coming from the shower. So it was time to take action, and after a

few beers, "Cockbite" Dulfer and a few others, barged into his room
with a plan to carry him down to the shower and scrub his hide good,
real good, maybe with a steel-bristled brush.

They found him lying on his bunk next to the window, and faster
than a teen's sex with his first woman, Oliver leapt up and jumped out
the open casement window. This was on the second floor, and their
eyes bugged out in fear. "He's F—g killed himself!" They figured he
was dead and they'd be cuffed and led to the stockade. They ran to
the window and saw that a small lean-to shed with a corrugated-tin
roof had broken his fall. Oliver scurried on down and ran off into the
distance wearing only his skivvies.

The second-floor residents never bothered him again. The question was, why did he jump in such a panic? Was it something more
than just the fear of a scalding shower?

He seemed a nice-enough guy, but he would disappear for days
from time to time and it was rumored he was in some kind of trouble,
maybe caught stealing in the barracks.

One incident had him shoved into a wall locker and sent sliding
down the barracks stairway. Another rumor had him charged with an
Article 112a, wrongful use or possession of a controlled substance.
When he would return to the barracks he would not explain himself,
becoming more mysterious all the time, and one day SP5 Wilkie
Ross was assigned to escort him when he was suddenly processing
out of our unit. Oliver apologized to Wilkie for getting him involved.
Involved? Oliver continued, "If they get me, they'll get you too. I'm
sorry." Wilkie didn't know it, but he was serving as protection for
Oliver. It turns out, Oliver had become an unwitting informant—a
"nark" as the Heads would have referred to him—and Battalion figured he would be in danger if he stayed at Tompkins. I don't know
who he fingered, accident or not, but the Dope Heads in our barracks

seemed concerned. Armiger, Kent, Hughes, and other Heads seemed to be distancing themselves from him.

We noticed an increase in Lifer activity on the third floor including some "unscheduled" inspections. Something was happening with Headquarters Company. Had they found the drug den in the fourth-floor attic? No. It turns out, Church and Armiger, two of the HQ Heads, had started an underground newspaper that was beginning to circulate through other units around Heidelberg including coffee houses frequented by GIs. The rag was protesting the Vietnam War and was promoting recreational use of drugs. The editors of this illegal paper were "dissidents" as the army saw them and free speech was not a right given to GIs by the UCMJ. They had apparently tracked the paper to Tompkins Barracks, but they couldn't get a handle on the perpetrators or where it was being printed. Maybe that's where Ollie had come in. I had seen an issue of the paper myself and thought nothing of it; free speech right? It seemed harmless to me. Michael O'Connell, my Topo Topics cartoonist, was the paper's primary illustrator, using his loose Pen & Ink style to satirize everything in the military. I thought how I would've enjoyed expressing _my_ World View in their paper instead of trying to sneak it through in an authorized version. The paper quickly disappeared from circulation, and Church and Armiger stayed under the radar, waiting for the right time to bring it out again. They never did.

O'CONNEL'S CARTOON STRIP IN TOPO TOPICS

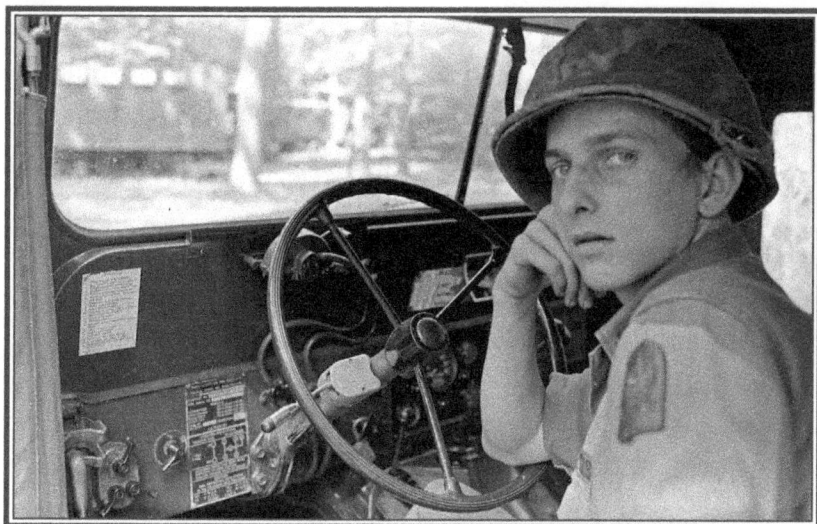

PFC MARK HUGHES–HEADED FOR AN EARLY OUT
–DRUGS AND JESUS DIDN'T SEEM TO MIX WELL–

DOOR POLICY REFINEMENTS

Removing the doors of suspected drug users didn't stem the tide of smoked-filled rooms and General Davidson decided to try a new approach—actually just the expansion of the same failed door policy—he ordered the removal of <u>all</u> the doors to the rooms of enlisted men! Yes, all of them. The Straights and Juicers were irate; the Heads just continued to puff away in the privacy of their attic den or in the woods off post. The result of this new policy was an increase in theft, noisy rooms that hindered a good nights sleep, and any semblance of personal privacy. Varying tastes in music would clash in the hallways along with GIs with simmering tempers. Black Sabbath would blast down the hall from 12" woofers at 2:00 in the morning. This led to the "Stereo Wars" as music from numerous rooms tried to drown out the music of the others—country, acid rock, Mantovani.

I went into my room and tried to listen to some 50's Rock & Roll on my Hi-Fi system. Ahab the Arab was now mixed with The Who's Pinball Wizard from down the hall. Wilkie Ross came in and plopped on the bed and shed his shiny black combat boots. "This door policy punishes the innocent as well as the guilty," he said.

"Do you want to hear Linda Ronstadt or Neil Diamond?" I asked as I turned on my JVC quadraphonic amplifier and Duel turntable.

"We innocents are immediately associated with drugs and the known drug users. We know who they are, why don't they—"

"How about Peter, Paul, and Mary?"

"This policy jeopardizes the security of all the valuables kept in our room. We've got expensive four-channel stereos and 100-watt speakers. Look at Big Al and Flash—their refrigerator, hot plate, coffee pot, cappuccino machine..."

"Olivia Newton-John, I'll put her on."

"Fine."

As Wilkie lay on his green bunk in his green fatigues and green wool socks fuming about the door policy, I stripped to my shorts as quickly as I could—none of that Olive Drab was going to rub off on me—and headed for the mess hall. From there, I was going to escape to the movies with Steve McQueen and James Coburn. Showing on the big screen was The Great Escape.

TOPO TOPICS IS SHUT DOWN

Captain Lough came to me one day and said printing the newsletter was costing too much.

"What do you mean?" I asked.

"Eleven-by-fourteen-inch pages, we're going to have to cut back. Too much paper."

"We've only been putting out an issue once every three months at twenty-four pages. I know the old paper was 8-1/2 by 11, but it ran monthly."

"You'll have to cut back to letter size."

"I can't do that, I have the next issue ready to go. The negatives have already been shot by Sergeant Mahan."

"Can't run it," said Lough, quite to the point, and turned away.

I made a quick calculation in my head and called after him, "Sir, this quarterly paper uses less paper and ink than the old monthly format."

"Can't run it."

"But, sir... you saw the paste-ups didn't you? You approved them?"

"I showed them to Colonel Williamson."

"You showed him <u>The Game of Army Life</u>?"—Most of the issue had been dedicated to a large board game with cards and instructions for a game played out as a new recruit starting in basic training, going through AIT, and trying to survive his stint in the army. To win, a player had to work his way around the circuitous track to the ETS goal line and that wasn't easy, what with all the extra duties and bad FTXs. It took up eight pages of the paper—"He didn't like it did he?"

Captain Lough didn't answer. He didn't have to.

That was the straw that broke the camel's back. It was March of '73 and I was entering my last year of service. How could they? I thought; it was a good game. It wasn't derogatory, it wouldn't cause the troops to riot, it was going to be fun to play and I knew the single men in the barracks would be cutting the newsletter apart to make the various cards to use in the game. Scissors would be in short supply. I had spent months on this game, completely designed and illustrated it. Stopping the presses was a personal blow to me. How could they? And the worst of it, I didn't believe Captain Lough was telling me the truth as to why I couldn't go ahead with the next issue. I was sure

THE GAME OF ARMY LIFE

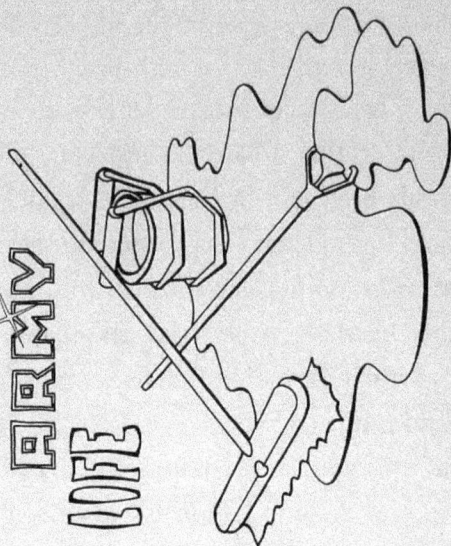

by don Kirk

RULES OF PLAY

☐ RECEIVE DRAFT NOTICE. START AT HOME WITH ALL YOUR MARBLES (25). THE OBJECT OF THE GAME IS TO SERVE YOUR TOUR OF DUTY AND REACH YOUR ETS DATE WITH MORE MARBLES THAN ANY OTHER PLAYER.

☐ IF YOU LOSE ALL YOUR MARBLES IT'S SOL AND YOU'RE OUT OF THE GAME. SHOULD YOU DECIDE THAT YOU DON'T WANT TO PLAY THE GAME ANYMORE, JUST GO AWOL.

☐ FOR PLAYING PIECES USE SMALL OBJECTS SUCH AS COINS, GUM WRAPPERS, AND SERVICE RIBBONS.

☐ PLAYERS (CALLED SOLDIERS IN THIS GAME) TAKE TURNS THROWING ONE DIE, MOVING THAT NUMBER OF SPACES FORWARD AND THEN CARRYING OUT THE ORDERS OF THE LAST SPACE LANDED ON.

☐ IF YOU HAVE ANY DOUBT AS TO THE RULES OF THIS GAME JUST GO TO THE AR's. GOOD LUCK, HOPE YOU MAKE IT PAL!

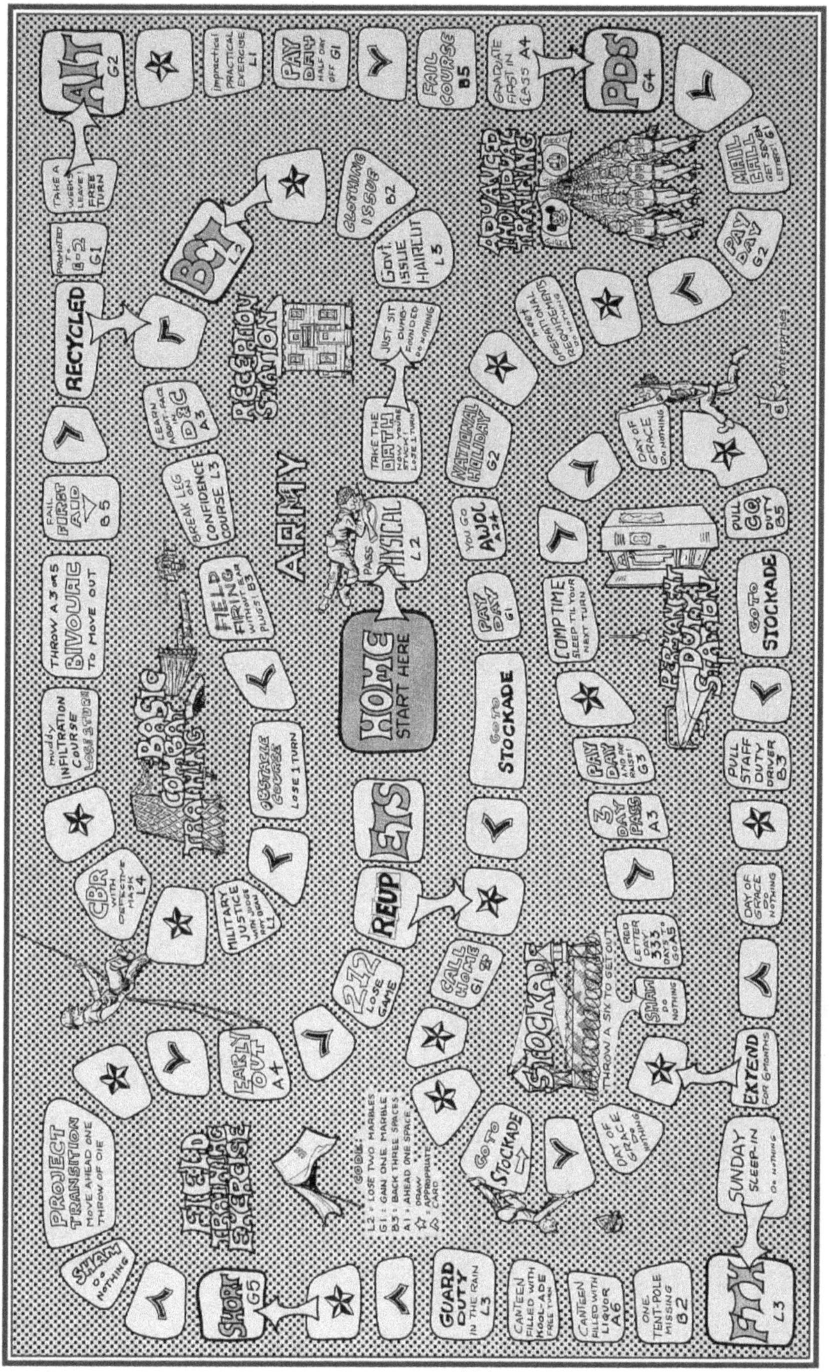
HOME
START HERE
ARMY
RECEPTION STATION
BASIC COMBAT TRAINING
ADVANCED INDIVIDUAL TRAINING
PERMANENT DUTY STATION
STOCKADE
THROW A SIX TO GET OUT
FIELD TRAINING EXERCISE
CODE:
L2 = LOSE TWO MARBLES
G1 = GAIN ONE MARBLE
B3 = BACK THREE SPACES
A1 = AHEAD ONE SPACE
DRAW APPROPRIATE CARD
RECYCLED
REUP
ETS
AIT G2
PDS G4
BCT L2
FTX L3
SHOP G5
GO TO STOCKADE
PASS PHYSICAL L2
SUNDAY SLEEP-IN DO NOTHING
EXTEND FOR 6 MONTHS
COMP TIME SLEEP TIL YOUR NEXT TURN
NATIONAL HOLIDAY G2
CLOTHING ISSUE B2
GOVT. ISSUE HAIRCUT L3

THE QUARTERMASTER & LAUNDRY BREAKS HALF THE BUTTONS ON YOUR FATIGUES, AND MELTS THE OTHER HALF. LOSE 1 MARBLE

YOU'RE GIVEN A THREE DAY PASS FOR THE WEEKEND BUT MONDAY TURNS OUT TO BE A NATIONAL HOLIDAY!!! LOSE THREE MARBLES

FIELD EXERCISE! YOU FALL ASLEEP IN YOUR FOXHOLE WHILE ON GUARD DUTY. THE O.D. DROPS IN!! LOSE 2 MARBLES

YOU DECIDE TO RE-UP FOR FOUR YEARS LOSE ALL BUT 10 MARBLES AND GO BACK 40 SPACES

THE EXTERMINATORS ARE AT THE MESS HALL SPRAYING FOR ROACHES LOSE 2 MARBLES

YOU FINALLY LEARN HOW TO MAKE HOSPITAL FOLDS ON YOUR BUNK, AND HOW TO SLEEP ON TOP OF THE BLANKETS!! YOU DON'T HAVE TO MAKE BED EACH MORNING! MOVE AHEAD 4 SPACES

EXTRA DUTY YOUR NAME SHOWS UP THREE TIMES ON THIS WEEK'S DUTY ROSTER LOSE 3 MARBLES

POLICE ☆ CALL ON SATURDAY A HIGH WIND BLOWS THE CITY DUMP INTO THE PARADE FIELD!!! LOSE 3 MARBLES

AN OFFICER TELLS YOU THAT TRUCKS ARE BEST FOUND ON THE TOP OF FLAG POLES! SO, YOU CLIMB UP THE POLE TO PULL MAINTENANCE!! GO BACK 5 SPACES FOR DREAMING THIS BUNK

COMICS ... BUY TEN MORE MARVEL COMICS TO READ ON CQ DUTY... GAIN 1 MARBLE

POST CLEANUP THIS WEEKEND ... LOSE 2 MARBLES

FORMS and Abbreviations ... LOSE 1 MARBLE

IN-RANKS INSPECTION THE CO THINKS YOU SHINED YOUR BOOTS WITH A HERSHEY BAR ... BRILLO PAD ... GAIN 1 MARBLE

YOU 'GET OVER' BY CARRYING A CLIPBOARD ... YOUR PLATOON SERGEANT WILL THINK YOU'RE BUSY, AND THIS WON'T GIVE YOU ANY DETAILS... MOVE AHEAD 7 SPACES

POINT DETAIL YOU SPILL A FIVE GALLON BUCKET OF PAINT ON THE DAY-ROOM FLOOR. BUT TO SOLVE THE PROBLEM YOU JUST PAINT THE REST GAIN 2 MARBLES

PAINT DETAIL YOU'RE DETAILED TO PAINT THE BILLETS ROOMS SO YOU PAINT FLOWERS ON THE WALLS GAIN 5 MARBLES

YOU SEE A 'LIFER' WEARING A MICKEY MOUSE WATCH FREAK OUT AND GAIN SIX MARBLES

YOU HAVEN'T BEEN PAID FOR THE LAST FOUR MONTHS. THE FIRST SERGEANT TELLS YOU: IF YOU HAVE A PERSONAL PROBLEM... SEE THE CHAPLAIN

YOU'RE CHOSEN FOR TWO WEEKS TDY OVER $200!! IN POCKET MONEY, HOTEL ACCOMMODATION AND YOU GET TO WEAR CIVILIAN WEAR GAIN 5 MARBLES AND 7 SPACES

TAKE TEN DAYS LEAVE FOR REST, RELAXATION, AND FREEDOM! MOVE AHEAD 10 SPACES

YOU RECEIVE AN ARTICLE 15 for MISSING FORMATION 7 DAY RESTRICTION LOSE 1 TURN

IT WAS FUN WHILE IT LASTED THIRTY DAYS AWOL 30 DAYS HARD LABOR LOSE 7 MARBLES

This card counts as a 3 DAY PASS IT CANCELS OUT ONE SPACE OF YOUR CHOICE KEEP CARD UNTIL NEEDED

TAKE TWO WEEKS LEAVE BECAUSE YOU'RE TIRED OF PLAYING MICKEY MOUSE GAMES. MOVE AHEAD 14 SPACES

HEALTH & WELFARE INSPECTION THEY SEARCH YOUR ... SILVERWARE AND SWITCH ... KILO HASHISH! ADVANCE 6 SPACES!

SHOW IT OR NOT? YOUR PLATOON LIFER SERGEANT WHO WEARS CLIP-ON TIES AND COMBAT BOOTS ... ZIPPERS... LOSE 6 MARBLES

YOU GET THE WORD THAT THERE'S GOING TO BE A BIG DIRTY DETAIL TODAY SO YOU WEAR YOUR GREENS INSTEAD OF FATIGUES ... GREENS!! GAIN 5 MARBLES

YOU GET INTO A FIGHT, AND END UP IN FRONT OF THE I.G. THEY GIVE YOU AN ARTICLE 15 for WILLFULLY DESTROYING MILITARY PROPERTY! LOSE 2 TURNS

A GENERAL IS TO YOUR AREA IN 15 MINUTES. THROUGH YOUR OPERATIONS OFFICER TELLS YOU TO CLEAN UP THE AREA AND LOOK BUSY... LOSE 1 ARTICLE 15. LAUGH YOUR HEAD OFF!

THIS CARD SERVES AS A PSYCHOLOGICAL WEAPON GAIN AS YOU READ IT. ... THINK YOU REALLY HAVE SOMETHING GOOD! HEHE! (snicker snicker)

TAKE YOUR MILITARY DRIVER'S LICENSE TEST. THROW DIE FOR RESULTS. 1-3 = FAILED - GET BACK ON BUS! 4-6 = PASSED - GET ... DRIVER RUSTED BACK 6

YOU RECEIVE AN ARTICLE 15 for WRITING A CHECK WITHOUT SUFFICIENT FUNDS 14-DAYS RESTRICTION LOSE 2 TURNS

YOU GO TO, AND SUCCESSFULLY COMPLETE AIRBORNE SCHOOL. YOU'RE AWARDED 6 PROMOTION POINTS, A PAIR OF JUMP BOOTS, AND A CHANCE TO JUMP BEHIND ENEMY LINES! MOVE AHEAD 6 SPACES

IT'S IG TIME. GO THRU FIVE PHOTOS (PG.) FOR FULL-FIELD INSPECTION. THREE SATURDAYS OF ADDITIONAL DUTY. ... LOSE 6 MARBLES

YOU GO ON SICK CALL for PNEUMONIA THE DOCTOR GIVES YOU THREE ASPIRIN AND SENDS YOU BACK TO WORK. MARBLES 3

YOU PUT IN A REQUEST FOR A SECONDARY MOS AS A CUSTODIAL ENGINEER AND YOU GET IT!... GO BACK TEN SPACES!

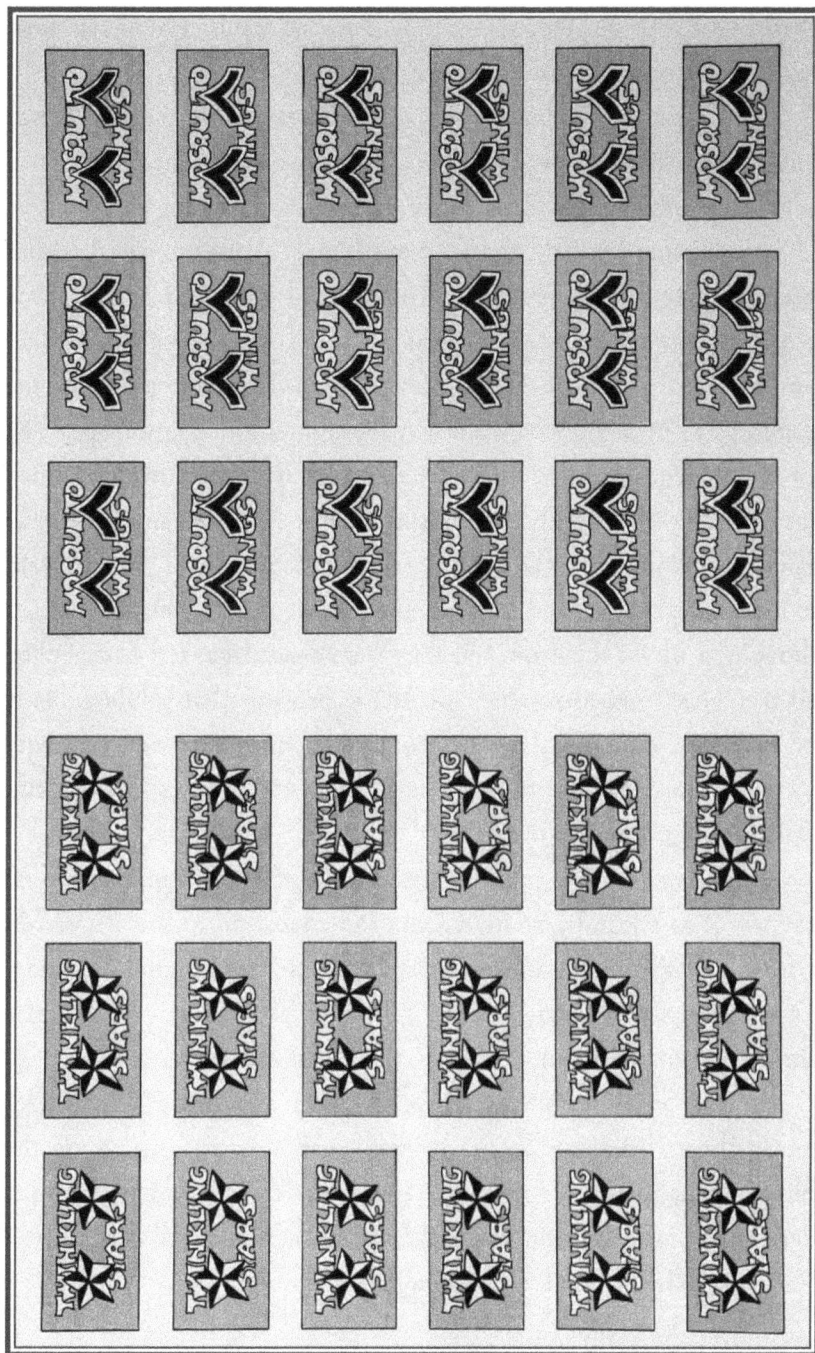

Williamson had put the kibosh to it. Too bad Church's underground rag had disappeared from the "magazine racks."

I told Mahan the bad news; he was heartbroken, thought it was going to be the best issue yet. He handed me the negatives.

"Sorry, keep these Kirk, maybe they'll have a change of heart."

Some time went by and Captain Lough asked me why I hadn't been working on the newsletter. I told him I quit. And I had. Many of the men asked me when the next issue of <u>Topo Topics</u> was coming out. I took that personal. I had failed them. I had big plans for the paper. I had even received word that the central office in Europe (<u>The Overseas Weekly</u>) liked the paper and wanted to meet me. So much for that. The only negative thing they had to say about my first issue: said I shouldn't put black borders around photos of people, said it meant they were dead, a newspaper convention to be followed. I thought, a life in the army and they were dead. I guess I had broken all the rules, tried to produce a better paper, one that would actually be read, one that would boost moral—but innovation and creativity was <u>not</u> allowed. The army was a staid, bureaucratically stifled system. Was I wrong? I didn't think so.

A brain couldn't help but get stagnant in this environment. What use was it to try and give my talents and education to the army? My efforts were essentially wasted. As SP5 Picklo was so fond of saying, "They can have my body, but not my mind." Big Al was right; it was time I quit giving them my mind—what little was now left of it.

I went to Woodburn's barracks room and heard "Bad, Bad, Leroy Brown" playing on his turntable. Woody was sitting on the bunk staring at Jim Croce's <u>Life and Times</u> album. Croce, with his dark curly hair and heavy mustache stared back up at Woody.

"Hey Kirk, I don't want to be here anymore."

"What now?"

"Just stuff."

"Maybe this will cheer you up. I've decided to let those extra roads on the Lampertheim map pass through final edit."

"What?"

"I see nothing, I know nothing."

Woody jumped up with an ear-to-ear smile on his face and stood at attention.

"Ya vol, mein Kommandant! 'FTA' on the Lampertheim!"

I went to my room and sat there quietly sketching a drawing in pencil. One was of a hand holding a revolver, finger squeezing on the trigger, the barrel pointing directly at the viewer—directly at me. I scribbled a caption underneath that read, "DROP DEAD OR I'LL SHOOT!" What choice did I have? I picked up another sheet of art board

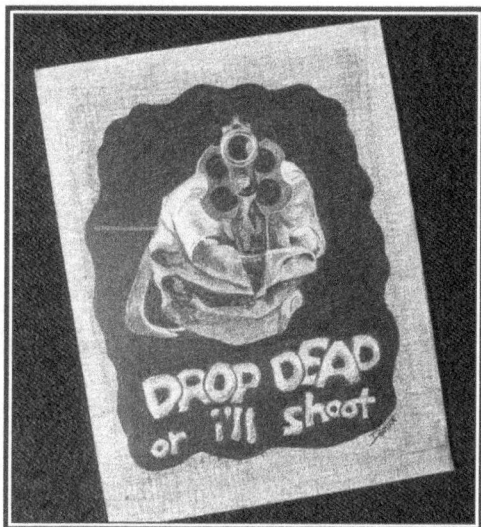

WHAT DID IT ALL MEAN?

and at the top of it drew a Victorian mansion on a distant hilltop. In the foreground, I sketched a man lying on his back in apparent agony, his mouth wide open, screaming bloody hell. A big featureless, glowing ball lay heavily on his chest.

A TANKED SOLDIER RUN AMUCK

About that time an American GI in the 3rd Armored Division at Coleman Kaserne in Gelnhausen went nuts and decided to take a joy ride with one of Uncle Sam's WWII tanks. He careened through the gate of Coleman with an M48A3 diesel-powered tank with a 90mm gun and hit Germany's narrow cobblestone streets. He wrecked havoc in the neighborhood with that 65-ton mass of steel, taking out street signs, crushing a few vehicles, and crashing

SIGMUND FREUD, ANY SUGGESTIONS?

through several walls before a parade of <u>Polizei</u> apprehended him. He tried to reverse the tank several times until he finally found himself stuck between two buildings. Word had it that he just wanted to get off the post and visit the nearest beer festival. Apparently he had finished all the bottles he had in his room. We thought this might be our own "Cockbite" Dulfer, but he was "partying" in his room at the time.

WADDELL, KIRK, AND THE BONG

Waddell invited me into his corner room on the North end of the second floor. He worked in the depot platoon, but the other map depot guys were at the other end of the long hall. Why was he there when the others were far away? I could only guess that's where he wanted to be to express his gang leadership, or, his supervising sergeant wanted him separated from the rest of the depot platoon to reduce his influence. There was no doubt that he was the "Depot Dudes" gang leader. One evening he invited me into his room and sat me down. The room was dark as a cave, the window blackened out, a smoky atmosphere engulfing the room, and drug paraphernalia strewn about. It was a small one-man room with a bunk bed at the far end. Another "depot dude" was also present, sitting under the top bunk smoking a joint. He barely acknowledged me.

Waddell: "Come on in Kirk, I wants to talk you."

Kirk: "Sure."

Waddell continued, "See this, you should try it. Blow a bowl with us."

"Don't do the heavy stuff."

"Oh no, man," replied Waddell, "Just water. Dis weed is cool and smooth. You'll forget you're at Tompkins."

The distant roommate finally spoke: "Yeah man."

I replied, "That's okay, thanks. I actually love my time here."

They both snickered.

I asked, "Waddell, how'd you get in this mapmaking company?"

Waddell replied, "When the recruiter axe me what I do, I tell him I sweep da floor of my town's newspaper. He figure I'm qualified to be a printer and sign me up."

Another "Airborne" Gilbert, I thought.

"Kirk, try it. It's okay, man, join us."

I realized the thing he was showing me was a water pipe—a bong, or some such illegal contraption. And it was handmade. A Motts Apple Sauce jar was wrapped in grey Duct tape with a plastic tube made from a dry erase marker sticking out of the top. A long clear plastic tube was also coming from the thing.

"What's the long tube for?" I asked.

"For use wid a government issue gas mask," replied Waddell, "for a really good hit, man."

My eyes widened.

"You won't need dat. This is mild stuff, man. Easy on ya. Good shit. Passes da time. Here, take a hit, man. Just put your mouth over dis tube and suck deeply, make her bubble—and don't exhale into da bong."

"I don't even smoke cigarettes. I have allergic rhinitis," I said.

"It's not a coffin stick, man."

I wanted to fit in, make friends with Waddell, but this was scaring me. What had I gotten myself into? But I didn't want to look like some wimp, so I took a light puff...and coughed.

"Hold it in. It's good shit, man." Waddell took a nice long puff himself. His eyes were bloodshot, a satisfying smile on his face. He pushed the bong back to me and I took another puff. Waddell seemed distant and the room just plain weird. His warbled, slowed-down speech no longer made sense. I wanted to get up and leave, but I felt totally out of control. I just sat there on the floor, Waddell standing over me, or was he now sitting at his desk, or over there now making coffee? Was his roommate smiling? Were they talking to each other? They seemed to be going about their own business as I just sat there, my head not of me. I seemed to be there for a very long time.

Waddell was trying to get me hooked, become a new customer. I now understood—without a doubt, he was a dealer.

Finally, I forced myself to stand up and spoke, "Thanks, Waddell, I'm uh, yes, cool, man." I searched for the door handle—there was no door—and meandered out, consciously trying to place one foot in front of the other. I returned to my room and fell-away asleep.

WACKJOB'S FREEDOM

Late one evening an OD-green military ambulance, with a large red cross on each side panel, arrived at Tompkins with red lights flashing and stopped in front of our barracks. We looked out the windows and then ran into the hall to see what was up. The two attendants grabbed their medical kits and hurried up the stairs to our floor and continued on up to Headquarters Company on the third. As the schizophrenic lights from the ambulance flashed their disturbing communiqué on the walls of our rooms, we stood in the hallway whispering questions to each other and waited for answers. After several prolonged minutes, the attendants came back down stairs, unloaded a gurney, and floated it up to the third floor. Soon the attendants hefted a burdensome gurney slowly back down the stairs, the carrier weighed down by a human-like form under a pastel-blue cloth. They passed our floor and we hurried back to the windows in our rooms. The gurney's wheels were down now as it was rolled up to the ambulance. The rear doors were opened and the gurney slid in. They didn't seem to be in any hurry as the NCO on duty signed a clipboard. They drove off without flashing lights and we returned to the halls. Michael Church came down from the third floor. He told us that Leonard "Looney Tunes" McMurray had again attempted suicide, but this time he didn't recover from efforts to resuscitate him. Sorrow spread quickly throughout the billets, but you could sense a peaceful air about the place. For a moment, our minds were as tranquil as seagulls floating on the updraft of a seashore cliff. We murmured such things as, "Looney Tunes finally succeeded. He made it! The son of a bitch made it! He's finally free of this man's f—g army."

A LAST REFUSAL

I would have missed a trip to London, England if I hadn't turned down yet another opportunity for a promotion. My tour trip with the Service Club to England had been booked for months, and it was the last they were to have, the Army having decided the tours were no longer to be. Chief Maxwell had put me in for SP5 once again and placed me on the roster to meet with a promotion board of officers and NCOs, but when I found out the scheduled date for the board would be while I was touring London, I said to the Chief, "seeing London is far more important than a promotion. I know it'll be my only chance for either option. I choose London." Well, Maxwell, lost it, and lost faith in me, the look on his crestfallen face was that of a devoted father who's pride in his son had just been shattered. Scotty and now me. He never tried to promote me again, it was finally clear to him I wasn't going to join the club and become a Lifer. I also think he took it as a personal affront to him and his beloved Army. I felt bad, couldn't take it back; the expression on his face, I'll never forget.

I remembered Picklo's motto: "You can have my body, but not my mind." I turned and walked away. This was the second time I had to choose between the Army and "the other." Remember, I also had to choose between and OCS (Officer Candidate School) exam and my final two exams to graduate A&M. The decision was simple, but painful and heartbreaking.

Frustrated with life at Tompkins, even with the opportunities I had been given and the many trips around Europe, I found myself in my underwear running up and down that long, noisy hallway in the barracks, screaming at the top of my lungs, "F-T-A!" And this was the second floor where the company commander's office was. Clearly, I had cracked, blew a 20-amp fuse. Even my roommate, Wilkie, said

I should tone it down—even as he hid and snickered loving every minute of it. I was behaving immaturely; I couldn't get over the fact that I was here against my will, conscripted as it were; I had a different plan for my life and they were screwing it up. If I had felt I was doing something worthwhile, felt actually needed—my talents put to good use—then maybe things might have been different.

PLAYING THE GAME

The doors were still off the rooms—all the rooms—USAREUR having seen no reduction in drug use—and we were about to fall out for morning formation after having had our meager breakfast in Wallow's Mess, and it was noisy as hell in the hallway. No peace, I thought to myself, can't even brush my teeth quietly. I lay down my toothbrush and slapped a sound-effects record on my Duel. I dropped the needle down on the cut of a lighthouse foghorn and turned the sound up all the way. Four 100-watt speakers blared down the hallway. I think the building shook and plaster began to crack. The commotion in the halls came to an abrupt halt. I repeated the horn three more times and shut down my system. People in their rooms came out in the hall to see what was up. Pineapple and Captain Peal came out of the orderly room. It was a showstopper. I was treating the Army like a game. I was living The Game of Army Life, but not playing by even its rules. I left my room, looking around feigning bewilderment, "Who done that?"

Wilkie said the guys could count on expecting the unexpected

from me. He said they liked that about me. I didn't understand why. He said I was the class clown, providing entertainment for them; I could be silly and play around with them like a bunch of boys on a school playground. A shy kid like myself with low self-esteem, no, I wasn't a class clown, I was just letting off steam, to relieve the pain of being there. If they hooked into it, all the well, maybe they could survive this hellhole too.

One morning at the Ramp, I went around the tables shaking everyone's hand and instead of saying "good morning," "congratulations," or "good job men," I quietly said "F-T-A," and a few of them looked at me strangely, but the rest gave me a firm hand and nodded "right-on." They began to verbalize and cheer as they watched me go from person to person, waiting to see everyone's reaction—platoon sergeants, privates, and all—and then they saw me approach Chief Maxwell and there was a sudden hush of electricity in the air. I put out my hand to Max, he raised his, and we shook, and like one of those vibrating joy buzzers of stinging surprise, I said "F-T-A." He jerked his hand away and his eyes shot daggers at me. Everyone saw it and quietly returned to their work. They were probably thinking, <u>Kirk has finally gone off the deep end.</u> I knew I was close. I was thinking, maybe Wackjob or Mark Hughes had the best approach.

PAULA

One day we got our first female recruit from the Woman's Army Corps (WAC) assigned to our photomapping platoon, and as expected by the Pentagon, she upset the apple cart. Paula Jacques was her name, of average looks, a bit homely, but she was still something feminine to look at. She had long hair and sure beat the gray floors and green walls of our environment. She even smelled good in her form-fitted green fatigues. She billeted with other woman at another post; there were no facilities for her at Tompkins (for her protection). It was known that a lot of those girls were lesbians—and the military, a place in heaven for them—but it wasn't long before the rumor mill was grinding out a story that Paula had slept with one of our own, and then another, with tension building as Paula teased another sex-starved GI. At first the whole platoon had perked up and production had increased, but you could see the guys hanging around Paula's desk (I guess they were trying to imagine what Paula looked like wearing only her dog tags). Frank Dulfer was the latest beneficiary of her wholesome gifts, and every morning the guys surrounded his table to find out his latest escapades with her. He would always crack a sheepish smile and not surrender too many details. It made Paula mysterious and desired by all. Rumor had it that the post theatre projection room where Dulfer worked at that time (he had replaced Lovely), was their heat-of-passion rendezvous point during movie presentations. But I can tell you, each projector reel was only ten minutes long. On the other hand, I can think of no better place to be left alone on a military post. I think when Cockbite was working, more film than usual had a hole burned in the film or a projector change-reel cue missed (those flashing blips on the screen). When the screen went white you could bet Cockbite was busy up there. Eventually, Paula began to flirt with me—yes me—and I wondered how she decided the order of her conquests. It soon became obvious to us that she was a sex-mad nympho who intended to take us all on. We didn't see anything wrong with that seeing as how The World was three thousand miles away, but to her, the battalion contained hundreds of sex-starved men she could get her hooks into as easy as shooting fish in a barrel. In her cute, flirtatious way she was so much as saying to me, "You're next, baby, very soon now." But my turn was prolonged, as Cockbite, with almost a daily smirk on his face, didn't seem to be willing to let go. It wasn't until Cockbite went back to the states on emergency leave when his dad passed away, that he relinquished her, and it wasn't me, but the good-looking blond-headed "Chilibean" Childress who filled the void left behind by Dulfer. He successfully handled Cockbite's duties in the projection room—both of them. Tokuhisa and Maxwell were becoming noticeably irritated at the distraction Paula had become, disrupting workflow with far too many eruptions, er interruptions. Then one day a new rumor surfaced, that maybe she had syphilis and was trying to get back at all men for something one man did to her in the past. The mood around the Ramp changed and Paula, one day, never returned, having been transferred elsewhere, hopefully to an all-female WAC unit, well, no, that would have been a treasure trove of sex-starved women.

Luckily, no one in our platoon had to see the doctor.

PAULA AND HER LATEST CONQUEST "CHILLIBEAN" CHILDRESS

GIs comment on drug crackdown

Usareur's anti-drug program doesn't seem to impress the troopies who have to live with it . . .

Recently initiated policies which deprive many Usareur soldiers of their privacy for the purpose of discouraging drug use have stirred heated discussions among EM, NCOs, and officers alike.

The Weekly wanted to find out GI sentiment toward the regs, whether troopers think the measures are effective, how strictly the policy is being enforced in their units and whether soldiers feel the rules are constitutional.

Here are the comments we got:

Pvt (E-2) Kurt Steinhaus, Ansbach: It takes away your personal rights and your privacy. Everything's back to the old Army; it takes away VOLAR. It may be legal but the Army really doesn't go by legality anyway. There's nothing we can do but just sit back and ride it out. Probably IG complaints — that'll just let them know how we feel about it, let them know the troops don't like it. Maybe that will stop it.

Spd Bruce Dawes, Ansbach: It's a sack of shit. How's that

cause of it. When I was home on leave I read an article about it and that almost stopped me from coming back.

Pfc Jerry Henderson, Amberg: I think it sucks, man. No privacy, taking away your personal possessions —, it's like taking your rights away from you. You can't even go to your own room anymore and sleep without somebody coming in. It's unconstitutional, they can take your stereo and clothes away. Just because they're taking doors away that's not going to stop the drug problem. There's going to be a severe drop in morale and somebody's going to get hurt. A pig will come in the room and somebody's going to get mad. Put it this way: what if you had a private house and the government decides to take your door away? It's the same thing.

Pfc Daniel Bateman, Baumholder: I think they suck. One of the lifer E-6s or E-7s comes through the billets at two a.m. and turns on the lights and har-

people are too intelligent to put up with this bullshit.

Spd David Fulton, Eschborn: They're a hassle. It's a waste of time in our unit because few men use drugs and most GIs are smart enough not to keep the shit in the barracks. Those regs aren't going to help that much. As far as not being allowed to lock the doors, yes, that's legal because it's a fire hazard. It's left up to the discretion of the commander and he can back it up with fire regs. I think the drug rules will be in for some time. But we haven't seen

Henderson — Dawes — Romano — Bateman

any cutdown in drug use; the majority of people are smart enough to hide it or use it off post.

Spd Joseph White, Frankfurt: They stink. They're trying to make it seem dreary and lifeless in the billets and they're taking

Related stories appear on page 7 and page 12

stitution. Any part of the drug policy can be taken as harassment; one thing that has our troops up in the air is not being able to have partitions in their rooms. The drug problem is, I feel, bad enough that something

effective just because of more emphasis on drug use. I don't see how you can deny a man to have incense and black lights; it's not too terribly constitutional. I haven't yet been able to figure out where UCMJ fits into the Con-

reason why you should want to lock your door when you're in the room unless you're doing something illegal. All they're doing is cracking down and having inspections to catch guys that have drugs; it's the Army's right to pull inspections. The only person who objects are those who like to burn incense but don't use drugs or those who do smoke drugs. It's illegal to smoke drugs and they can take whatever measures they want to stop it. But, of course, I'm prejudiced because I'm an MP. When they make drugs legal, then the measures would be unconstitutional.

Spd Richard Logan, Frankfurt: It looks like punishment be-

"USAREUR'S ANTI-DRUG PROGRAM DOESN'T IMPRESS THE TROOPIES WHO HAVE TO LIVE WITH IT..."

OPERATION ORANGE PEEL

I was into my last year of enlistment—that extra year I had signed up for to avoid a vacation in Vietnam—and I was fed up with the system. I would debate with some of the officers, that the people weren't the problem; it was the system that was broke, the vertical chain of command, the reticence by commanders to send anything up that chain, to keep that "status quo." I tried to explain how a more horizontal structure would lead to more creative solutions to problems. They said it wouldn't work. They needed strict military discipline with a clear chain of command to fight a war. I said we had to buy Rapidiograph pens on the Economy out of our own pockets, because Supply couldn't get them as long as they weren't in the system. (So why weren't they in the system if that's what we needed?) So what if it took us three times as long to do our job. Fed up, I had a plan, a formal protest. My many carefully crafted and argued cases formally presented in official letter form usually fell on deaf ears. The whole company was not getting sleep because of the noisy halls, and the theft of cameras and Hi-Fi equipment was on the rise with the "no doors on billets rooms drug-fighting policy." We had had enough. With several members of our mapping and headquarters platoons, I secretly drew up a plan that was weeks in the making. The plan was code-named "Orange Peel"—an idea of Wilkie's—and we worked out the details. Our duffle bags with pup tents and sleeping bags were stored in a trailer at the Ramp (packed for quick mobilization, with mess kit, towels, and extras like playing cards and candy bars) and they had to be secretly moved to our barracks and stored there, hidden (in the Dayroom and Dope Den), until the day of the protest. It was to be on a Friday afternoon after work, and when that day came, quietly and without fanfare, and without anyone apparently giving orders, pup tents began popping up like daisies around the quadrangle's flagpole. Two shelter halves were required to make up a pup tent, and that required a pairing of troops, a certain amount of coordination. The stars and stripes on this breeze-less day hung there like a wet noodle. Up popped five more tents, then ten, then fifteen. PFC Church from headquarters sat in front of his tent writing poetry as if with not a care in the world. It beat pounding on a typewriter. In another tent, a couple of "Dudes" were smoking pot. Waddell was standing outside the tent taking deep breaths, "I'm diggin' it, man." At least no one had yet decided to make a cook fire.

SP4 Kent, a little bleary-eyed, came up to me, "Looks like we've a good showing."

"It scares me," I said. "Just keep your shit wired tight, Kent."

"I can hold my breath."

"Kirk, this is loony, you can't buck the system," said political cartoonist Michael O'Connel from Headquarters.

It was now four-thirty Friday and the officers—who all lived off Tompkins on the Economy or at Patrick Henry Village—were leaving for the weekend when they saw the commotion in the quadrangle. "Who authorized this?" asked the 'butter bars,' the company

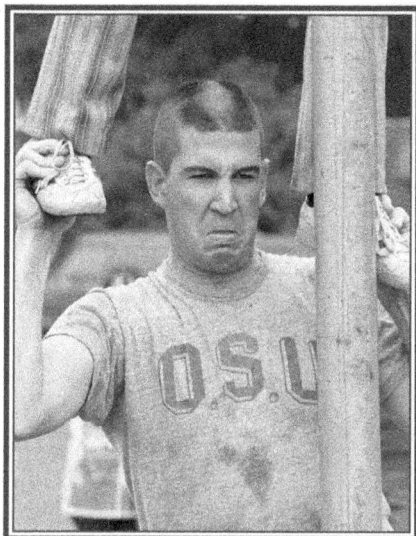

CAPTAIN PORR

commanders, the majors, and eventually 'the old man' himself, Battalion commander Lt. Col. Williamson, his tobacco pipe hanging from his lips, foul smoke curling into the air. Officers in all sizes came out of the woodwork like cockroaches after dark, scratching their heads and shuffling their feet as they came out onto the parade ground. Captain Porr from S-3, an athletic, straight-arrow with a flat-topped crew cut, looking as if he had just gotten out of combat training, ask the first question.

"Lieutenant Sneed, what's this all about, what are these men doing here?"

"Beats me Capt'n Porr, I didn't get a memo on this."

"Is this Repro's doing? I see some African-American men here."

"I don't know."

"Where's Repro's platoon sergeant? Get him out here!"

"Yes sir," replied Sneed and scurried off.

Another officer type approached. It was Sergeant Major Swenson, special staff, office of the commander, man of large stature with lots of ribbons on his Class-A uniform.

"What's going on here, Capt'n?"

"I don't know," replied Porr.

"You don't know? Have you talked to any of these men?" demanded Swenson, "Who's in charge?" Swenson seemed a little "tipsy." I figured he kept a liquor flask in his shirt pocket like "Airborne" Gilbert.

"I'll find out," answered Captain Peal, our company commander, a quiet, unassuming man who wanted to do the best job he could— but not make waves—jumped out of his shorts and approached the men as they continued to stake their tents, roll out their sleeping bags, and prepare an area to build a campfire. Well, at least they hadn't started digging a latrine; after all, it was the quadrangle—and right under the American flag.

"What's going on here, private?" asked Captain Peal, "What platoon you from?"

"Repro."

"Who's in charge?"

TOMPKINS BARRACKS, HEADQUARTERS BUILDING ON LEFT

"I dunno, sir. We's just protestin'."

"You're what?"

"Protestin'."

"You don't protest in the military. You go through channels. What channels did you go through?"

"Channels, sir? My roomy ask me to come."

"Who told him?" Peal shifted his weight uncomfortably from one leg to the other. He normally spent his days sitting at a deck in a straight-backed gray metal chair with a worn cushion having a hemorrhoid-inducing split across the middle.

"A guy down the hall."

"You don't know his name?"

"Yous'll 'ave ta ax my roomy, sir."

Frustrated, Captain Peal moved on into the group—many of them from Headquarters company—only to hear a number of varying complaints: the cancellation of three-day weekend passes, lack of entertainment activities on the post, the bad location of the dumpsters requiring a long walk before breakfast (surprise, surprise!), the daily room inspections requiring hospital corners on bed covers, and an empty, sanitized trash can, excessive and unnecessary extra duties, and the lack of enough to eat. It was clear the men were upset, but to Peal, their protest didn't have a focus, an objective on which he could launch an attack. Finally, one of the protestors gave Peal _my_ name, and, in seconds, he was on me like flies to a mess kitchen.

"What's this all about, Kirk? Do I know you Kirk? Have you pulled CQ duty? When was the last time you pressed your fatigues?"

"Uh, yes, no sir, not recently, I've permanent Alert Driver Duty."

"I see, permanent, that's going to change. What's this all about?"

"The doors sir, and the lack of food. A general unrest, sir."

"A general unrest? Looks like the beginning of the Bolshevik Revolution."

"No sir, the beginning of democracy."

"The U.S. Constitution doesn't apply in the military."

"I'm finding that out."

"Article One, Section 8 of the U.S. Constitution authorized Congress to do it," said Peal.

"Do what, sir?"

"Write the Uniform Code of Military Justice. The military can legally operate under different laws."

"Legally operate under different laws?"

"Yes."

"Well I'll be a monkey's uncle." I didn't actually say that out loud, but couldn't believe there were exceptions to the constitution.

"I hear they won't let you print Topo Topics, Kirk. Has this protest got something to do with that?"

"No, sir. Captain Lough said my twenty-four pages per issue was costing too much."

Peal looked confused, I continued:

"I've only been able to put out an issue quarterly. The old letter-sized Topo Topics, published monthly, uses a lot more ink and paper than mine does. The real reason for cutting it off, well sir, it was mostly a large board game called The Game of Army Life.

"The Game of Army Life?"

"Yes, sir, a little harmless entertainment for the troops. I guess Headquarters didn't like it."

"I want to see this game."

"Now, sir?"

"No, when this thing is over."

"It is pretty funny, sir. Sergeant Mahan has the negatives if you'd like to—"

PLASTIC ARMY MEN PLAYING "THE GAME"?

Captain Peal turned and hurried away. I mumbled to myself, you're in it sir, you're playing it. I could see Peal reporting my comments to the other officers. Grouped in a small circle, mumbling to each other, it looked like they were preparing for a Circle Jerk—a bunch of elderly boy scouts preparing for an assault on friendly weapons. They seemed totally confounded by events, lacking an SOP for handling such a situation. Befuddled, they just wanted to go home. I wondered if a real enemy had thrown them a curve—like instead of attacking head on, coming up the rear, flanking them, coming from above or below—could they handle it? I didn't think so. They always got a "heads up" (advance warning) when an FTX was to happen; they wouldn't be able to move out in two hours if they really had to. The surprise IGs (General's Inspections) were never a surprise even to the enlisted troops. "The IG's coming," they'd say, "roll your socks, line them in ranks and files in your drawers—uniformity men uniformity—dust above the doors, clean the windows, use hospital corners, I want

245

your blankets tight enough to bounce a quarter, and shine all those boots so I can see my face in them." Yes, we had two years of boot camp at Tompkins. I had learned to save time in the mornings by pinning my wool blanket to the underside of my bunk, and then sleeping on top of it, using an extra blanket I kept stowed in my locker because every day was an inspection day for us at Tompkins.

Frank Dulfer, Woody, O'Neill, and Kenneth Arey approached. Woody was running floss through his teeth and Dulfer was saying "You've got bad breath, Woody! Bad bad breath!" At that, Woody seesawed his floss even faster. "Cockbite" Dulfer was mumbling something like, "In case of Russian attack, women, children, and Carto first."

"Kirk," said Dulfer, "you better lock and load, they're gonna be commin' back."

"I've got 270 days and a wakeup."

"What's going on here, Kirk?" asked O'Neill.

Dulfer had to jab, "O'Neill, you're standing in a hole again."

We all stood there looking at the bewildered officers who were glancing, ever so often, at us from their circle jerk. Arey now repeated O'Neill's question, "What's happening, Kirk?"

"A discombobulated befuddlement," I replied.

"Huh?" asked Possum with a wrenching smile.

"FUBAR," said Cockbite with a half grin, "F—d up beyond all recognition. These frickin' lifers are clueless."

"Oh," replied Possum.

"They've got a situation, don't know what to do about it," I said.

"It's the stockade for us," said Dulfer, "I've seen it, don't want to go."

"The place ain't big enough for all of us,"said Arey.

"They'll take just the ringleaders," said Cockbite, "like you,

Possum Shit."

"I'm not the—I've a chance for promotion comin' up!"

"Don't sweat it Possum," I said, "they'll just take me."

"Mutually Assured Destruction," added Dulfer matter-of-factly.

"What?" I asked.

"Mad, M-A-D, goin' frickin' mad, that's where we're headed."

Bill Fauri from my platoon approached, his thick octagonal glasses in his hands as he wiped them with his O.D. green handkerchief.

"Kirk, you've still got time to stand down and make a threat assessment, follow protocol. You can expect collateral damage in addition to the direct losses you'll sustain from this half-baked scheme."

"You're gonna reenlist <u>aren't you</u>, Bill?"

"Not in a million squared eons, Kirk. When they return, you need to work toward a conflict resolution."

"Sounds like a plan—I think," added "Possum Shit" Arey.

I looked at Arey sideways.

We all looked at the officers standing on the sidelines.

Finally, Captain Peal returned; his usually quite, unassuming demeanor now a bit suspect:

"What are you demanding?" he asked of me.

"Not demanding anything, sir."

"Then what the F—?"

"The door policy for one."

"I can't let you stay here."

"These men are just trying to get your attention."

"They've got it, believe me, but I've got headquarters breathing down my neck. You can't stay here; it's that simple. How about it if you went to the soccer field over there outside the quadrangle? We'll let you spend the night there. We can't have protests in the Army."

"Does the UCMJ have an article that covers protests?" I asked.

"I don't know."

"Then maybe it's lega—"

"I don't want a court case."

I was tense, apprehensive, and the other men were gathering around and expecting me to stand up to the Lifers and refuse any deals. A gaggle of Officers were now standing shoulder to shoulder along the sidelines as if waiting for a Thanksgiving Day parade, and standing clear in my mind was the stockade where I had pulled guard duty that cold wintry day. Yeah, I had influence, but I didn't really want to piss anyone off, I had just nine months to go, and stockade time would surely be tacked on to that, so I agreed to move our camp. The enlisted men moved reluctantly, continuing to try to get their complaints heard. We spent a quiet night just off the quadrangle and the next day packed up and returned our equipment to our trailers. Very anti-climatic to say the least, but apparently we had been noticed. Possum was very happy with the deal.

THIS JUST IN FROM THE OVERSEAS WEEKLY

We made headlines in <u>The Overseas Weekly</u> and the doors were soon put back on our rooms and Sergeant Billy "Ass Crack" Wallow, Fire Chief Gunter Schmidt, and Sergeant Major Philip Swenson, mysteriously disappeared from Tompkins Barracks. When we asked about them, the official line was that they had been transferred to other duty stations. And quite mysteriously, we soon had much larger meal portions at the mess hall. You see, it turns out, they were in cahoots with each other to sell our food rations on the black market in Germany (Article 108, wrongful disposition of military property). They had apparently been doing it for some time, more than a year, maybe two, and the three men were removed from Tompkins before we found out and could "string 'em up"—or so the Battalion apparently feared we might do. (Note: Gunter Schmidt was probably contributing his take to the Nazi underground!)

CAMOUFLAGED VANS

As early as the first week of Basic Training, they had my number. Our first assignment, once we had our haircut and gear put away, was to print our name three times on white one-inch masking tape and stick the tape to our bunk, footlocker, and wall locker. I printed mine neatly in a neat architectural-style block letters and the platoon leader saw how sharp they were and ordered me to print <u>everyone's</u> names (so our platoon would look sharp). That came to 150 name tags. Fine, done, the company commander sees my work and wants me to redesign their day room, all this while doing the classes, rifle training, PT, and KP duty.

So, when I first arrived at the Ramp, sure enough, I was assigned to paint some needed outdoor signs on plywood. How they got my number, I'll never know. As mentioned earlier, one of my "OFF LIMITS" signs was placed on the fenced-in area full of junked cars.

SOLDIER APPLYING PATTERN WITH CHALK

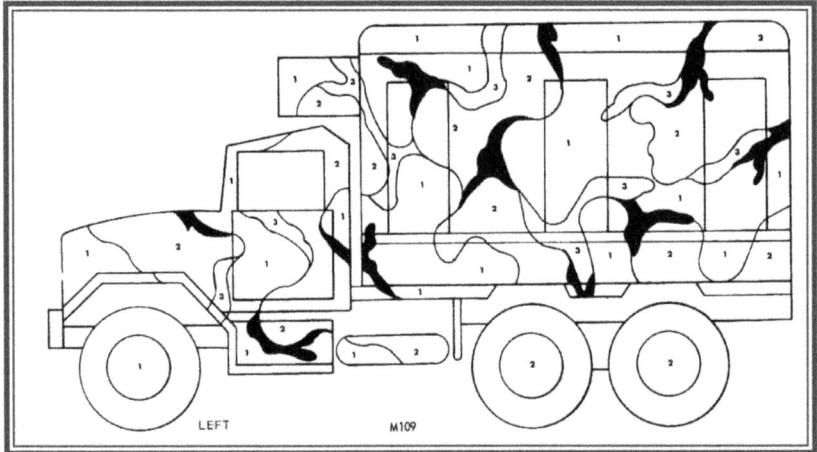

Figure 3-10. 2-1/2T Van, (M185 instrument shop) (sheet 3 of 5).

Source: TECHNICAL BULLETIN TB 43-0147
"COLOR MARKING AND CAMOUFLAGE PATTERNS USED ON MILITARY EQUIPMENT MANAGED BY USATROSCOM, HEADQUARTER,
DEPARTMENT OF THE ARMY, DECEMBER 1975"

5-TON VAN AFTER CAMOUFLAGING
(Note: no diagram was provided for van side when open, so make it up)

So now I was well into the last few months of my incarceration at
Tompkins, when "Pineapple" Tokuhisha handed me a small pile of
8-1/2 x 11 sheets of paper with some sketches on them. He didn't say
much, looked at me, and with his eyes said, "here buddy, new task,
have at it." He grabbed my other hand and dropped a box of chalk
in my palm then said, "you don't have to paint them, just do the
outlines," and turned away, then turned back and added, "This comes
from USAREUR Headquarters. All the vehicles in the European
Theater have to be the same."

I flipped through the sheets and they were elevations of our military vehicles, the jeep, 3/4-ton, deuce-and-a-half, 5-ton, and so on.
On the inked sketches were squiggly marks that looked like a bad
pattern for a rock wall with letters in each rock shape. It hit me:
it was the pattern to be followed in the process of repainting our
Olive Drab, WWII equipment, a four-color camouflage pattern using

THE NEWLY CAMOUFLAGED VEHICLES
–AT LEAST SOME COLOR WAS INTRODUCED TO THE RAMP–

black, brown, a sand color, and dark green. It was my job to mark off the pattern with chalk on <u>all</u> the vehicles in our Company; the other guys would get to paint them. I looked at the sheets again, I understood the function of camouflaging: vehicles photographed from the air, or seen at a distance, could then blend in with the landscape by both using colors similar to the terrain and by distorting the vehicle's form—like throwing netting over a vehicle. For the camouflaging to work, the straight edges of the equipment must appear distorted (there are no straight lines in nature). After glancing at the drawing for no more than a minute, I saw a glaring flaw. I folded one sheet and placed a vehicle's elevation adjacent to the adjoining side view and the rock-like outlines didn't match, not by line, not by color. It was obvious to me that each elevation was laid out independent of the others so that the camouflaging effect was lost. The straight edges of the vehicles would still read as edges (corners weren't cut off with a patch of color and internal shadows were not extended). I ran back to Pineapple and told him of my discovery. He looked and looked and finally understood, but then said, "Make what changes you have to to make it work."

"But Toke," I said, "This plan is for everyone in Europe, I change mine, and the uniformity is gone."

"That's their problem."

"But what about other units that don't catch this mistake?"

"We've got a deadline, make it work." He turned and walked away down the ramp, polished boots squeaking.

There was always something strange about pressed fatigues and spit-shined combat boots; it made sense for a Class-A uniform, but an outfit designed for working in?

So, here was another example of how problems encountered "in the field," and creative solutions to those issues, never went back up the chain of command to help all the units. A field expedient fix of an engine problem in one unit—that could save lives or thousands of dollars—usually just sat there, unknown to the rest of the Army. Something was wrong with the system. (In August 1975, one year after I left the Army, the US Army Combat Arms Training Board published a circular—TC5-200—that described an improved and standardized method of camouflaging.)

THE SHORT TIMER

It was April of '74 and I was now "short" with only 85 days and a wake up. When a GI was "short" he let everyone know it and the closer he got to his ETS date, the louder he got, to the point of obnoxiousness. At the Ramp we even had a large board covered with Mylar where the Short Timers where listed with their days left. When they were short they could get out of some of the extra duties, or at least they tried. It was known as the "short-timer's disease" and if too

TB 43-0147

CHAPTER 3

COLOR, MARKING AND PATTERNS OF

CAMOUFLAGE EQUIPMENT

Section I. CAMOUFLAGE PATTERN PAINTING

3-1. General *a.* This section describes an improved method of camouflaging military equipment and how to apply it to existing equipment. This improved method is simple, and field tests have proved that it works well in confusing the enemy observer and enhancing battlefield survivability. It consists of painting newly developed patterns on the equipment, using only four colors. The patterns (different for each model of vehicle or item of equipment) have been carefully worked out by a team of camouflage experts and scientists. Unlike older camouflage patterns, this is a general all-purpose pattern. By changing only one of the four colors, or at the most, two, the same basic pattern can be made to work equally well in different seasons of the year or on different types of terrain.

b. This section describes the new patterns and where they can be obtained, what colors and kinds of paint are to be used for various conditions, and how the patterns are to be painted on the equipment. It also shows a sample pattern and how a few common items of equipment look when they have been pattern painted.

c. This section does not give basic information on paint application; if needed, this should be obtained from TM 43-0139, Painting for Field Use. Basic information on camouflage can be found in TM 5-200, Camouflage Materials.

d. The instructions in this section apply only to the first pattern painting of existing solid-color vehicles and related equipment. These will be painted with the color combination appropriate to the season or terrain in the operational area of the equipment. Repainting of patterns in different colors to adapt them to different seasons or types of terrain will be up to the appropriate commander.

d. These new designs also lend themselves to touchup painting with better results than are now obtainable from touchup of the current OD vehicles. Slight mismatches in color will not be as noticeable as they are on a solid-colored vehicle except from very close inspection. Likewise, minor abrasions and scaling of surfaces will be equally inconspicuous.

3-3. Advantages *a.* The new system of pattern painting has the following major advantages:

(1) Provides ground and air observation in the target acquisition role.

(2) Can be applied by troops with minimum training, effort and equipment.

(3) Has effectiveness under combat conditions, but also presents a good military appearance in garrison.

(4) Uses colors from the standard camouflage chart (fig. 3-1) and thus avoids color mixing or tinting in the field to obtain the specified color. TB 43-0147

(5) Uses standard camouflage paints identifiable by National stock number (NSN) or Military Specification Number.

(6) Combines effectively with other camouflage techniques such as use of natural foliage.

(7) Permits the changing of one or two colors to adapt it to seasonal and geographic changes (and avoids the need to completely repaint the vehicle for such changes)

3-2. Reason for Pattern Painting *a.* All military vehicles and equipment have characteristic shapes and interior shadows. These so-called signatures contrast with natural surroundings and make the object conspicuous. Pattern painting does much to break up the signature characteristics by using lusterless paint to reduce the glare of headlights, color to reduce contrasts with the soil and vegetation, and pattern shape, size, and placement to distort the vehicle's form. The paint also reflects near infrared radiation. The patterns, designed for each type of vehicle, have color areas that cut off corners; avoid straight, vertical, and horizontal lines; and extend internal shadows in shapes similar to natural features and vegetation.

b. Pattern painting is not a magic, cure-all camouflage technique. However, it makes the item much harder to see and to recognize as a military object. It also provides an excellent base for further, more complete camouflage. If properly sited, the pattern-painted vehicle will need much less work to camouflage than a solid colored vehicle.

c. The theory behind this new pattern-painting design is to provide a system that can be adapted to various geographical and seasonal changes by the changing of one or, at most, two colors. For instance, the forest green can be changed to sand for desert operations, or the field drab changed to dark green and the sand to field drab for temperate climate terrain in summer. By using the appropriate color from the standard camouflage color chart (figure 3-1) in conjunction with the pattern-painting design, a good color combination for almost every terrain can be obtained.

border lines can vary as much as 2 inches from the standard pattern without causing loss of effectiveness.

b. The camouflage pattern consists of wavy irregular patches of color applied to the vehicle. The colors used for the patterns have been selected from the standard camouflage colors as shown in figure 3-1. The standard colors are:

Abbreviation	Color
W	White
DS	Desert sand
S	Sand
EY	Earth yellow
ER	Earth red
FD	Field drab
EB	Earth brown
OD	Olive drab
LG	Light green
DG	Dark green
FG	Forest green
BL	Black

c. The patterns use only four of these colors, for any geographic or climatic conditions. The only exception-winter arctic, which is solid white. When changing from one geographic or climatic condition to another, the shape of the pattern itself does not change; only one or two of the colors that make up the pattern change. Figure 3-2 shows the combinations of colors to be used

Source: **TECHNICAL BULLETIN TB 43-0147**
COLOR MARKING AND CAMOUFLAGE PATTERNS USED ON MILITARY
EQUIPMENT MANAGED BY USATROSCOM, HEADQUARTERS, DEPART-
MENT OF THE ARMY, DECEMBER 1975

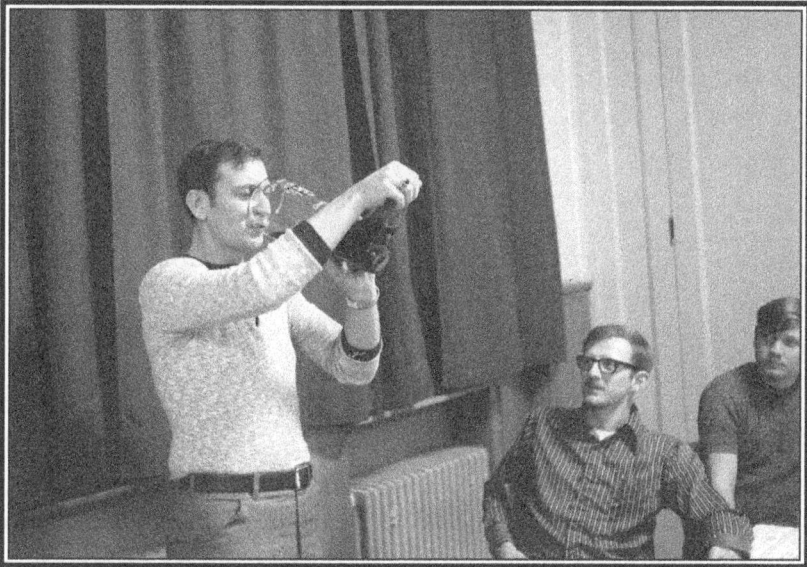

CW2 MAXWELL CELEBRATING AT SHORT TIMER'S PARTY
–DRINKING FROM A SHORT TIMERS GLASS BOOT–

many people from the same platoon were soon to leave, it was hard
to get any work done. The Short Timers would take all the leave they
had coming to them, they'd be given time to process out, and they'd
not be asked to start a mapping job there wasn't time to finish. That
usually left them with mox-nix work or running errands (which always
took much longer than it should have). Picklo was a master at it.

It was apparently a tradition to give a party to those going back
to The World and a glass boot filled with a gallon of beer was given
every short timer to drink. He'd try to chug it all down, and then pass
around what was left. We did that at the ramp for everyone leaving,
except me. Maxwell asked me if I wanted a boot and I said no, I didn't
drink. "Okay," was his offended response, it was one last punch to his
tender, liver-damaged gut. "I'm sorry," I said, "but I'm not one of the
boys." I was once again rejecting army traditions and its way of life.

A DEPARTING SHORT TIMER WAS SUFFICIENT REASON
TO GET DRUNK (LILBURN AT LEFT, WOODY IN MIDDLE)

EPILOGUE

And so my short career in the Army came to an end. I wasn't court martialed, or given a Section 8 due to insanity, but my top-secret clearance was pulled. Someone up there at the Pentagon must have heard about "Operation Orange Peel." And Captain Peal, he found out the code name of our protest and was going around asking everyone, except me, why it was called that. Did it have something to do with him? Maybe an affront to him? What had he done wrong to deserve the wrath of his troops? I don't guess he ever got a straight answer. (The code name referred to the orange peel-coat we used to scribe our map details and had nothing to do with him.)

I heard after I was out, a rumor that the chain-smoking Jim McKay had quit smoking, at least the weed variety, but shot himself in the foot while cleaning his weapon and was assigned a desk job in Supply without his pistol. But I also heard he had reenlisted and

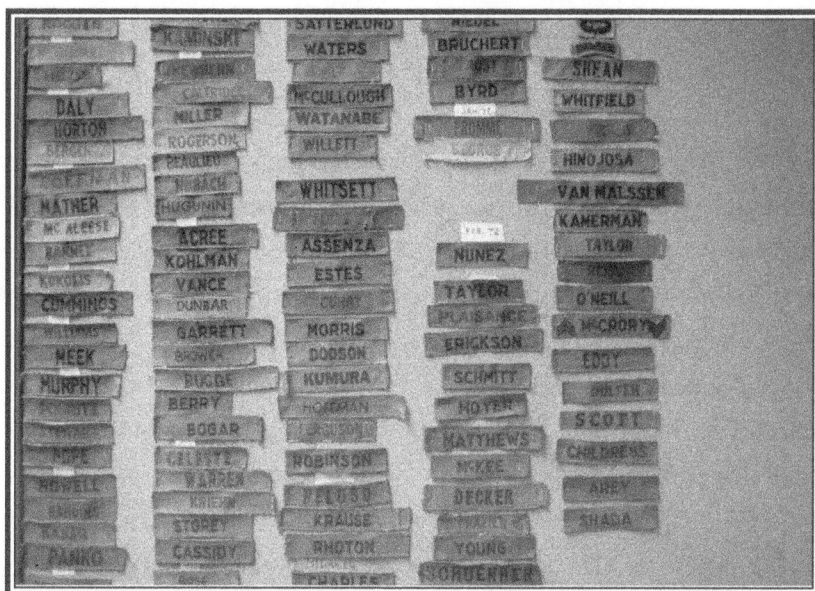

THE NAMETAGS OF SOLDIERS ROTATED OUT

become an instructor at the Defense Mapping School in Ft. Belvoir and I doubt that he would have shot himself in the foot during classroom instruction, but then again...

"Arab" Shada and the Jewish Kim Frost were both transferred to a Topo unit at Fort Shafter in Hawaii where their feud continued.

SP5 Gilbert went to the NCO academy, got drunk, got into a fight, and got his jaw broke. After getting his jaw wired shut and after months of drinking through a straw, he was sent back to our "carto" unit without ever finishing the academy. He apparently preferred becoming a professional alcoholic instead of a professional NCO.

And as for PFC Mark Hughes, the drugs he consumed on his short Army tour got him all screwed up and that got him an Early Out. Soon after, I heard he died from liver damage caused by the medications he was taking for paranoid schizophrenia. He never got his G.E.D. He was one kid, I figured, should never have joined the army. If it wasn't the army that screwed him up, the environment at Tompkins surely did.

SP5 Wilkie Ross re-enlisted to get out of Germany and took the $10,000 dollars in return for five more long years (it had to have been the green socks and green T-shirts he slept in). He <u>was</u> sent back to the states (to the 524th at Fort Hood), but as luck would have it, the Army sent him right back to Tompkins Barracks. By then the barracks just across the quadrangle was billeted with WACs who were assigned to administrative and clerical positions at the various military posts around Heidelberg. He bought a P.O.V. and managed several trysts with the girls. Sergeant Foskey got a game point with Wilkie, but I succeeded in getting SP5 Glenn O'Neill to get out, a point for me, but then it wasn't long—back home at Bryan, Texas—that he realized his mistake and re-enlisted (I had to subtract a point). He felt out of place back in Bryan, felt he wasn't prepared for civilian life. He joined the Army Reserves only to find out it was a country club for the area's rich and famous draft dodgers. The Army was all he knew, so he reenlisted for three more years only to find the politics of getting along with superiors too much and got back out. While still in, he married the company clerk, had a couple of kids, and then got divorced. Later he remarried, had two more kids, and established a career as a machinist building "cool gadgets" in various departments (like Physics and Oceanography) at Texas A&M University. His interest in cars grew from matchbox toys to full-scale antique autos and hot-rod T-buckets.

The new Information Officer at Battalion Headquarters begged me to edit the unit newsletter again—there had been no issues published, of any size, since my resignation—and I replied as succinctly and unmistakably as I could and "bite me" was my not so cordial answer, something "Cockbite" Dulfer might have proudly said. During my days as a Short Timer, I got the go ahead to do some of the things I had long ago petitioned for. One had to do with the aesthetics of gas and steam pipes at the Ramp. Haphazard steam pipes, electrical conduit, valves, and wall furnaces ran along the back wall of the vehicle bays, and they were all painted a dismal gray in a cheerless gray warehouse with a gloomy gray sky visible through murky gray skylights. We worked in that environment day in and day out, no wonder we were dreary and depressed all the time. I had written a letter suggesting the piping be painted bright colors (pastels of orange, red, blue, yellow, and pink—yes pink) to create a kind of sculptured art mural all along the walls. I envisioned quite a thing of beauty, and they finally, actually approved it. I got to select the colors and, of course, had to do the painting myself (after all, I was short), which was fine by me because I had complete control over the color scheme—pipe elbows orange, valve handles red, water lines blue,

A FURNACE ON THE RAMP PAINTED PINK AND BLUE

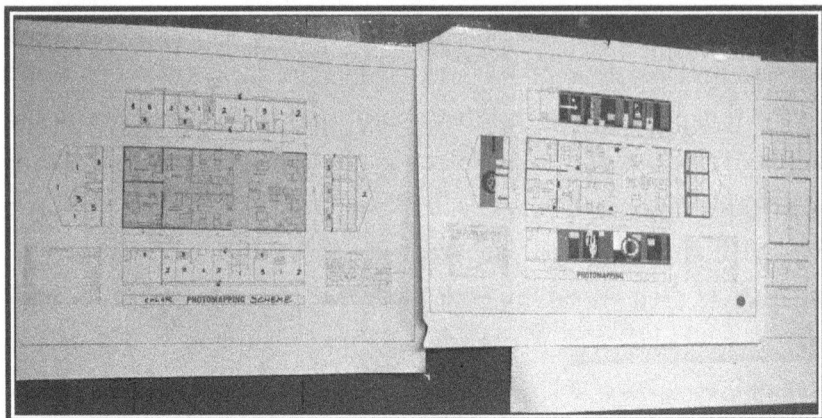

MY PLANS FOR A NEW "OPERATIONS" AT THE RAMP

furnaces pink, walls yellow. Yes, really, they actually let me do it, no olive drab or gray! I was then asked to design a new operations work area and suggested a furniture layout and color scheme before my last ride in a 3/4-ton to Frankfurt, where I was told to hand in <u>all</u> my gear: scuffed black combat boots, wrinkled green fatigues, worn out green

BUILDING THE NEW OFFICE AREA AT THE RAMP

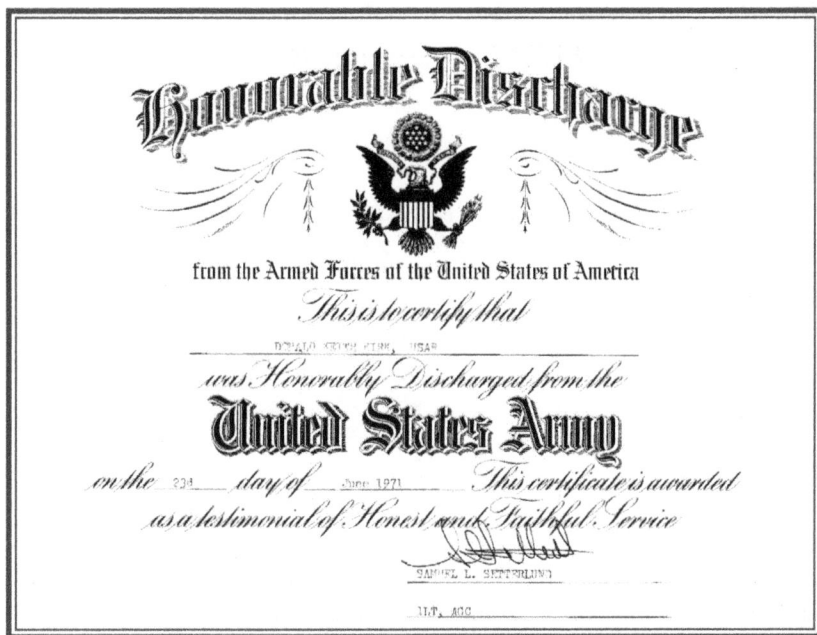

AN HONORABLE DISCHARGE
–A TESTIMONIAL OF HONEST AND FAITHFUL SERVICE–

socks, green T-shirts, even my green fatigue jacket with "KIRK" sewn to it. Wearing my Class-A uniform with a Weapons Qualifications Metal and National Defense Service Ribbon, I hopped on the Freedom Bird back to The World.

Floyd "Bean" Wever stayed in the military, got married, had two kids, went to Fort Rucker for flight school, but was medically grounded so became a Warrant Officer in Terrain Analysis. After twenty years of fun in the Army he retired and got a real job working in aviation-related jobs.

Paul Balcavage left the Army after his stint and volunteered for the home-town recruiter program, but after six months he had recruited no one. He considered reenlisting to become a helicopter pilot, but "Cockbite" Dulfer talked him out of it: "Even if you're a

CERTIFICATE OF APPRECIATION

DONALD KEITH KIRK SPECIALIST FOUR UNITED STATES ARMY
24 JUNE 1971 TO 18 JUNE 1974

I extend to you my personal thanks and the sincere appreciation of a grateful nation for your contribution of honorable service to our country. You have helped maintain the security of the nation during a critical time in its history with a devotion to duty and a spirit of sacrifice in keeping with the proud tradition of the military service.

I trust that in the coming years you will maintain an active interest in the Armed Forces and the purpose for which you served.

My best wishes to you for happiness and success in the future.

Richard Nixon

COMMANDER IN CHIEF

A CERTIFICATE OF APPRECIATION SIGNED BY TRICKY DICK
–SOMETHING I'D BE PROUD TO HANG ON MY BATHROOM WALL–

pilot in a Huey, you're still gonna get shot at, dummy." Vietnam was still in play. He married his high-school sweetheart and then divorced her after seven years. Using the GI bill, Paul got a civil engineering degree and remarried.

Wilkie Ross became a Staff Sergeant before he ETS'd out of the 63rd at Ft. Brag after eight years of service. Two marriages later and several state jobs, he settled into a job with the Department of Veterans Affairs in hospital administration saying he "possessed an extraordinary amount of personal pride while working with and helping our nation's veterans to have better lives."

Frank "Cockbite" Dulfer ETS'd about the same time I did, went back to college (taking it seriously this time) and joined the National Guard. He was sent to Fort Knox for armor officer training, drove and fired a tank(a full-sized one), and eventually climbed to the rank of Brigadier General in the New Jersey Army National Guard (and he did it with marbles in his mouth).

It looked like those snot-nosed kids the Army "hired" became useful citizens to society after all. At the time, I never really thought about all the talent that A Company had there in one place, with not only "artistic" and hand-eye-coordination skills, but some of the smartest and most capable people out there. They <u>were</u> the creme of the crop (or the Army made them that way). As a group, we could have been a real force to reckon with if we had more to do than just scribe maps. Imagine a civilian company with that talent.

When I got back to the States, 55-MPH speed limits were the law of the land and Ray Stevens' "The Streak" was at the top of the charts. And I found men wearing these ugly polyester "Leisure Suits." "You've got to be kidding," I said. Sherbet-colored plaid jackets and slacks, sticky and hot in the Texas sun, "What happened to cotton for God's sake?" My OD-green fatigues didn't seem so bad after all. And jackets worn over turtle-neck sweaters? White dudes wearing Afro's! What had The World come to? Watergate was in full swing and there was talk of impeaching my favorite president, "Tricky Dick" Nixon. "Flesh Gordon," and "Young Frankenstein" filled theatre seats. "Towering Inferno" was on fire and "All in the Family," "Happy Days," and "M.A.S.H." were hits on the boob tube. The Vietnam War was winding down and it was going into the "lost" column. I became a free-lance building designer, artist, writer, and filmmaker and in no case was I required to wear a uniform (including a suit. I did wear one for funerals and weddings—the same one).

When I arrived at Tompkins Barracks, I was a SP4, when I left, I was a SP4, that should tell you something, but it doesn't quite. When I was in college, the Architecture department required a course on photography and one of the professors, a white-haired, laid-back has-been of an architect, who taught a class in perspective, was assigned to teach the photography class. He had no course curriculum, no cameras for us to use, and he didn't care whether or not we attended any of his classes. As a group we didn't much care either, we were too busy with design projects. The end of the semester came and no one had done anything or learned any photography and yet Professor Pledger—that was his name—decided he had to give us some kind of exam to pass us. He told us to come up with a photo assignment, anything we wanted, just turn it in before the end of the year and he'd give us all passing grades. I was infuriated. I still didn't have a camera and I certainly hadn't learned anything. Why should I get a passing grade? So I didn't—I couldn't in all good conscious—turn anything in, and so he gave me an "incomplete." I chanced on him just before I left the campus, and he told me I had to turn something in,—anything, for him to pass me. The gall. No, hell no, I wouldn't turn anything in. I got an "F" and was the only one to get one. I never saw anyone else's assignments. The next year, to get the required credit, I took a real photography course in the Journalism department. I learned so much that the camera became an appendage. No, I would stay a SP4; I had a well-entrenched value system. I couldn't accept a grade, any grade, for coursework I didn't do and I couldn't accept a promotion from an organization I didn't fully support.

In the army, I could never see the big picture; I never understood my importance or place in the army. I never appreciated what I was given, nor the people who tried to groom me for a life in the military because I had preconceived feelings about being there against my will. I became a bitter person, disillusioned about my government and never able to trust it again. My anger against the government raged on for years after my honorable discharge. I know, because three years later, in June 1977, the army sent me a letter officially discharging

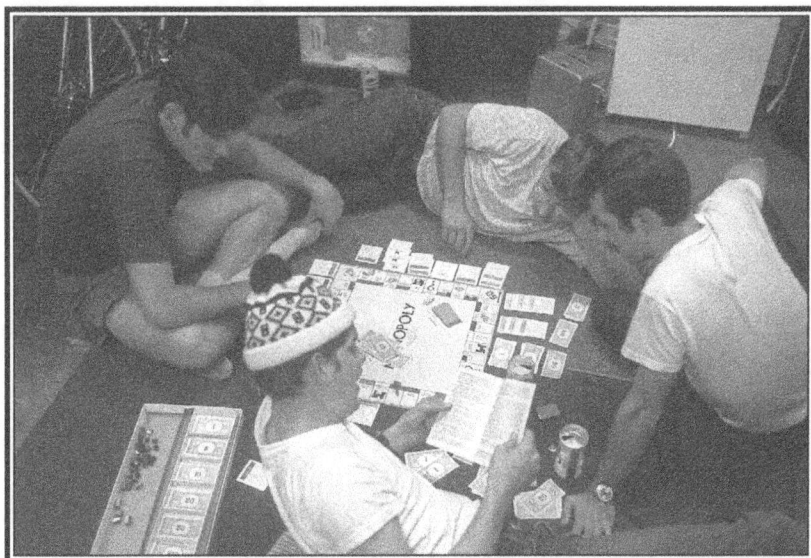

LEARNING A BOARD GAME, BUT IT'S JUST MONOPLY–SOLDIERS AT
TOMPKINS WOULD NEVER GET THE OPPORTUNITY TO PLAY "THE
GAME OF ARMY LIFE" –EXCEPT IN REAL LIFE–AT TOMPKINS BARRACKS.
(TAYLOR, DULFER, O'NEILL AND WEVER)

me (I hadn't known I wasn't already discharged) and asked me if I
wanted my 201 file (military records) sent to me, that they would be
destroyed if I didn't reply. Hell, no, I didn't reply; I wanted to forget.
These were the government's copies of everything that happened to
me while I was serving that unwelcome stint: my medical file, evalu-
ations, letters of appreciation (laughable and almost all identical),
my top-secret clearance that I never received because of Operation
Orange Peel, and who knows what else. Looking back, it would have
been nice to see the official reason for rescinding that top-secret clearance.

To me the army was a joke. The people I liked, the system I
didn't. I did my job with enthusiasm, and instead of hanging around
the barracks, I saw some of Europe. ROTC at Texas A&M had
already soured me to the idea of a military career. Being drafted by

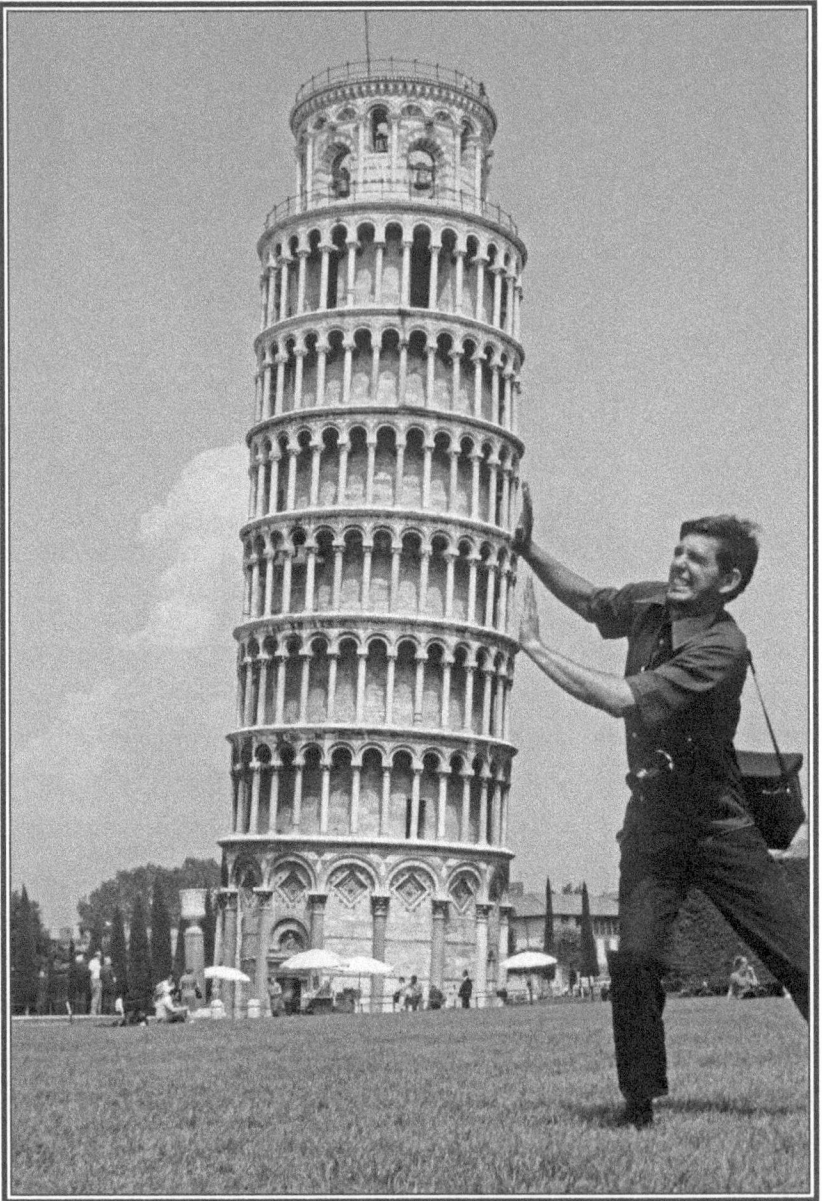

THE OBLIGATORY SHOT OF ME
HOLDING UP THE TOWER OF PIZA
–LIFE'S ALL ABOUT BALANCE–
(Glenn O'Neill photo)

"Tricky Dick" when there was an architectural firm ready to hire me and the used-car Army recruiter didn't help matters. I was primed for discontent, though some of it was justified. I did realize I was a lucky soldier to have been sent to Germany and not Vietnam.

THE END

P.S. I didn't know it at the time, but Tompkins Barracks was just an extension of the demoralized troops in Vietnam. Frustration, anger, and fear had spread through the military ranks and around the world, affecting all of our military, affecting Tompkins, affecting me.

For the Second Edition:
Thanks to all who gave me feed back and new stories, and thanks for being friends. And thanks for your service to this country.
    —Don "SP4" Kirk

PFC DULFER POSING ON A 3/4-TON (Frank Dulfer collection)

PHYSICAL AND MENTAL STATUS
ON RELEASE FROM ACTIVE SERVICE

For use of this form, see AR 635-5; the proponent agency is The Adjutant General's Office.

NAME - LAST NAME - FIRST NAME - MIDDLE INITIAL AND SERVICE NUMBER/SOCIAL SECURITY ACCOUNT NUMBER

SP4 KIRK DONALD K

DATE

74 06 18

DB

MENTAL STATUS

ENLISTMENT OR RE-ENLISTMENT WITHOUT MENTAL RETEST IS AUTHORIZED PROVIDED ENLISTMENT OR RE-ENLISTMENT IS ACCOMPLISHED WITHIN ONE YEAR AFTER DATE OF SEPARATION. YOUR RECORDED APTITUDE AREA SCORES ARE AS FOLLOWS:

COA - NONE
COB - NONE
EL - 135
GM - 122

MM - 124
CL - 133
GT - 130
RC - 94

IN - 128
AE - 100
AFQT - SCORE IS 31 OR ABOVE
[X] YES [ ] NO

OTHER TEST SCORES RECORDED IN ITEM 25, DA FORM 20:

MOB-1 - 148
OCT-1 - 118
ALAT-1 - 17
RETESTED (Date)

ARC-1 - 55
ACS - 133
T&D - NONE
ON AQB (WACB) IN ACCORDANCE WITH PARAGRAPH 4-20, AR 601-210.

DATE TESTED: 28 JUN 71

PHYSICAL STATUS

YOUR PHYSICAL CONDITION ON _____74 06 18_____ IS SUCH THAT YOU ARE CONSIDERED PHYSICALLY
(Date of Separation)

QUALIFIED FOR SEPARATION OR FOR RE-ENLISTMENT WITHOUT RE-EXAMINATION, PROVIDED YOU RE-ENLIST WITHIN 3 MONTHS AND STATE THAT YOU HAVE NOT ACQUIRED NEW DISEASES OR INJURIES DURING THE INTERVAL PERIOD WHEN NOT A MEMBER OF THE MILITARY SERVICE.

YOUR PHYSICAL PROFILE AT DATE OF SEPARATION IS:

TYPED NAME, GRADE, AND ARM OR SERVICE OF PERS OFFICER | SIGNATURE

FLOYD K. MAERTENS, 2LT, ASSISTANT ADJUTANT

STATEMENTS OF PHYSICAL AND DEPENDENT STATUS AT TIME OF ENLISTMENT

PHYSICAL STATUS

HAS THERE BEEN ANY CHANGE IN YOUR PHYSICAL CONDITION SINCE YOU WERE SEPARATED?
[ ] YES [ ] NO (If yes, describe below).

DEPENDENT STATUS

HAS THERE BEEN ANY CHANGE IN YOUR DEPENDENT STATUS SINCE YOU WERE SEPARATED?
[ ] YES [ ] NO (If yes, describe below).

DATE | SIGNATURE

INSTRUCTIONS: Prepare in triplicate. Original and duplicate will be given to individual concerned. Triplicate will be filed in individual's DA Form 201.

DA FORM 1811 SEP 66   PREVIOUS EDITIONS OF THIS FORM ARE OBSOLETE.

DA FORM 1811: STATE OF MIND
–PHYSICAL AND MENTAL STATUS ON RELEASE FROM ACTIVE DUTY–

2L/DM/XX-JM

THIS IS AN IMPORTANT RECORD
SAFEGUARD IT.

1. LAST NAME-FIRST NAME-MIDDLE NAME	2. SEX	3. SOCIAL SECURITY NUMBER	4. DATE OF BIRTH	YEAR	MONTH	DAY
KIRK DONALD KEITH	M			48	Ø3	Ø2

5. DEPARTMENT, COMPONENT AND BRANCH OR CLASS	6a. GRADE, RATE OR RANK	b. PAY GRADE	7. DATE OF RANK	YEAR	MONTH	DAY
ARMY RA	SP4	E4		71	11	Ø9

8a. SELECTIVE SERVICE NUMBER	b. SELECTIVE SERVICE LOCAL BOARD NUMBER, CITY, STATE AND ZIP CODE	c. HOME OF RECORD AT TIME OF ENTRY INTO ACTIVE SERVICE (Street, RFD, City, State and ZIP Code)
41 9 48 199	LB#9 SAN ANTONIO TEXAS 78211	8831 SAGEBRUSH SAN ANTONIO TEXAS 782Ø4

9a. TYPE OF SEPARATION	b. STATION OR INSTALLATION AT WHICH EFFECTED			
RELIEF FROM ACTIVE DUTY	FORT JACKSON SOUTH CAROLINA 292Ø7			

c. AUTHORITY AND REASON	d. EFFECTIVE DATE	YEAR	MONTH	DAY
------		74	Ø6	18

e. CHARACTER OF SERVICE	f. TYPE OF CERTIFICATE ISSUED	10. REENLISTMENT CODE
HONORABLE	NONE	---

11. LAST DUTY ASSIGNMENT AND MAJOR COMMAND	12. COMMAND TO WHICH TRANSFERRED
USAREUR CO A 649TH ENGINEER BN (E1-WH1UAOA)	USAR CON GP (REINF) RCPAC 97ØØ PAGE BLVD, ST LOUIS, MO 63132

13. TERMINAL DATE OF RESERVE/WAS OBLIGATION	14. PLACE OF ENTRY INTO CURRENT ACTIVE SERVICE (City, State and ZIP Code)	15. DATE ENTERED ACTIVE DUTY THIS PERIOD		
YEAR MONTH DAY		YEAR	MONTH	DAY
77 Ø6 23	SAN ANTONIO TEXAS 78211	71	Ø6	24

16a. PRIMARY SPECIALTY NUMBER AND TITLE	b. RELATED CIVILIAN OCCUPATION AND D.O.T. NUMBER	18. RECORD OF SERVICE	YEARS	MONTHS	DAYS
81D2Ø 71-11-Ø4 MAP COMPILING SCORE 113 73-Ø2	PHYSICAL GEOGRAPHER Ø29.Ø88	(a) NET ACTIVE SERVICE THIS PERIOD	Ø2	11	25
		(b) PRIOR ACTIVE SERVICE	ØØ	ØØ	ØØ
17a. SECONDARY SPECIALTY NUMBER AND TITLE	b. RELATED CIVILIAN OCCUPATION AND D.O.T. NUMBER	(c) TOTAL ACTIVE SERVICE (a + b)	Ø2	11	25
		(d) PRIOR INACTIVE SERVICE	ØØ	Ø1	21
NONE	NONE	(e) TOTAL SERVICE FOR PAY (c + d)	Ø3	Ø1	16
		(f) FOREIGN AND/OR SEA SERVICE THIS PERIOD	Ø2	Ø6	11

19. INDOCHINA OR KOREA SERVICE SINCE AUGUST 5, 1964	20. HIGHEST EDUCATION LEVEL SUCCESSFULLY COMPLETED (In Years)
☐ YES ☒ NO	SECONDARY/HIGH SCHOOL ____ YRS (1-12 grades) COLLEGE 4 YRS

21. TIME LOST (Preceding Two Yrs)	22. DAYS ACCRUED LEAVE PAID	23. SERVICEMEN'S GROUP LIFE INSURANCE COVERAGE	24. DISABILITY SEVERANCE PAY	25. PERSONNEL SECURITY INVESTIGATION	
NONE	47 DAYS	☒ $15,000 ☐ $5,000 ☐ $10,000 ☐ NONE	☒ NO ☐ YES AMOUNT	a. TYPE ENTNAC	b. DATE COMPLETED 71-Ø7-27

26. DECORATIONS, MEDALS, BADGES, COMMENDATIONS, CITATIONS AND CAMPAIGN RIBBONS AWARDED OR AUTHORIZED

NATIONAL DEFENSE SERVICE MEDAL

27. REMARKS

COUNTRY OF LAST OVERSEA SERVICE: GERMANY
TIME LOST: NONE
MAP COMPILING

28. MAILING ADDRESS AFTER SEPARATION	29. SIGNATURE OF PERSON BEING SEPARATED
SEE#8C	*Donald K. Kirk*
30. TYPED NAME, GRADE AND TITLE OF AUTHORIZING OFFICER	31. SIGNATURE OF OFFICER AUTHORIZED TO SIGN
ETHEL P. SAULS, 2LT, ASSISTANT ADJUTANT	*Ethel P. Sauls*

DD FORM 214 1 NOV 72 — PREVIOUS EDITIONS OF THIS FORM ARE OBSOLETE. — THIS IS AN IMPORTANT RECORD SAFEGUARD IT. — REPORT OF SEPARATION FROM ACTIVE DUTY

DD FORM 214: DISCHARGE PAPERS
–"RELIEF" FROM ACTIVE DUTY–

COMMON ARMY ACRONYMS

The military soldier often talks in code, officially and unofficially.

AAFES—Army and Air Force Exchange Service
AIT—Advanced Individual Training
APC—Armored Personnel Carrier
APO—Army Post Office
ASAP—As Soon As Possible
AWOL—Absent Without Official Leave
BCT—Basic Combat Training
CO—Commanding Officer
CONUS—Continental United States
CWO—Chief Warrant Officer
CQ—Charge of Quarters
DOD—Department Of Defense
EER—Enlisted Efficiency Report
ETC—Engineer Topographic Center
ETS—Expiration of Term of Service
FNG—F----g New Guy
FTA—F--- The Army
FTX—Field Training Exercise
FUBAR—F----d Up Beyond All Recognition
GPV—General Purpose Vehicle (the 3/4-ton Jeep)
HQ—Headquarters
IG—Inspector General
KIA—Killed In Action
MOS—Military Occupational Specialty
MP—Military Police
NCO—Non-Commissioned Officer
OCS—Officer Candidate School
PCS—Permanent Change of Station
PDS—Permanent Duty Station

PFC—Private First Class
P.O.V.—Privately Owned Vehicle
PT—Physical Training
PX—Post Exchange
POW—Prisoner Of War, Privately Owned Weapon
REFORGER—REturn of FORces to GERmany
ROTC—Reserve Officer Training Corps
SMLM—Soviet Military Liaison Mission
SNAFU—Situation Norman: All F-----d Up
SOL—Shit Out of Luck
SOP—Standing Operating Procedure
TDY—Temporary Duty Assignment/Temporary Divorce for a Year
TOC—Tactical Operations Center
TTMICP—Theatre Topographic Map Inventory Control Point
UCMJ—Uniform Code of Military Justice
USAREUR—United States Army Europe/Seventh Army
VOLAR—VOLuntary ARmy
XO—Executive Officer

ENTRANCE, SCHLOSSGARDEN, SCHWETZINGEN

THE NARROW STREETS OF MONACO
–A BEAUTIFUL PLACE ON A HUMAN SCALE BECAUSE IT WAS
BUILT BEFORE THE AUTOMOBILE–

MISS AMERICA USO SHOW AT TOMPKINS BARRACKS
BOB HOPE DIDN'T MAKE THIS TRIP, BUT THE GIRLS MADE UP FOR HIM

THE FIRST EVER MISS AMERICA USO SHOW TO VISIT
EUROPE. ONE-AND-ONE-HALF HOURS OF DANCING, SONGS,
COMEDY AND MUSIC. MISS AMERICA PAMELA ELDRED AND SIX
STATE CHAMPIONS HOSTED THE PROGRAM, FALL 1972.

TEARING DOWN CAMP AND LOADING TENTS
–LETS DO IT AGAIN IN SIX MONTHS, MAYBE MAKE A CAREER OF IT–

THE VERY PRACTICAL 3/4-TON–OUR FAVORITE VEHICLE
–WISH I HAD ONE IN CIVILIAN LIFE–

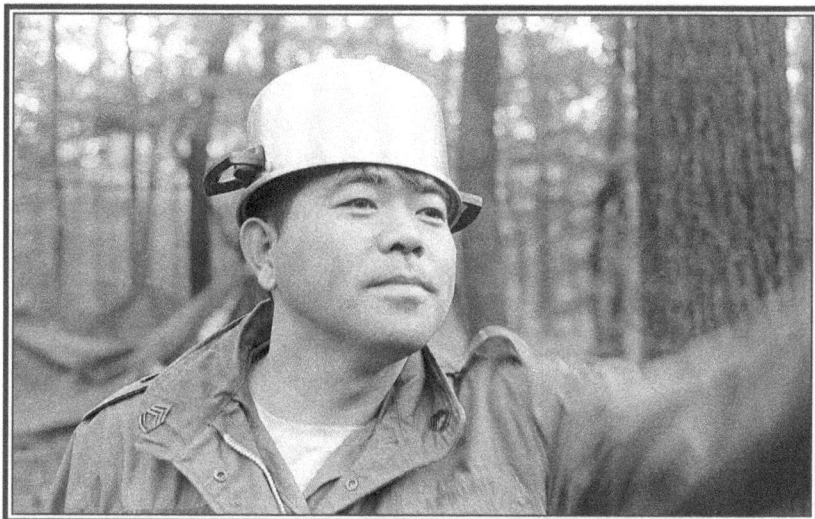

ONWARD AND UPWARD THROUGH THE BEEF STEW
–PLATOON SERGEANT "PINEAPPLE" TOKUHISA–

A GUNG-HO RANGER, TOM "AIRBORNE" GILBERT
–SLEEPING IT OFF–

SP5 GLENN O'NEILL WILL REENLIST
–HIS SECOND TOUR DOESN'T GO SO WELL–
(Paul Balcavage Photo)

SP4 JIM McKAY BECAME AN INSTRUCTOR AT THE DEFENSE
MAPPING SCHOOL AND CONTINUED A HABIT OF REENLISTING
(Mike Kilman Photo)

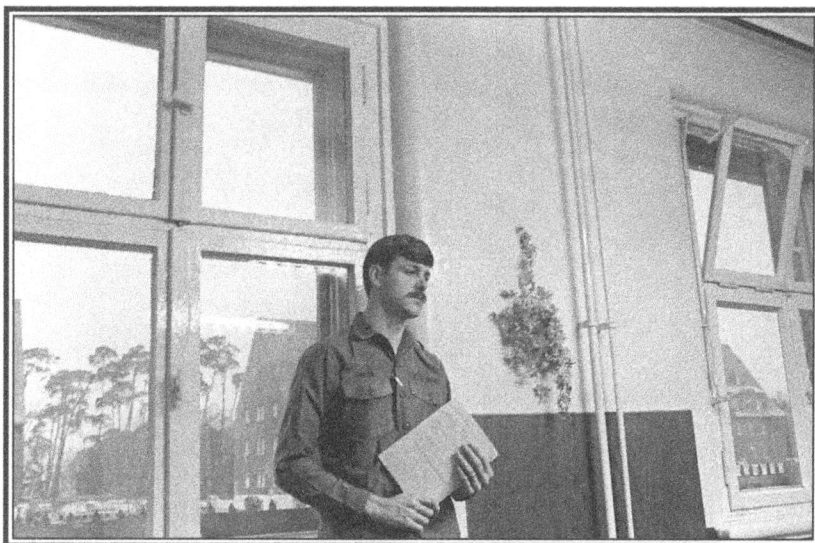

THE VOLKSMARCHING LT SNEED TEACHING
A BASIC LEADERSHIP COURSE AT TOMPKINS
(Mike Kilman Photo)

SP4 KILMAN GOT THE HIGHEST SCORE IN CLASS
FOR A LECTURE ON HOW TO USE A PUSH (AND PULL) BROOM
(Jim McKay Photo)

PSG TOKUHISHA AND CHIEF MAXWELL
TOP-NOTCH CAREER SOLDIERS
(Frank Dulfer Photo)

Subject: Tompkins Barracks
Date: October 23, 2009
To: SP4 Kirk

Hi Donald,

While on the web recently I came across your book about your life at Tompkins Barracks. I ordered up a copy and read it with great interest. I was stationed at Tompkins Barracks as a cartographer from 1982 to 1986 and was in the 630th Engineering Co., 649th Engineering Battalion. The life you depicted in your book was very similar to my experiences. While most of the army crap had not changed, some things at Tompkins had changed. The bowling alley had been demolished, a new club was built across the street north of the old one. Attitudes were a little different. Since none of us were drafted, we had nobody to blame but ourselves.

One story that may interest you. In 1985 my squad was responsible for updating the Lampertheim map. While field checking one day we found some roads on the map that were not on the ground. Trying to figure out what the hell was going on, one of our guys was looking at the scribecoat and realized that the roads spelled "FTA." Our entire platoon enjoyed the brilliance of this act and I am proud to let you know that the "FTA" roads were incorporated into the new map and lived on past 1986 when I left.

Thanks for a wonderful book that brought back some bad, but also many very good memories.

Mark Howlett
Kent Washington

"STANDING" GUARD AT FTX ENTRANCE
–PFC CHURCH WRITING HIS UNDERGOUND NEWSPAPER–

Subject: Tompkins Barracks
Date: February 24, 2008
To: SP4 Kirk

I've just finished your book. It brought back many, many memories. I knew Chief Maxwell and Sp4 Creech. I, too, was a draftee in the 656th(1966-68) and I was a terrible, bitter soldier. I agree with many of your sentiments, especially that the "vertical chain of command" was a severe problem. I got out in 1968 and after two disillusioned years at San Diego State, I went back into the Army. Yes, I became a "lifer." Our times overlapped in early 1973 when I deployed from Ft. Hood back to Tompkins as part of a REFORGER exercise—little had changed. I PCSd back to Tompkins in 1975 and much had changed. The Army was beginning to get over the effects of Vietnam and there were a lot more American Women at Tompkins, not only in the 649th but Military Personal Center Europe was billeted there. I got out of TOPO in 1977, switching to Military Intelligence, doing many interesting things in Special Ops and finally retiring after the first Gulf War. I realize that you have "literary license" but I take issue with some of the things you write about. You call Tompkins Barracks a "prison" and then write of all the places you visited [and that] makes little sense. To judge the Army and its soldiers by your experience is a sad mistake. Just as judging the Army of your era by the soldiers of WWII or Korea is an error. Still, thanks for the memories.

Mike Staggs

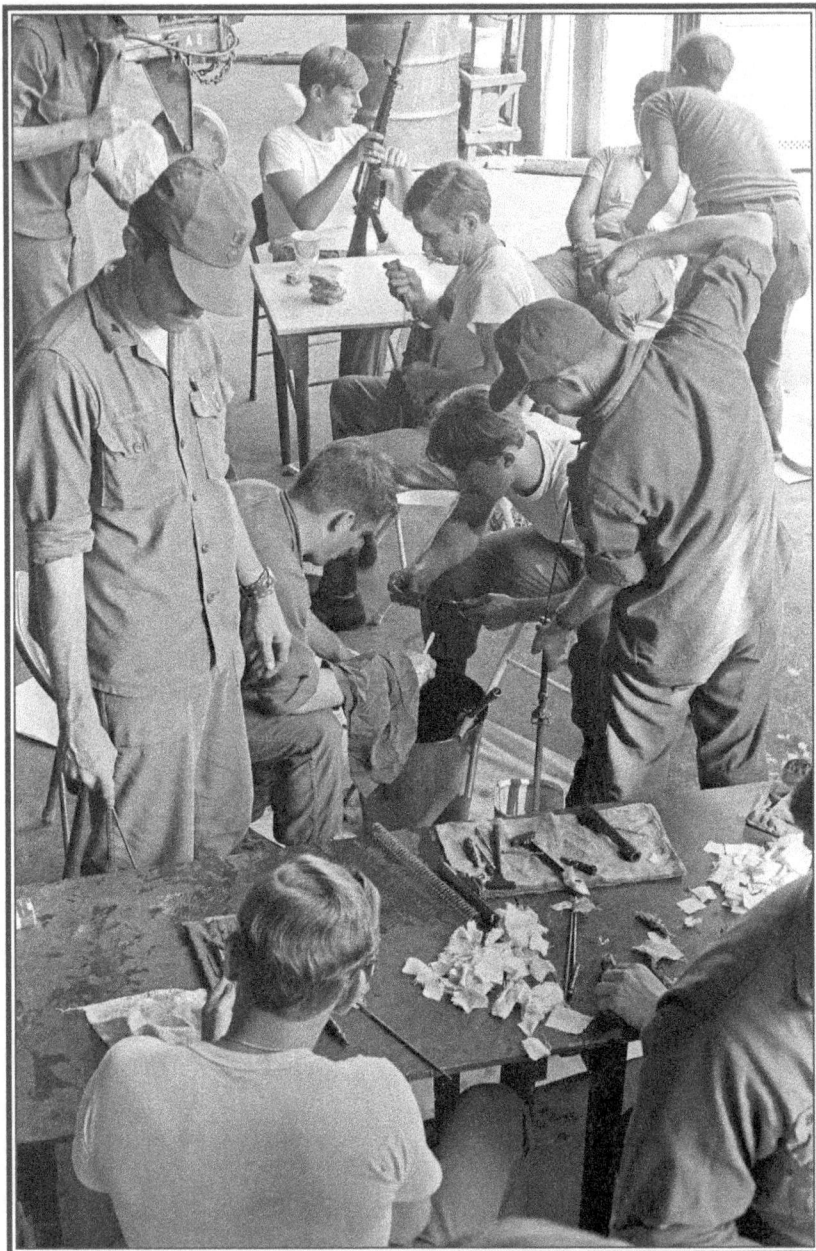

WEAPONS CLEANING AT THE RAMP
–ON A COLT, OR IS IT, A MATTEL SEMI-AUTOMATIC–

Subject: SGT Decker
Date: October 3, 2012
To: Don

Just received a copy of Life at Tompkins Barracks today. Only had time to skim it so far, but it's going to be interesting. I never knew how Decker lost part of his finger. Other names in your book that I remember—Bean, Maxwell, Easter, Childress...I think we called Pineapple, "Toke-a-hasha." I arrived pretty much as you were leaving and finished out my last year at Tompkins in the 517th Terrain Detachment; first two mostly in the 30th at Ft. Belvoir. The army sucked, but other than that my time at Tompkins was a good time with some good people. And let's not forget Albert's. Anyway, I'll spend time reading it tonight. Glad you were able and willing to do this book.
Thanks, Tom Herrick

Letter: Frank Dulfer
Subject: Tompkins
Date: April 14, 2009
To: DK

I finished reading your "novel" last night. It brought back a lot of memories. Some of your stories I remembered, others I must have had a liter or two at the time, because I don't have any memory cells left. I still have a copy of Topo Topics. I remember you getting pissed-off about cancelling the paper at the time. I thought it was because you published a paper that was outside the "regs" for a unit our size. I didn't realize that LTC Williamson was punishing you for being such a radical. I didn't have quite as dismal a view of the Army as you did. Most of my memories are pretty positive.
Per Cartas Servemus, Frank Dulfer

PISS ON 'EM!
O'NEILL AS THE "MANNEKEN PIS."
–THE LEGENDARY "PEEING BOY OF BRUSSELS," BELGIUM.

Subject: Tompkins Barracks
Date: September 16, 2010
To: SP4 Kirk

I thought this was an appropriate email to pass on to the
Tompkins Barracks "inmates" —General Frank Dulfer.

PROUD TO BE IN YOUR COMPANY

When a Veteran leaves the "job" and retires to a better
life, many are jealous, some are pleased, and others,
who may have already retired, wonder if he knows what
he is leaving behind, but we already know.
1. We know, for example, that after a lifetime of camara-
   derie that few experience, it will remain as a longing
   for those past times.
2. We know in the Military, life is a fellowship that lasts
   long after the uniforms are hung up in the back of the
   closet.
3. We know even if we throw our uniform away, it will be
   on us with every step and breath that remains in our
   life. We also know how the very bearing of the man
   speaks of what he was, and in his heart still is.
   These are the burdens of the job. We will still look at
people suspiciously, still see what others do not see or
choose to ignore, and always we will look at the rest of
the Military world with a respect for what they do, evolv-
ing from a lifetime of knowing.
   Never think for one moment you are escaping from
that life. You are only escaping the "job" and merely
being allowed to leave "active" duty.
   So what I wish for you is that whenever you ease
into retirement, in your heart you never forget for one
moment that you are still a member of the greatest fra-
ternity the world has ever known.   —anonymous

CIVILIAN FRIENDS V.S. VETERAN FRIENDS

CIVILIAN FRIENDS get upset if you're too busy to talk to them for a week. VETERAN FRIENDS are glad to see you after many years, and will happily carry on the same conversation you were having the last time you met.

CIVILIAN FRIENDS keep your stuff so long that they forget it's yours. VETERAN FRIENDS borrow your stuff for a few days and then give it back.

CIVILIAN FRIENDS know a few things about you. VETERAN FRIENDS could write a book with direct quotes from you.

CIVILIAN FRIENDS will leave you behind if that's what the crowd is doing. VETERAN FRIENDS will kick the crowd's ass that left you behind.

CIVILIAN FRIENDS are for a while. VETERAN FRIENDS are for life.

CIVILIAN FRIENDS have shared a few experiences. VETERAN FRIENDS have shared a lifetime of experiences no citizen could ever dream of.

CIVILIAN FRIENDS will take your drink away when they think you've had enough. VETERAN FRIENDS will look at you stumbling all over the place and say, "You better drink the rest of that before you spill it!" Then they'll carry you home safely and put you to bed.

CIVILIAN FRIENDS will talk crap to the person who talks crap about you. VETERAN FRIENDS will knock the hell out of them for using your name in vain.

A veteran—whether active duty, retired, or reserve—is someone who, at one point in his life, wrote a blank check made payable to "The Government of the United States of America" for an amount of "up to and including my life." And military spouses, dependents, and families are as much veterans as their spouses.

From one Veteran to another, it's an honor to be in your company.

COMPANY A PHOTOMAPPING PLATOON
656 ENGINEER BATTALION
TOMPKINS BARRACKS, SCHWETZINGEN, GERMAN 1973
READY TO SERVE

FOR IMMEDIATE STARS & STRIPES DISTRIBUTION

APPROVED USAREUR

TOP LEFT: VanMalssen, Bailey, Gilbert, O'Neill, Picklo, Fauri, Balcavage, Lilburn

THE U.S. ARMY'S MEN OF ACTION SERIES, DOD PUBLICITY PHOTO 2MJ6A, PHOTO BY PFC DULFER

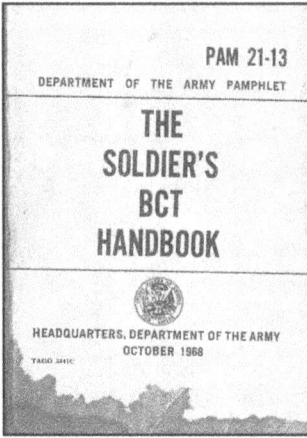

PAM 21-13
DEPARTMENT OF THE ARMY PAMPHLET

THE SOLDIER'S BCT HANDBOOK

HEADQUARTERS, DEPARTMENT OF THE ARMY
OCTOBER 1968

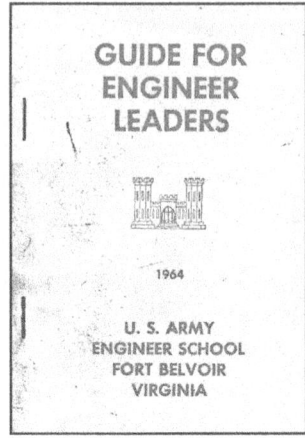

GUIDE FOR ENGINEER LEADERS

1964

U. S. ARMY
ENGINEER SCHOOL
FORT BELVOIR
VIRGINIA

JOHN "WOODY" WOODBURN
(Frank Dulfer Photo)

DON "DK" KIRK
(Frank Dulfer Photo)

THE MEDIEVAL TOWN OF ROTHENBURG, GERMANY

THE RHINE RIVER, GERMANY
DOTTED WITH CASTLES, IT FLOWS NORTH FROM THE SWISS
ALPS TO THE NORTH SEA IN THE NETHERLANDS

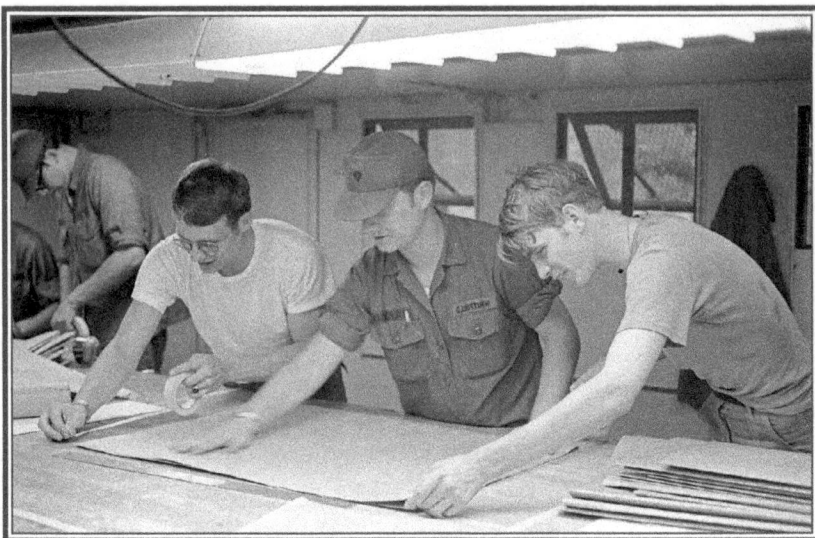

LAYING OUT MAP FLATS FOR TRACING
–FAURI, WHITFIELD, WEVER–

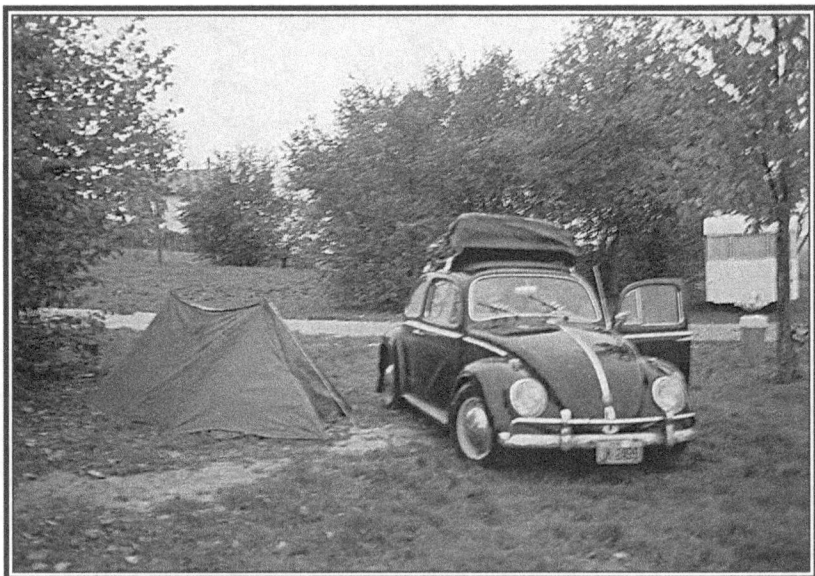

TRAVELING IN GLENN O'NEILL'S P.O.V.
–AN INEXPENSIVE WAY TO SEE EUROPE–

RECOMMENDED CHANGES TO EQUIPMENT TECHNICAL PUBLICATIONS

SOMETHING WRONG WITH THIS PUBLICATION?

THEN. . .JOT DOWN THE DOPE ABOUT IT ON THIS FORM, CAREFULLY TEAR IT OUT, FOLD IT AND DROP IT IN THE MAIL!

FROM: (PRINT YOUR UNIT'S COMPLETE ADDRESS)

DATE SENT

PUBLICATION NUMBER	PUBLICATION DATE	PUBLICATION TITLE

BE EXACT. . .PIN-POINT WHERE IT IS

IN THIS SPACE TELL WHAT IS WRONG AND WHAT SHOULD BE DONE ABOUT IT:

PAGE NO.	PARA- GRAPH	FIGURE NO.	TABLE NO.

PRINTED NAME, GRADE OR TITLE, AND TELEPHONE NUMBER

SIGN HERE:

DA FORM 1 JUL 79 2028-2

PREVIOUS EDITIONS ◆ ARE OBSOLETE.

P.S.—IF YOUR OUTFIT WANTS TO KNOW ABOUT YOUR RECOMMENDATION MAKE A CARBON COPY OF THIS AND GIVE IT TO YOUR HEADQUARTERS.

Source: TB 43-0147, TECHNICAL BULLETIN
COLOR, MARKING AND CAMOUFLAGE PATTERNS USED ON MILITARY EQUIP-
MENT MANAGED BY USATROSCOM, HEADQUARTER, DEPARTMENT OF THE
ARMY, DECEMBER 1975

WHERE IS THE FORM FOR RECOMMENDED
CHANGES TO THE UNITED STATES ARMY?
(OR RECOMMENDED CHANGES TO THIS BOOK!)

www.ingramcontent.com/pod-product-compliance
Lightning Source LLC
Chambersburg PA
CBHW021849090426

42811CB00033B/2190/J